HOW THE Brain Learns Mathematics

HOW THE Brain Learns Mathematics

David A. Sousa

For information:

Corwin Press
A Sage Publications Company
2455 Teller Road
Thousand Oaks, California 91320
www.corwinpress.com

Sage Publications Ltd.
1 Oliver's Yard
55 City Road
London EC1Y 1SP
United Kingdom

Sage Publications India Pvt. Ltd.
B 1/I 1 Mohan Cooperative Industrial Area
Mathura Road, New Delhi 110 044
India

Sage Publications Asia-Pacific Pte. Ltd.
33 Pekin Street #02-01
Far East Square
Singapore 048763

Printed in the United States of America.

Library of Congress Cataloging-in-Publication Data

Sousa, David A.
How the brain learns mathematics/David A. Sousa.
p. cm.
Includes bibliographical references and index.
ISBN 978-1-4129-5305-4 (cloth)
ISBN 978-1-4129-5306-1 (pbk.)
1. Mathematics—Study and teaching—United States. 2. Learning, Psychology of. 3. Learning—Physiological aspects. I. Title.

QA13.S66 2008
510.71—dc22 2007024839

This book is printed on acid-free paper.

08 09 10 11 10 9 8 7 6 5 4 3 2

Acquisitions Editor:	Robb Clouse
Editorial Assistant:	Jessica Wochna
Production Editor:	Sarah K. Quesenberry
Proofreader:	Caryne Brown
Typesetter:	C&M Digitals (P) Ltd.
Cover/Graphic Designer:	Lisa Miller

Contents

About the Author

David A. Sousa, EdD, is an international educational consultant. He has made presentations at national conventions of educational organizations and has conducted workshops on brain research and science education in hundreds of school districts and at several colleges and universities across the United States, Canada, Europe, Asia, and Australia.

Dr. Sousa has a bachelor of science degree in chemistry from Massachusetts State College at Bridgewater, a master of arts in teaching in science from Harvard University, and a doctorate from Rutgers University. His teaching experience covers all levels. He has taught high school science, served as a K–12 director of science, and was Supervisor of Instruction for the West Orange, New Jersey, schools. He then became superintendent of the New Providence, New Jersey, public schools. He has been an adjunct professor of education at Seton Hall University and a visiting lecturer at Rutgers University. He was president of the National Staff Development Council in 1992.

Dr. Sousa has edited science books and published numerous books and articles in leading educational journals on staff development, science education, and brain research. He has received awards from professional associations and school districts for his commitment and contributions to research, staff development, and science education. He received the Distinguished Alumni Award and an honorary doctorate in education from Bridgewater (Massachusetts) State College.

Dr. Sousa is a member of the Cognitive Neuroscience Society. He has appeared on NBC's *Today* show and on National Public Radio to discuss his work with schools using brain research. He makes his home in south Florida.

A mathematician, like a painter or a poet, is a maker of patterns. If his patterns are more permanent than theirs, it is because they are made with ideas.

—Godfrey Harold Hardy

A Mathematician's Apology

Acknowledgments

Corwin Press gratefully acknowledges the contributions of the following individuals:

Patricia Allanson
Seventh/Eighth-Grade Mathematics Teacher
Deltona Middle School
Deltona, FL

Carol Amos
Mathematics Teacher
Twinfield Union School
Plainfield, VT

Jim Barta
Associate Professor, Elementary Education
Utah State University
Logan, UT

Janice Bradley
Project Coordinator, Mathematically Connected Communitities
New Mexico State University
Las Cruces, NM

Deborah Gordon
Third-Grade Teacher
Madison School District
Phoenix, AZ

Elizabeth Marquez
Mathematics Assessment Specialist
Educational Testing Service
Princeton, NJ

Renee Ponce-Nealon
Third-Grade Teacher
FSUSD, Tolenas Elementary School
Fairfield, CA

Daniel Raguse
President
The Math Learning Center
Salem, OR

Rita Smilkstein
Faculty Emerita (English), North Seattle Community College
Invited Faculty, Western Washington University's Woodring College of Education
Seattle, WA

Kimberly C. Smith
Eighth-Grade Mathematics Teacher and Mathematics Department Chair
A. Laurin Welborn Middle School
High Point, NC

Robert Sylwester
Emeritus Professor of Education
University of Oregon
Eugene, OR

Mary L. Thoreen
NBCT, Mathematics Teacher
Wilson Middle School
Tampa, FL

Keith H. Weber
Assistant Professor
Graduate School of Education
Rutgers University
New Brunswick, NJ

Introduction

Numbers rule the universe.

—Pythagoras

EVERYONE CAN DO MATHEMATICS

Human beings are born with some remarkable capabilities. One is language. In just a few years after birth, toddlers are carrying on running conversations without the benefit of direct instruction. Over the next few years, their sentences become more complex, and their vocabulary grows exponentially. By the age of 10, they understand about 10,000 words and speak their native language with 95 percent accuracy.

Another innate talent is number sense—the ability to determine the number of objects in a small collection, to count, and to perform simple addition and subtraction, also without direct instruction. Yet, by the age of 10 some of these children are already saying, "I can't do math!" But you never hear them saying, "I can't do language!" Why this difference?

Children often say, "I can't do math!" But you never hear them say, "I can't do language!" Why this difference?

One reason is that spoken language and number sense are survival skills; abstract mathematics is not. In elementary schools we present complicated notions and procedures to a brain that was first designed for survival in the African savanna. Human culture and society have changed a lot in the last 5,000 years, but the human brain has not. So how does the brain cope when faced with a task, such as multiplying a pair of two-digit numbers, for which it was not prepared? Thanks to modern imaging devices that can look inside the living brain, we can see which cerebral circuits are called into play when the brain tackles a task for which it has limited innate capabilities. The fact that the human brain *can* rise to this challenge is testimony to its remarkable ability to assess its environment and make calculations that can safely land humans on the moon and put a space probe around a planet hundreds of millions of miles away.

Why Is Learning Mathematics So Hard?

Succeeding in high school mathematics is still no easy feat. The results of the 2005 National Assessment of Educational Progress (NAEP) mathematics tests of 9,300 twelfth-grade students revealed that more than 39 percent fell below the proficient level in basic mathematics skills. Because the 2005 test had significant changes from earlier versions, direct comparisons to previous test results cannot be made. Nonetheless, no educator or parent can feel reassured by results showing nearly 40 percent of high school seniors performing below the minimum proficiency levels in basic mathematics. For fourth graders, the average score was three points higher, and for eighth graders the average score was one point higher in 2005 than in 2003, on a 0 to 500–point scale. These increases were barely significant (NAEP, 2007).

Explanations for this lackluster performance abound. Some say that learning mathematics is difficult because it is so abstract and requires more logical and ordered thinking. Others say that the various symbols used in mathematics make it similar to tackling a foreign language. Education critics maintain that only a few students are really developmentally incapable of handling mathematics and that the poor performance stems mainly from inadequate instruction. They cite the so-called "math wars" as hindering major progress in mathematics curriculum development similar to what the "reading wars" did to reading instruction during the 1990s.

Response From Mathematics Educators

The National Council of Teachers of Mathematics (NCTM) published the *Principles and Standards for School Mathematics* in 2000, proposing five process standards and five content standards for prekindergarten through Grade 12 mathematics instruction (NCTM, 2000). Since then, interpretation of the standards in the elementary and middle school grades became so broad that NCTM decided to refocus the curriculum at those grade levels.

In 2006, NCTM released *Curriculum Focal Points,* which identifies three important mathematical topics at each level, prekindergarten through Grade 8, described as "cohesive clusters of related knowledge, skills, and concepts," which form the necessary foundation for understanding concepts in higher-level mathematics. The publication is intended to bring more coherence to the very diverse mathematics curricula currently in use. It provides a framework for states and districts to design more focused curricular expectations and assessments for PreK to Grade 8 mathematics curriculum development. Whether this new effort will succeed in improving student achievement in mathematics remains to be seen. In the meantime, teachers enter classrooms every day prepared to help their students feel confident enough to master mathematics principles and operations. One thing seems certain: Students who are poor in mathematics in their early years remain poor at mathematics in their later years.

ABOUT THIS BOOK

I am often asked to give specific examples of how the fruits of scientific research have made an impact on educational practice. That question is a lot easier to answer now than it was 15 years ago because recent discoveries in cognitive neuroscience have given us a deeper understanding of the brain. Thanks to brain-scanning technology we now have more knowledge about our short-term and long-term memory systems, the impact of emotions on learning, how we acquire language and motor skills, and how the brain learns to read. But it is only recently that researchers have begun to examine closely the neural mechanisms involved in processing arithmetic and mathematical operations.

Questions This Book Will Answer

This book will answer questions such as these:

- What innate number capabilities are we born with?
- How much number manipulation and basic arithmetic can young children learn without direct instruction?
- Why do Asian languages allow their native speakers to learn counting sooner and faster than English-speaking children?
- What kind of number word system could help English-speaking children learn to count easier and faster?

- Why is learning mathematics so difficult for so many students?
- What are the implications of the current research in how we learn to calculate for everyday classroom practice?
- How does the brain manage to deal with abstract mathematics concepts?
- What strategies are effective in teaching students with reading difficulties to learn mathematics?
- How can we tell if a student's difficulties in mathematics are the result of environmental factors or developmental deficits?
- What strategies should teachers of mathematics consider when planning lessons?
- What have brain imaging studies revealed about the nature of dyscalculia?
- How can elementary and secondary school classroom teachers successfully detect mathematics difficulties?
- What instructional strategies work best with students who have difficulties in mathematics?
- How can teachers use research on how the brain learns mathematics to design an instructional model for teaching PreK through Grade 12 mathematics?

Chapter Contents

Chapter 1 — Developing Number Sense. Children's ability to determine quantities begins soon after birth. This chapter examines the components of this innate number sense and how it leads to counting and basic arithmetic operations. It looks at the regions of the brain that work together and manipulate numbers and the ways in which language affects how quickly and how easily children learn to count.

Chapter 2 — Learning to Calculate. Because counting large numbers is not a survival skill, the brain must learn mathematical concepts and procedures. This chapter explores the various developmental stages that the brain must go through to understand number relationships and manipulations, such as in multiplication. It discusses why the brain views learning to multiply as an unnatural act, and it suggests some other ways to look at teaching multiplication that may be easier.

Chapter 3 — Reviewing the Elements of Learning. This chapter presents some of the recent findings from cognitive neuroscience, including discoveries about memory systems, the nature and value of practice and rehearsal, lesson timing, and the benefits of writing in mathematics classes. Gender differences as well as learning and teaching styles are also discussed.

Chapter 4 — Teaching Mathematics to the Preschool and Kindergarten Brain. Although young children have an innate number sense, certain instructional strategies can enhance those capabilities and prepare children to be more successful in learning arithmetic operations. This chapter suggests some of those strategies.

Chapter 5 — Teaching Mathematics to the Preadolescent Brain. Here we look at the development and characteristics of the preadolescent brain and how they affect the individual's emotional and rational behavior. The chapter offers suggestions on how lesson plans can be modified, from the primary grades on up to middle school, to take into account the nature of this developing brain so that more of these students will be successful in learning mathematics.

Chapter 6 — Teaching Mathematics to the Adolescent Brain. Similar to the previous chapter, we review the nature of the adolescent brain and suggest what considerations need to be made to adapt lessons to meet their needs. Included here are discussions of mathematical reasoning as well as instructional choices, such as layering the curriculum and graphic organizers, that can be very effective strategies for making mathematics relevant to today's students.

Chapter 7 — Recognizing and Addressing Mathematics Difficulties. Numerous suggestions are offered in this chapter to enable teachers to identify and help students overcome their difficulties in learning mathematics, including math anxiety. This chapter discusses the major differences between the environmental and developmental factors that contribute to mathematics difficulties. It presents some tested strategies that teachers of all grade levels can use with students who are poor at mathematics to help them understand number operations and gain a more accurate and deeper understanding of mathematical concepts.

Chapter 8 — Putting It All Together: Planning Lessons in PreK–12 Mathematics. What is mathematics? How do we use the important findings discussed in the previous chapters in daily practice? This chapter suggests ways to incorporate this research into the planning of mathematics lessons and presents a four-step instructional model for teaching PreK through Grade 12 mathematics.

Other Helpful Tools

At the end of each chapter, you will find a page called **Reflections,** an organizing tool for helping you remember important ideas, strategies, and resources you may wish to consider later.

I have included some information on the history of mathematics that I thought might be interesting and attach a human aspect to this topic. As in all my books, I have referred to the original scientific research and listed those citations whenever possible.

Look for the ✓. Most of the chapters contain suggestions for translating the research on learning mathematics into instructional practice. These suggestions are indicated with a checkmark (✓). Any time you see this symbol it means, Here is a strategy to consider!

This is not a book of activities in mathematics. Rather, this book is designed to help teachers decide which books and activities are likely to be effective in light of current research on how the brain learns mathematics.

At the back of the book is an extensive listing of Internet **Resources** that offers a wide range of activities for teachers and students at all grade levels.

This book is not meant to be a source book for mathematics activities PreK through Grade 12. Rather, it is meant to suggest instructional approaches that are compatible with what cognitive neuroscience is telling us about how the brain deals with numbers and mathematical relationships. Of course, there are some suggested activities that represent my view of how these research findings can be translated into effective classroom practice. But these are meant to suggest the *type* of activity rather than be the definitive activity. There are hundreds of books and computer programs on the market, as well as Internet resources, loaded with mathematics activities, games, and worksheets. This book is designed to help the teacher decide which of those books and activities are likely to be effective in light of current research.

The information presented here was current at the time of publication. However, as scientists continue to explore the inner workings of the brain, they will likely discover more about the cerebral mechanisms involved in learning mathematics. These discoveries should help parents and educators understand more about the nature of mathematics, mathematics difficulties, and effective mathematics instruction. Stay tuned!

ASSESSING YOUR CURRENT KNOWLEDGE OF HOW WE LEARN MATHEMATICS

The value of this book can be measured in part by how much it enhances your knowledge about how humans learn mathematics. This might be a good time for you to take the following true-false test and assess your current understanding of some concepts related to mathematics and mathematics instruction. Decide whether the statements are *generally* true or false and circle T or F. Explanations for the answers are found throughout the book in special boxes.

1. T F The brain comprehends numerals first as words, then as quantities.
2. T F Learning to multiply, like learning spoken language, is a natural ability.
3. T F It is easier to tell which is the greater of two larger numbers than of two smaller numbers.
4. T F The maximum capacity of seven items in working memory is valid for all cultures.
5. T F Gender differences in mathematics are more likely due to genetics than to cultural factors.
6. T F Practicing mathematics procedures makes perfect.
7. T F Using technology for routine calculations leads to greater understanding and achievement in mathematics.
8. T F Symbolic number operations are strongly linked to the brain's language areas.
9. T F Secondary school students' attitudes about mathematics have improved dramatically in recent years.

WHAT'S COMING?

What innate number capabilities are we born with? Are schools taking advantage of these capabilities when teaching arithmetic operations? How does our native language affect our ability to learn to count? The answers to these intriguing questions are found in the next chapter.

Chapter 1

Developing Number Sense

Wherever there is a number, there is beauty.

—Proclus (A.D. 410–485)

BABIES CAN COUNT

In 1980, Prentice Starkey (1980) persuaded 72 mothers to bring their young babies to his laboratory at the University of Pennsylvania for a novel experiment. While seated on its mother's lap, each baby, aged between 16 and 30 weeks, observed slides projected on a screen. The slides contained two or three large black dots spread out horizontally. Starkey varied the spacing between the dots so that neither the total length of the line nor the density of the dots could be used to discriminate their number. After numerous trials, Starkey noticed that the average fixation time of 1.9 seconds for a two-dot slide jumped to an average of 2.5 seconds (a 32 percent increase) for a three-dot slide. Thus, the babies detected the change from two to three dots.

In a follow-up experiment, Strauss and Curtis (1981) at the University of Pittsburgh repeated this format but used colored photographs of common objects instead of dots. The objects varied in size and alignments, so that the only constant was their number. The babies continued to notice the difference between slides of two and three objects (Figure 1.1). Similar experiments with infants have been conducted by various researchers, even as recently as 2006 (Berger, Tzur, & Posner, 2006). They all yield the same finding: In the first few months of life, babies notice the constancy of objects and detect differences in their numerical quantities. Babies, of course, do not have

Figure 1.1 Researchers used slides similar to these to prove that infants can discriminate between the numerosities of 2 and 3. The slides with the dots are similar to those used by Starkey (1980), and slides with objects are representative of the experiments conducted by Strauss and Curtis (1981).

a sophisticated concept of counting, but they do have a conception of quantity, or what scientists call *numerosity.*

Is numerosity innate, or is it something the babies were able to learn in their first few months? Newborns can distinguish two objects from three, and perhaps three from four. Their ears notice the difference between two sounds from three. It seems unlikely that newborns could gather enough information from the environment to learn the numbers 1, 2, and 3 in just the few months after birth. Thus, this ability seems to have a strong genetic component.

More support for the notion that numerosity is prewired in the brain comes from case studies of patients who have lost or never had a sense of numbers. Butterworth (1999), for example, describes a patient who had a stroke that left her language and reasoning abilities intact but destroyed her ability to estimate or determine the number of objects in any collection. After another patient had an operation to remove a tumor from the left side of her brain, numbers had no meaning for her. Once again, this patient's language ability and general intelligence were unaffected, but she could not even be taught finger addition. The multiplication tables were just a nonsense poem to her. Butterworth also describes a man who apparently never had number sense, although he earned a college degree in psychology. He had to use his fingers for simple arithmetic and resorted to a calculator for other computations, although the answer had no meaning for him. He was unable to tell the larger of two numbers or to quickly count just three items in a collection.

Dehaene (1997) examined how one's sense of numbers can be disrupted after a stroke. One patient counted about half the items in a collection and then stopped counting because she thought she counted them all. Another patient would count the same items over and over again, insisting there were 12 items when there were only four. Here, too, language ability and general intelligence were not affected. These are just a few examples from a large collection of case studies that lead to one conclusion: We are born with a built-in number sense!

What Is Number Sense?

Tobias Danzig (1967) introduced the term "number sense" in 1954, describing it as a person's ability to recognize that something has changed in a small collection when, without that person's knowledge, an object has been added or removed from the collection. We have number sense because numbers have *meaning* for us, just like words and music. And as in the case of learning words, we were born with it or, at the very least, born with the ability to acquire it without effort at a very young age. Mathematician Keith Devlin (2000) refined the definition by suggesting that number sense consisted of two important components: the ability to compare the sizes of two collections shown simultaneously, and the ability to remember numbers of objects presented successively in time.

> *Because we are born with number sense, most of us have the potential to be a lot better at arithmetic and mathematics than we think.*

Because we are born with number sense does not necessary mean that we all can become great mathematicians. But it does mean that most of us have the potential to be a lot better at arithmetic and mathematics than we think. If this is true, then why do so many students and adults say they "can't do math"? We will answer this fascinating question later.

Animals Also Have Number Sense

The discovery that infants have a number sense came as no surprise to researchers who work with animals. For more than 50 years, experiments have shown that birds (Koehler, 1951), rats (Mechner & Guevrekian, 1962), lions (McComb, Packer, & Pusey, 1994), and chimpanzees (Woodruff & Premack, 1981) possess both of the number sense abilities described earlier by Devlin.

Of course, different species of animals exhibit their number sense at varying levels of sophistication. Many birds, for example, display a sense of numerosity in the number of times they repeat a particular note in their song. Even members of the same species will learn the number of repetitions common to their location, which may be six repetitions in one woodland and seven in another.

Rats and lions seem to have the ability to *estimate* and *compare* number. The ability of animals to compare the numbers of objects in collections has an obvious survival advantage. It would help a group of animals to know whether to defend their territory if the defenders outnumber the attackers, or to retreat if there are more attackers. Note that I am referring to the animals as "estimating" and "comparing" numbers, not "counting." No one believes that animals actually count by number, as in 1...2...3 or 11...12...13. Rather, most researchers accept that many animals recognize the difference between one and two objects; after that it is probably just "more than two."

What about chimpanzees, our closest relatives on the evolutionary tree? Experiments show that chimpanzees can do basic arithmetic. For instance, in an experiment using chocolate bars, chimpanzees recognized that 3 bars + 4 bars = 7 bars and 5 bars + 1 bar = 6 bars. They also recognized that 6 is less than 7. Again, the chimpanzees were not actually counting to 6 or 7, but most likely were comparing visual scans to recognize that one sum was *greater* than the other (Woodruff & Premack, 1981).

The numerical estimating ability shown in rats and chimpanzees resembles the innate number sense of human infants. Animals can count in that they can increase an internal counter each time an external stimulus occurs, such as a rat pressing a lever to get food. But their representation of numbers is a fuzzy one. Humans can do much more. After just a few months of age, toddlers discover numbers and number words in a precise sequence, and they quickly begin to extend an innate ability to the point where they can eventually measure exact quantities, even into the billions.

Why Do We Have Number Sense?

Number sense became an innate ability in humans and other animals most likely because it contributed to their survival. Animals in the wild must constantly assess dangers and opportunities in their environment. To do so, they need cerebral systems than can rapidly compute the magnitude of any challenge. As primitive humans went searching for food, they also had to determine quickly whether the number of animals they spotted represented an opportunity or a danger, whether they were moving too fast, were too big to capture, or were just too far away. A mistake in these calculations could be fatal. Consequently, individuals who were good at determining these magnitudes survived and contributed to strengthening their species' genetic capabilities in number sense.

Humans and other animals developed an innate number sense because it contributed to their survival.

Piaget and Number Sense

Contemporary research on number sense dramatically undermines Jean Piaget's constructivist views of 50 years ago. He asserted that newborns enter the world with a clean cognitive slate (remember *tabula rasa*?) and, by gathering information from their environment, they gradually construct a coherent understanding of the world around them. Piaget (1952, 1954) conducted experiments and concluded that children younger than 10 months of age had no recognition that physical objects are permanent, what he called "object permanence." He also believed that children did not possess number sense and that they were unable to grasp the concept of number conservation—the idea that rearranging items in a collection does not change their number—until about five years of age. Furthermore, Piaget and his fellow constructivists suggested that children do not develop a conceptual understanding of arithmetic until they are seven or eight years of age.

Piaget's work had great influence on educational thought because his conclusions were based on experimental psychology. Many educators interpreted Piaget's work as meaning that the child is not ready for arithmetic until the age of six or seven. Teaching arithmetic earlier would be counterproductive because it might result in distorted number concepts. The child's frustration in learning even simple arithmetic operations too soon would only generate feelings of anxiety about mathematics. According to Piaget, it was better to start teaching logic and the ordering of sets because these ideas are necessary for acquiring the concept of number. These notions are still prevalent in many of today's preschools.

Does this persistent Piagetian approach make sense? Researchers today recognize that many of Piaget's experimental procedures with children were flawed, thus leading to erroneous conclusions. We noted earlier how birds and rats easily recognize a certain number of objects as well as their spatial configuration. And chimpanzees spontaneously choose the larger of two numerical quantities of food. Why, then, would human children have to wait until the age of four or five to gain the same arithmetic capabilities of other animals? We already know the answer: They don't. Human infants are at least as gifted as animals in arithmetic, and their ability to acquire number concepts grows rapidly within their first year of life.

LEARNING TO COUNT

Although infants are born with the same rudimentary number sense observed in rats and chimpanzees, they possess two arithmetic capabilities that quickly separate them from other animals. One is the ability to count. The other is to use and manipulate symbols that represent numeric quantities.

Recognizing the number of objects in a small collection is part of innate number sense. It requires no counting because the numerosity is identified in an instant. Researchers call this process *subitizing* (from the Latin for "sudden"). But when the number in a collection exceeds the limits of subitizing, counting becomes necessary.

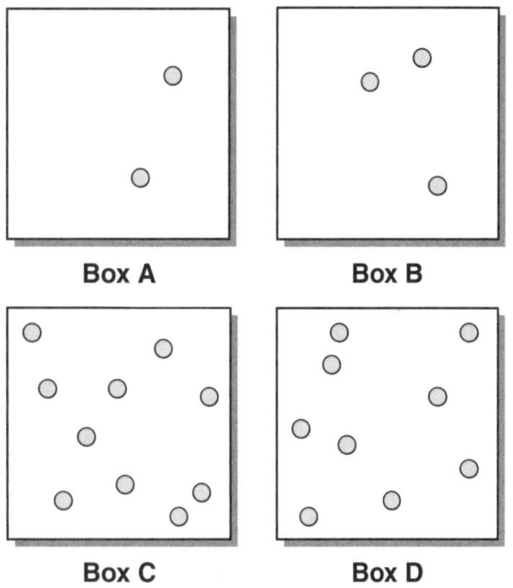

Figure 1.2 We can easily perceive the difference between two and three items through subitizing. But as the number of items increases, we resort to counting to arrive at an accurate total.

Subitizing

Our innate visual processing system allows us to comprehend the numerosity of a collection. It works instantly and accurately to quantify groups of four or fewer objects without actually counting them. But subsidization loses accuracy as the number in the collection increases. With more objects, the process slows down as we abandon subitizing and resort to counting or estimation based on visual patterns we discern in the collection. Why is that? It is likely that subitizing is a primitive cerebral process while counting involves more sophisticated operations.

Indeed, recent PET scan studies seem to indicate just that. When participants in the studies were subitizing one to four items, areas in the visual cortex were activated while areas involving attention were quiet. While counting five to eight items, however, numerous brain networks were recruited, including those involved in visual attention in the top area of the brain and cognitive processing in the front regions of the brain. These results suggest that subitizing is a low-key subconscious (neuroscientists call it *preattentive*) operation while counting provokes significant cerebral activity (Piazza, Mechelli, Butterworth, & Price, 2002; Sathian, Simon, Peterson, Patel, Hoffman, & Grafton, 1999).

Figure 1.2 shows the difference between subitizing and counting. Look at boxes A and B. The eyes can immediately detect the difference between two and three items in these boxes without counting. How many dots are there in box C? And how many in box D? Chances are you had to resort to counting to determine the number of dots in each box. This suggests that subitizing may well be the developmental prerequisite skill necessary to learn counting. If that is the case, then we should examine subitizing more closely and determine if reinforcing this skill in children will help them learn counting easier.

Types of Subitizing

Clements (1999) describes two types of subitizing: perceptual and conceptual. *Perceptual subitizing* involves recognizing a number without using other mathematical processes, just as you did when looking at boxes A and B in Figure 1.2. This innate cerebral mechanism is very likely the same used by animals, and accounts for some of the surprising capabilities of infants described earlier in this chapter. Perceptual subitizing also helps children separate collections of objects into single units and connect each unit with only one number word, thus developing the process of counting.

Conceptual subitizing allows one to know the number of a collection by recognizing a familiar pattern, such as the spatial arrangement of dots on the faces of dice or on domino tiles. Other patterns may be kinesthetic, such as using finger patterns to figure out addition problems, or rhythmic patterns, such as gesturing out one "beat" with each count. Creating and using conceptual subitizing patterns help young children develop the abstract number and arithmetic strategies they will need to master counting (Clements, 1999; Steffe & Cobb, 1988). Those children who cannot conceptually subitize are likely to have problems learning basic arithmetic processes. Can this innate ability of subitizing be strengthened through practice? The answer is yes. You will find suggestions for how to teach subitizing in Chapter 4.

Creating and using conceptual subitizing patterns help young children develop the abstract number and arithmetic strategies they will need to master counting.

Counting

Origins of Counting

No one knows when and how humans first developed the idea of counting beyond the innate sequence of "one, two, and many." Perhaps they began the way young children do today: using their fingers. (This system is so reliable that many adults also do arithmetic with their fingers.) Our base-10 number system suggests that counting began as finger enumeration. The Latin word *digit* is used to mean both *numeral* and *finger.* Even evidence from brain scans lends further support to this number-to-finger connection.

When a person is performing basic arithmetic, the greatest brain activity is in the left parietal lobe and in the region of the motor cortex that controls the fingers (Dehaene, Molko, Cohen, & Wilson, 2004). Figure 1.3 shows the four major lobes of the brain and the motor cortex. The area within the dotted oval is highly activated when a person is doing arithmetic. This area includes both a part of the parietal lobe and the section of the motor cortex that controls finger movement.

This raises an interesting question. Is it just a coincidence that the region of the brain we use for counting includes the same part that controls our fingers? Or is it possible that counting began with

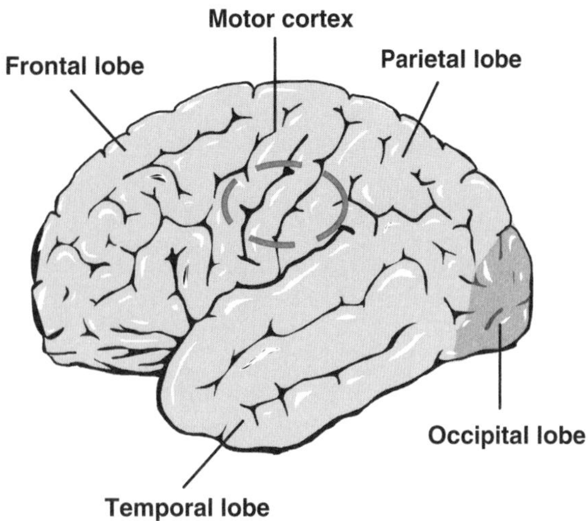

Figure 1.3 This view of the left side of the brain shows the four lobes and the motor cortex. The area within the oval is highly activated when a person is doing arithmetic. This area includes part of the parietal lobe and the section of the motor cortex that controls the fingers.

our fingers, and the brain later learned to do counting without manipulating them? Some researchers speculate that if our human ancestors' first experience with numbers was using their fingers, then the region of the brain that controls the fingers would be the area where more abstract mental arithmetic would be located in their descendants (Devlin, 2000).

Assuming fingers were our first counting tools, we obviously ran into a problem when counting collections of more than 10 objects. Some cultures resorted to using other body parts to increase the total. Even today, the natives of the Torres Straits Islands in New Guinea denote numbers up to 33 by pointing to different parts of their body, including fingers, arms, shoulders, chest, legs, and toes. Naming the body part evokes the corresponding number. Thus, the word *six* is literally "wrist," and *nine* is "left breast." They use sticks for numbers larger than 33 (Ifrah, 1985). But this process is hopeless for numbers beyond 30 or so. Eventually, some cultures used a physical tally system, such as making notches on a bone or stick. Notched bones have been discovered that date back about 40,000 years. According to the fossil record, this is about the same time that humans started to use symbolic representations in rock carvings and cave paintings (Devlin, 2000).

Finger counting and physical tallies show that these cultures understood the concept of numerosity, but that does not imply they understood the abstract concept of *number*. Archeologists, such as Denise Schmandt-Besserat (1985), suspect that the introduction of *abstract* counting numbers, as opposed to markings, appeared around 8,000 BC and were used by the highly advanced Sumerian society that flourished in the Fertile Crescent of what is now Iraq and Syria. They used tokens of different shapes to represent a specific quantity of a trade item, such as a jar of oil or loaf of bread. They used symbolic markings on clay tablets to keep running totals of items in commerce. It was not really a separate number system, but it was the first use of a symbol system that set the stage for the functional, abstract numbers we use today.

Our present numbering system was developed over two thousand years by the Hindus, and attained its present form in about the sixth century. In the seventh century, it was introduced to Europe by Persian mathematicians and thus became known as the "Arabic system." This ingenious invention now enjoys worldwide acceptance for several reasons.

- Each number has its own word, and the number words can be read aloud. Saying a number, such as 1776 *(one-thousand seven-hundred and seventy-six),* clearly reveals the numeric structure of units, tens, hundreds, and thousands.

- The numerical system is not just symbols but also a *language,* thereby allowing humans to use their innate language fluency to handle numbers.

- It is concise and easily learned.

- We can use it to represent numbers of unlimited magnitude and apply them to measurements and collections of all types.

- It reduces computation with numbers to the routine manipulation of symbols on a page.

In fairness, I should mention that the original idea of denoting numbers by stringing together a small collection of basic symbols to form number words came from the Babylonians around 2000 BC. But the system was cumbersome to use because it was built on the base 60, and thus did not gain wide acceptance. Nonetheless, we still use it in our measurements of time (60 seconds make one minute, etc.) and geography (60 seconds make one degree of latitude and longitude).

Beginning to Count

Wynn (1990) was among the first researchers to examine how young children conceptualize the how and why of counting. She discovered that by the age of 30 months, most children have seen someone counting on numerous occasions. They also demonstrate the ability to count different types of sounds on a videotape. So, quite early on and without explicit teaching, they understand that counting is an abstract procedure that applies to all kinds of visual and auditory objects.

By the age of three, most children recognize that there are separate words to describe the quantity of something—that is, they answer the question of "how many." Children also know that number words are different from those that describe the size, shape, or color of objects and that they hold a specific place in the sequence of describing words. They learn to say "three big dogs," but never "big three dogs." At this stage, they know that "three" is a number, but they may not know the precise value that it represents. That will come to them later with experience and practice.

For the young mind, counting is a complex process that uses a one-to-one principle. It involves saying number words in the correct sequence while systematically assigning a number word to each object being counted. Eventually, children recognize that the last number in the counting sequence tells them the total number of objects in the collection, a concept known as the *cardinal principle*. Students who do not attain the cardinal principle will be delayed in their ability to add and subtract with meaning. As a result, these students always recount each item when adding. They recognize addition as an increase in number but do not start from the last number counted. In Chapter 4, you will find some suggestions on how to help children learn to count.

How Language Affects Counting

Cultural Variations in Working Memory Capacity

Every time the results of international test scores in mathematics are released, children from the United States usually perform dismally compared to children from other nations, particularly those from Asia. Differences in classroom instruction and curriculum may be partly to blame. But cultural differences in computational ability may have their roots in the words that different cultures use to represent numbers.

Read the following list of numbers aloud: 7, 5, 9, 11, 8, 3, 7, 2. Now cover the list and take about 20 seconds to try to memorize the list. Now recite them again without looking at the list. Did you get them all correct? Chances are that if your native language is English, you might have gotten only about four or five in the correct order. But if you are Chinese, you may have gotten all of them correct. Why is that? When you try to remember a list of numbers by saying them aloud, you are using a verbal memory loop, a part of immediate memory that can hold information for only about two seconds. This forces you to rehearse the words to refresh them in the loop. As a result, your memory span is limited by how many number words you can say in less than two seconds. That time span is too short for most people to say aloud the 12 syllables contained in the eight numbers you were trying to remember. Of course, if you can recite faster, you will remember more.

Chinese numbers are very brief. Most of them can be recited in less than one-fourth of a second. Pronouncing their English equivalents takes about one-third of a second. This difference might seem trivial to you, but it is very significant to researchers. Studies of languages as diverse as English, Hebrew, Arabic, Chinese, and Welsh show a correlation between the time required to pronounce numbers in a given language and the memory span of numbers in its speakers. People in Hong Kong, where the Cantonese dialect of Chinese is spoken, have a number memory span of about 10 digits, as opposed to the seven in speakers of English and other Western languages.

One factor contributing to this difference is the finding from brain imaging studies that native Chinese speakers process arithmetic manipulation in areas of the brain different from those of native English speakers. Researchers speculate that the biological encoding of numbers may differ in the two cultures because their languages are written so differently, resulting in vastly dissimilar visual reading experiences (Tang et al., 2006).

Surprisingly, the magical number of seven items, long considered the fixed span of working memory, is just the standard span for a special population of humans—namely, Western adults on whom about 90 percent of psychological studies have been focused. No doubt there is a biological limit to the capacity of working memory, but that limit also appears to be affected by culture and training. The cultural variations in memory span suggest that Asian numerical notations, such as in Chinese and Japanese, are more easily memorized than our Western notations because they are more compact (Miller, Smith, Zhu, & Zhang, 1995).

> *The magical number of seven items, long considered the fixed span of working memory, is just the standard span for Western adults. The capacity of working memory appears to be affected by culture and training.*

There are some tricks that adults can use to increase digit memory span. These tricks can also be taught to young students at the appropriate age.

✓ Memorize numbers by saying them aloud and using the shortest words possible. The number 76,391 is easier to remember as "seven-six-three-nine-one" (6 syllables) rather than as "seventy-two thousand three hundred and ninety-one" (13 syllables).

✓ Chunking numbers into groups is another useful strategy. Ten-digit telephone numbers are easier to remember when they are divided into the three-digit area code, followed by two groups of three and four digits.

✓ Look for ways to tie parts of the number you are memorizing to other numbers that are familiar to you, such as your area code, postal zip code, address, or Social Security number.

English Words Make Learning Arithmetic Harder

Although the base-10 system has taken over most languages, how we say numbers in different languages runs the gamut from simple to complex. English has many inconsistencies in its number

> *Because of language differences, Asian children learn to count earlier and higher than their Western peers.*

words. Ten has three forms: *ten, -teen,* and *-ty. Eleven* and *twelve* fit no pattern, and the ones are stated before the tens in the numbers 13 through 19. Chinese and Japanese hold the prize for simplicity. Not only is their number syntax easy to learn and remember, but their syntax perfectly reflects the decimal structure. English syntax does not. As a result, Asian children learn to count earlier and higher than their American and Western peers and can do simple addition and subtraction sooner as well. By age four, Chinese children can generally count up to 40, while American children of the same age can barely get to 15, and it takes them another year to get to 40.

How do we know the difference is due to language? Because children in the two countries show no age differences in their ability to count from 1 to 12. Take a look at Figure 1.4. The curves represent the percentage of children who could correctly count up to a certain number. Note the marked separation of the counting curves just past the number 12. Differences appear only when English-speaking children encounter the special rules for forming number words.

Here's why. In Chinese, for example, the nine short names for the numbers 1 through 9 respectively are *yi, èr, san, si, wu, liù, qi, ba,* and *jiu.* The four multipliers are 10 *(shi),* 100 *(bai),* 1,000 *(qian),* and 10,000 *(wàn).* Composing a number past 10 is simple: 11 is ten one *(shi yi),* 12 is ten two *(shi èr),* 13 is ten three *(shi san),* and so on up to 20, which is two ten *(èr shi).* This logical system continues: 21 is two ten one *(èr shi yi),* 22 is two ten two *(èr shi èr),* 30 is three ten *(san shi),* and 40 is four ten *(si shi).* For numbers past 12, Chinese children just keep applying the simple rules that worked for 1 to 12. (Japanese has an almost identical counting system.) Chinese needs only 11 words to count from 1 to 100, but English requires 28.

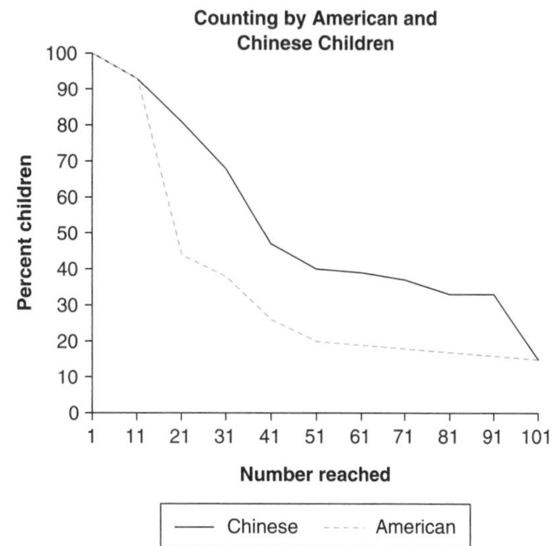

Figure 1.4 The chart shows the percentage of American and Chinese children reciting numbers as far as they could. More Chinese children could count much further than their American peers. (Adapted from Miller, Smith, Zhu, & Zhang, 1995 with permission of the publisher and author.)

American children often try to apply logical number rules but find that after correctly reciting *twenty-eight,* and *twenty-nine,* they have made a mistake when they continue with words like *twenty-ten* and *twenty-eleven.* These types of grammatical errors in number syntax are almost nonexistent in Asian countries.

The number word differences affect the experiences that Asian and American children will have with arithmetic in their early school years. Because the system of spoken Chinese numerals directly parallels the structure of written Arabic numerals, Chinese children have much less difficulty than their American peers in learning the principles of place value notation in base 10. For instance, when asked to form the number 25 with unit cubes and bars of 10, Chinese children readily select two bars of 10 and five units. American children, however, laboriously count out 25 units, and fail to take advantage of the shortcut provided by groups of 10. If given a bar of 20 units, they use it more frequently than two bars of 10. This indicates that they seem to give attention to the surface meaning of 25, while Chinese children are exhibiting a deeper understanding of the base-10 structure (Dehaene, 1997).

I should also note that the French and German languages have their own peculiarities. For instance, 70 in French is *soixante-dix* (sixty-ten), and 97 is an awkward *quatre-vingt-dix-sept* (four-twenty-ten-seven). German has its unique reversal of decades and units in its number words. The number 542 is said as *funf hundert zwei und vierzig* (five hundred two and forty).

To summarize, the Western language systems for saying numbers pose more problems for children learning to count than do Asian languages. The Western systems are harder to keep in temporary memory, make the acquisition of counting and the conception of base 10 more difficult, and slow down calculation. Unfortunately, no one realistically expects that Western counting systems will be modified to resemble the Asian model. But educators should at least be aware of these significant language problems, especially when they are comparing the test results in mathematics of Asian and English-speaking elementary students.

The Mental Number Line

During the last 40 years or so, numerous experimenters have made some intriguing discoveries when they have asked people to compare numbers. One of the earliest experiments consisted of measuring the time it took for adults to decide which was the larger of two Arabic digits. When two digits were far apart in values, such as 2 and 9, the adults responded quickly, and almost without error. But when the digits were closer in value, such as 5 and 6, the response time increased significantly, and the error rate rose dramatically. Furthermore, responses for an equal distance between numbers slowed down as the number pairs became increasingly larger. That is, the response time was greater when comparing digits 3 and 4 than for digits 2 and 3, and greater still for digits 8 and 9 (Moyer & Landauer, 1967). Subsequent experiments consistently yield similar results (Figure 1.5).

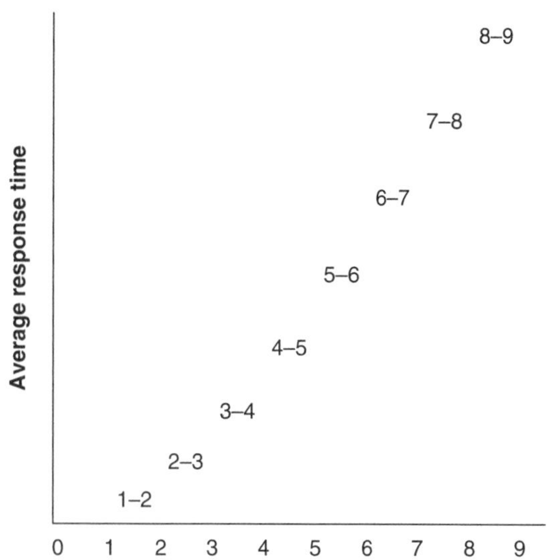

Figure 1.5 This qualitative chart illustrates how the average response time increases for adults deciding which is the larger of the two digits in each pair as the value of the digits increases.

Another experiment measured the time it took adults to decide whether a two-digit numeral was larger or smaller than 65. Once again, the response time grew longer as the numerals got closer in value to 65 (e.g., Is 71 larger or smaller than 65?) and, conversely, became progressively shorter as the value of the numerals became more distant from 65 (e.g., Is 43 larger or smaller than 65?) (Dehaene, Dupoux, & Mehler, 1990). Similar results were found in more recent studies in which response times were measured for number comparisons in kindergartners (Temple & Posner, 1998), in second graders (Nuerk, Kaufmann, Zoppoth, & Willmes, 2004), and adults (Brannon, 2003).

These experiments lead to two conclusions:

- The speed with which we compare two numbers depends not just on the distance between them but on their size as well. It takes far longer to decide that 9 is larger than 8 than to decide that 2 is larger than 1. For numbers of equal distance apart, larger numbers are more difficult to compare than smaller ones.
- It takes much longer to decide on the larger of two numbers that are a small distance apart than to decide on the larger of two numbers that are a greater distance apart. It is easier to recognize that 74 is larger than 37 than to decide that 74 is larger than 73.

What can explain these findings? Researchers suggest that the brain comprehends each numeral and transforms it quickly into an internal quantity, ignoring the digit symbols representing that quantity. How easily the brain distinguishes two numbers depends not so much on their absolute numerical distance as their distance relative to their size. In other words, it appears that humans possess a mental number line, where we envision numbers as points on a line, with 1 on the left, 2 to its right, then 3, and so on. When we have to decide which of two numbers is larger, we mentally view them on our internal line and determine which one is on the right.

The mental number line is similar to the standard one we learn in elementary school, but with one important difference. On our mental number line, the numbers are not spaced out evenly as they are on the standard number line. Instead, the farther we go along the mental number line, the closer together the numbers appear to be. This explains the results of the number-comparison experiments described earlier. The increasing compression of numbers makes it more difficult to distinguish the larger of a pair of numbers as their value gets greater. We can decide which is the larger of 6 and 5 much faster than for the pair 65 and 64. Although both pairs have the same numerical difference of one, the larger pair appear closer together on our mental number line than do the smaller pair. As a result, the speed and accuracy with which we carry out calculations decrease as the numbers get larger. Figure 1.6 illustrates this phenomenon. (Incidentally, experiments with people whose native language is read from right to left, such as Arabic and Hebrew, possess mental number lines that also run from right to left. Apparently, our mental number line generally runs in the direction of our reading.)

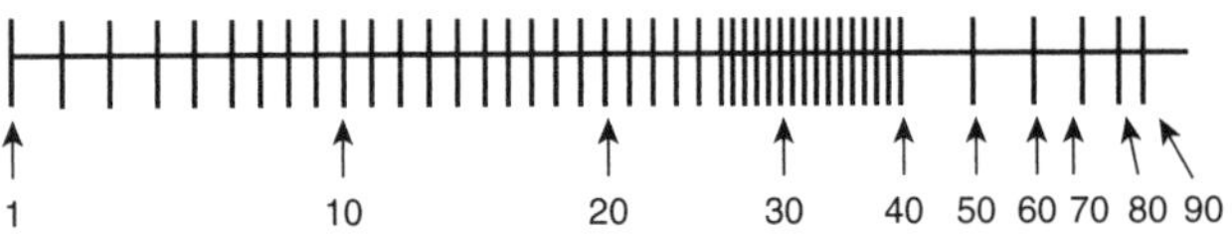

Figure 1.6 This illustration of the mental number line shows why the brain can decide that 10 is larger than 1 faster than it can decide that 80 is larger than 70.

Why are these findings important? The internal number line offers us a limited degree of intuition about numbers. It deals with only positive integers and their quantitative relationship to each other (there were no negative numbers in our ancestral environment). This probably explains why we have no intuition regarding other numbers that modern mathematicians use, such as negative integers, fractions, or irrational numbers. Yet all these entities posed significant challenges to the mathematicians of the past, and still present great difficulties to the students of today. These entities remain difficult for the average person because they do not correspond to any natural category in our brain. Small positive integers make such sense to our innate sense of numerosity that even four-year-olds can comprehend them. But the other entities make no such natural connection. To understand them, we have to construct mental models that provide understanding. Teachers do this when they discuss these topics. For example, when introducing negative numbers, teachers resort to metaphors such as money borrowed from a bank, temperatures below zero, or simply an extension of the number line to the left of zero.

> *The increasing compression of numbers on our mental number line makes it more difficult to distinguish the larger of a pair of numbers as their value gets greater. As a result, the speed and accuracy with which we carry out calculations decrease as the numbers get larger.*

Number Symbols Are Different From Number Words

One fascinating discovery about numerical symbols and number words is that the brain processes them in different locations. Brain imaging experiments and clinical case studies have convinced researchers that number symbols are hardwired in our intuitive number module in the left parietal

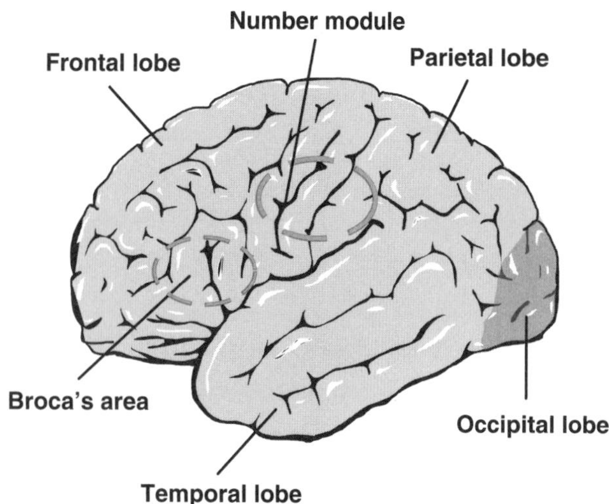

Figure 1.7 Broca's area in the left frontal lobe processes our language vocabulary, including number words. Number symbols, however, are hardwired in the number module located in the left parietal lobe.

lobe. Ordinary language number words, however, are stored in Broca's area, located in the left frontal lobe (Figure 1.7). Broca's area is where our language vocabulary is processed.

Clinical studies describe people who are unable to read words due to damage in Broca's area, but who can read aloud single or multi-digit numbers presented to them using numerals. Other patients with severe language impairments can hardly read or write, but do just fine on a standard arithmetic test if the questions are presented in a purely numerical form (Butterworth, 1999).

Our number system may indeed be a language, but it is a very special one that is handled in a different region of the brain from normal language. Devlin (2000) suggests that this separation of number symbols from number words is just what would be expected if our number symbols were derived from the use of our fingers (a parietal lobe process) and number words from ordinary language (a frontal lobe process).

The human brain comprehends numerals as quantities, not as words. This reflex action is deeply rooted in our brains and results in an immediate attribution of meaning to numbers.

The major implication here is that the human brain comprehends numerals as a quantity, not as words. Automatically and unconsciously, numerical symbols are converted almost instantly to an internal quantity. Moreover, the conversion includes an automatic orientation of numbers in space, small ones to the left and large ones to the right. Comprehending numbers, then, is a reflex action that is deeply rooted in our brains, resulting in an immediate attribution of meaning to numbers.

Expanded Notions of Number Sense

Mathematics educators have a much broader view of number sense than cognitive neuroscientists. We have already noted that cognitive neuroscientists view number sense as a biologically based innate quality that is limited to simple intuitions about quantity, including the rapid and accurate perception of small numerosities (subitizing), the ability to count, to compare numerical magnitudes, and to comprehend simple arithmetic operations. Dehaene (2001) is a major proponent of a single number sense—namely, the basic representation of quantity—rather than a patchwork of representations and abilities. He does suggest, however, that this core number sense becomes connected to other cognitive systems as a consequence of both cognitive development and education.

When Berch (2005) reviewed the literature in cognitive development, mathematics cognition, and mathematics education, he found that mathematics educators consider number sense to be much more complex and multifaceted in nature. They expand this concept to include skill sets that develop as a result of involvement with learning activities in mathematics. According to Berch, some of these abilities include

- Ability to recognize something has changed in a small collection when, without direct knowledge, an object has been removed or added to the collection
- Elementary abilities or intuitions about numbers and arithmetic
- A mental number line on which analog representations of numerical quantities can be manipulated
- An innate capacity to process approximate numerosities
- Ability to make numerical magnitude comparisons
- Ability to decompose numbers naturally
- Ability to develop useful strategies for solving complex problems
- Ability to use the relationships among arithmetic operations to understand the base-10 number system
- Ability to use numbers and quantitative methods to communicate, process, and interpret information
- Awareness of levels of accuracy and sensitivity for the reasonableness of calculations
- Desire to make sense of numerical situations by looking for links between new information and previously acquired knowledge
- Knowledge of the effects of operations on numbers
- Fluency and flexibility with numbers and understanding of number meanings
- Recognition of gross numerical errors
- Understanding of numbers as tools to measure things in the real world
- Inventing procedures for conducting numerical operations
- Thinking or talking in a sensible way about the general properties of a numerical problem or expression, without doing any precise computation

Portions of this more expansive view of number sense already appear

- as one of the five content standards of the National Council of Teachers of Mathematics *Principles and Standards for Mathematics* (NCTM, 2000),
- in contemporary mathematics textbooks, and
- as a distinct set of test items included in the mathematics portions of the National Assessment of Educational Progress (NAEP), the Trends in International Mathematics and Science Study (TIMSS), and the Program for International Student Assessment (PISA).

Can We Teach Number Sense?

Those who view number sense as an intrinsic ability will argue that the elementary components are genetically programmed, have a long evolutionary history, and develop spontaneously without explicit instruction as a young human interacts with the environment. However, most of these researchers do not view number sense as a fixed or immutable entity. Rather, they suggest that the neurocognitive systems supporting these elementary numerical abilities provide just the foundational structure needed for acquiring the expanded abilities cited by mathematics educators. And they recognize that both formal and informal instruction can enhance number sense development prior to entering school.

Berch (2005) notes that the abilities and skills associated with the expanded view of number sense cannot be isolated into special textbook chapters or instructional units, and that their development does not result from a set of activities designed specifically for this purpose. He agrees with those mathematics educators who contend that number sense constitutes a way of thinking that should permeate all aspects of mathematics teaching and learning. It may be more beneficial to view number sense as a by-product of other learning than as a specific goal of direct instruction.

Gersten and Chard (1999) suggest that the innate qualities of number sense may be similar to phonemic awareness in reading development, especially for early experiences in arithmetic. Just as phonemic awareness is a prerequisite to learning phonics and becoming a successful reader, developing number sense is a prerequisite for succeeding in mathematics. They further propose that number sense is the missing component in the learning of early arithmetic facts, and explain the reason that rote drill and practice do not lead to significant improvement in mathematics ability.

Just as phonemic awareness is a prerequisite to learning phonics and becoming a successful reader, developing number sense is a prerequisite for succeeding in mathematics.

Because Gersten and Chard (1999) believe that number sense is so critical to success in learning mathematics, they have identified five stepping-stones that allow teachers to assess a child's understanding of number sense. Their five levels are

- **Level 1.** Children have not yet developed number sense beyond their innate notions of numerosity. They have no sense of relative quantity and may not know the difference between "less than" and "more than" or "fewer" and "greater."
- **Level 2.** Children are starting to acquire number sense. They can understand terms like "lots of," "six," and "nine," and are beginning to understand the concepts of "less than" and "more than." They also understand lesser or greater amounts but do not yet have basic computation skills.
- **Level 3.** Children fully understand "less than" and "more than." They have a concept of computation and may use their fingers or objects to apply the "count up from one" strategy to solve problems. Errors occur when the child is calculating numbers higher than five, because this requires using the fingers of both hands.
- **Level 4.** Children are now relying on the "count up" or "counting on" process instead of the "counting all" process they used at the previous level. They understand the conceptual reality of numbers in that they do not have to count to five to know that five exists. Assuming they can count accurately, children at this level are able to solve any digit problem.
- **Level 5.** Children demonstrate retrieval strategies for solving problems. They have already automated addition facts and are acquiring basic subtraction facts.

Teaching Number Sense at All Grade Levels

Gurganus (2004) agrees that number sense is analogous to phonemic awareness. However, she takes the broader view and notes that, unlike phonemic awareness, number sense develops throughout a student's mathematics education and applies to a wide range of concepts. Here are her suggestions to teachers for promoting number sense across the grade levels.

✓ **Pair numbers with meaningful objects.** To help young students view numbers as values rather than labels, associate numbers with concrete objects. For example, there are two wheels on a bicycle, three wheels on a tricycle, and four wheels on a car.

✓ **Use language to gradually match numbers with objects and symbols.** Model using talk to create sentences about number activities so that students can use self-talk to describe these relationships. For instance, "Two blocks and three more blocks give us five blocks."

- ✓ **Incorporate counting activities.** Ask younger students to count to 10 and back. Challenge older students to count by 2s, 5s, 10s, and even 3s, 4s, or 7s. Counting up and back builds understanding of number relationships and magnitudes. Have students challenge each other to guess a counting pattern. For example: "500, 525, 550, 575—What is my pattern?"
- ✓ **Provide experiences with number lines.** Create a large number line across the classroom floor using colored tape (Figure 1.8). Have students move from number to number to show counting, operations, or even rounding. Draw number lines using whole numbers, integers, or decimals.

Figure 1.8 Different number lines placed on the floor of the classroom with tape can help students understand number relationships.

- ✓ **Plan meaningful estimation experiences**. Students need to recognize that many things cannot and need not be measured precisely. Provide lots of practice with estimation. Stress that estimation is not guessing but that there should be a reasonable range for the estimation based on experience. For example, "How many students do you think ate in the cafeteria today?"
- ✓ **Measure and then make measurement estimates.** Have students use measurement tools to measure length, area, volume, mass, temperature, and other attributes of meaningful things in their environment. Young students can start with measuring the teacher's desk or distances on the classroom floor. After some practice, ask students to estimate before they measure. This builds a stronger sense of measurement units and what they represent.
- ✓ **Use number charts.** Charts in different arrangements (e.g., 1 to 100) offer many opportunities for students to explore number patterns. Cover up specific numbers on the charts and challenge students to discover the underlying relationships of difficult concepts such as factors and primes.
- ✓ **Introduce materials that involve numbers or number representations.** Ask students to examine items such as dice, dominoes, playing cards, coins, clocks, and rulers. Ask them to search for ways they can adapt these items for counting, pattern making, number operations, and number comparisons.

✓ **Read literature that involves numbers.** Books such as *The Mud Flat Olympics,* by James Stevenson (1994), or *Anno's Counting Book,* by Anno Mitsumasa (1977), provide a different way to take a mathematical journey.

✓ **Create magic number squares.** Show students how to determine the missing numbers and have them create new squares to challenge their classmates (Figure 1.9).

	2	3	13
5		10	
	7		12
4			

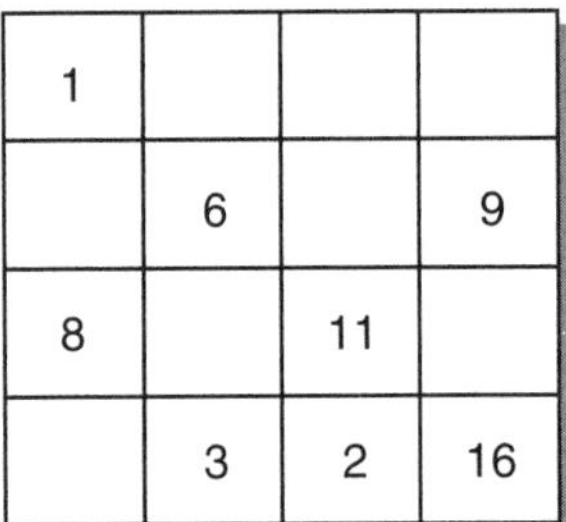

1			
	6		9
8		11	
	3	2	16

Figure 1.9 Number squares come in many different configurations and are enjoyable ways to learn addition. In these examples, rows, columns, and diagonals must add up to 34.

✓ **Manipulate different representations of the same quantity.** Model moving back and forth between decimals, fractions, and percentages (e.g., 0.25 = 1/4 = 25%). Point out the same length in millimeters, centimeters, and meters (e.g., 35 mm = 3.5 cm = 0.035 m).

✓ **Explore very large numbers and their representations.** Students love the sound of large numbers, like billion and trillion, but often have difficulty conceptualizing them. Use calculators to investigate the effects of squaring and other exponents. Where appropriate, express large numbers with scientific notation (e.g., 500,000 can be written as 5×10^5).

✓ **Collect and chart data.** At every grade level, students can collect meaningful data. Ask the students to use concrete objects whenever possible, such as counting each type of bean in a mixture or the number of marbles of each color in a collection. Also ask the students to examine the data using graphs, formulas, and other comparisons.

✓ **Compare number representations in other cultures.** Students can gain insights into number relationships by exploring how other cultures count, use symbols for numbers, and solve algorithms. Students often find these activities fascinating. They can read about gesture counting and the various symbols and systems that various cultures have used to represent numbers (see Zaslavsky, 2001).

✓ **Set up spreadsheets.** Commercial spreadsheets are a great way for teaching students how to encode formulas for cells that will compute and compare values within other cells. Ask "What if. . .?" questions and manipulate values within the spreadsheet.

✓ **Solve problems and consider the reasonableness of the solution.** Remind students that the last step in problem solving should be to ask, "Does this answer make sense?" Have them practice selecting solutions by estimation without actually working out the problems.

✓ **Find everyday, functional uses of numbers.** Explore every opportunity for students to see the practical applications of mathematics. For example, they could follow their favorite sports team's averages, track a company on the stock market, look for sales at the department store, or determine distances on a road map for the school field trip. Whenever possible, ask the students to graph, compare, predict, and discuss their data and measurements.

✓ **Explore unusual numbers.** Older students might find adventure in special numbers with intriguing patterns. Examples are Fibonacci and the golden ratio; abundant, perfect, and weird numbers; and number patterns that form palindromes.

✓ **Model the enjoyment of numbers and number patterns.** Research studies show repeatedly that the teacher is the most critical factor in establishing a climate for curiosity and enjoyment of mathematics. Keep learning and searching for new ways to have fun with numbers. The Internet is a valuable resource for number games. See the **Resources** section of this book.

More suggestions for teaching number sense to students in the primary grades will be found in Chapter 5.

Quantities to Words to Symbols

In an effort to describe how number sense emerges, researcher Sharon Griffin (2002) created a model showing that the development of number sense goes through three major phases. First, the visual processing system recognizes objects in a collection. For small collections, the numerosity can be determined quickly and without counting through our innate capacity to subitize. As the quantity of objects in a collection grows larger, we move to the second phase and create number words to communicate an exact count in our native language to others.

The third phase emerges when we realize that writing number words for large quantities is tedious and that they do not lend themselves to mathematical manipulation. Therefore, we create numerical symbols and operational signs. At the beginning, the flow from one stage to the next is linear. But with practice, all three phases interact whenever the brain performs mathematical operations (Figure 1.10).

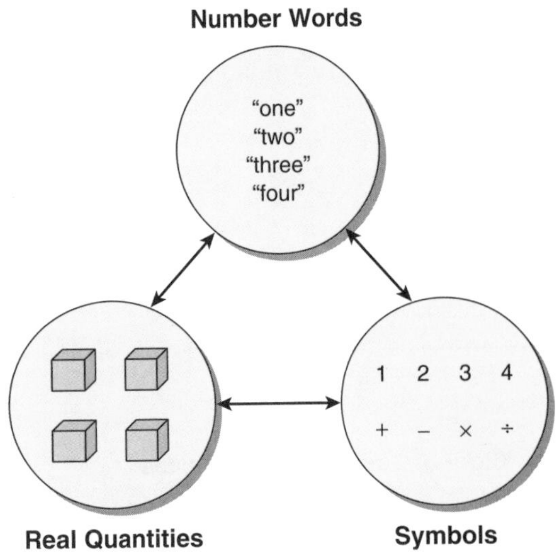

Figure 1.10 Researcher Sharon Griffin created a model that shows the development of number sense from recognizing real-world quantities to creating number words to describe those quantities and, finally, symbols and operational signs to represent and manipulate quantities. With practice, all three interact when the brain processes mathematical operations. (Adapted with permission from Griffin, 2002)

Gardner's Logical/Mathematical Intelligence

Many readers may be familiar with the theory proposed in 1983 by Howard Gardner of Harvard University that humans are born with a variety of capabilities that allow them to succeed in their environment. His idea—known as the theory of multiple intelligences—was that we possess at least seven (now up to 10) different intelligences. The original seven intelligences he proposed are musical, logical/mathematical, spatial, bodily/kinesthetic, linguistic, interpersonal, and intrapersonal. Soon after he added naturalist, and several years later spiritualist and emotionalist. Gardner defined intelligence as an individual's ability to use a learned skill, create products, or solve problems in a way that is valued by the society of that individual. This novel approach expanded our understanding of intelligence to include divergent thinking and interpersonal expertise. He further differentiated between the terms *intelligence* and *creativity*, and suggested that in everyday life people can display intelligent originality in any of the intelligences (Gardner, 1993).

This theory suggests that at the core of each intelligence is an information-processing system unique to that intelligence. The intelligence of an athlete is different from that of a musician or physicist. Gardner also suggests that each intelligence is a continuum and semiautonomous. A person who has abilities in athletics but who does poorly in music has enhanced athletic intelligence. The presence or absence of music capabilities exists separately from the individual's athletic prowess.

Is Logical/Mathematical Intelligence the Same As Number Sense?

According to Gardner, the logical/mathematical intelligence uses numbers, sequencing, and patterns to solve problems (Figure 1.11). Thus, it deals with the ability to think logically, systematically, inductively, and to some degree deductively. It also includes the ability to recognize both geometric and numerical patterns, and to see and work with abstract concepts. Students strong in this intelligence:

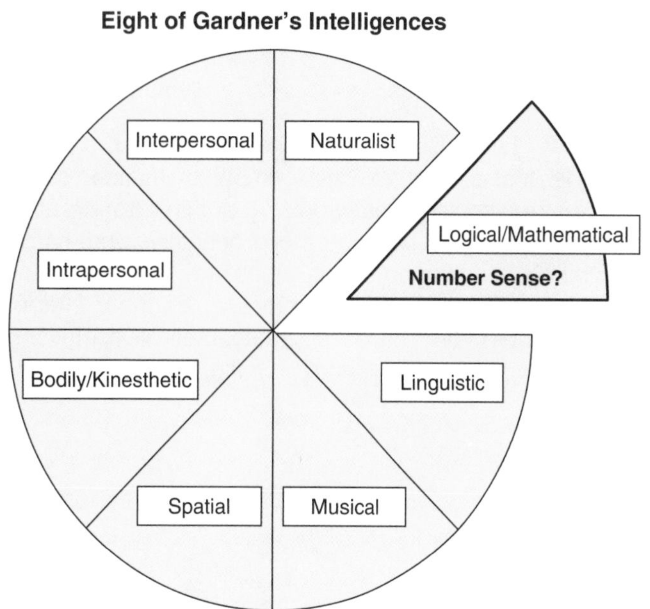

Figure 1.11 This chart shows eight of Gardner's ten intelligences (Gardner, 1993). Is it possible that the logical/mathematical intelligence is the same as number sense?

- Can easily compute numbers mentally
- Like to be organized
- Are very precise
- Have a systematic approach to problem solving
- Recognize numerical and geometric patterns
- Like computer games and puzzles
- Like to explore and experiment in a logical way
- Are able to move easily from the concrete to the abstract
- Think conceptually

Gardner made clear that intelligence is not just how a person thinks, but also includes the materials and the values of the situation where and when the thinking occurs. The availability of appropriate materials and the values of any particular culture will thus have a significant impact on the degree to which specific intelligences will be activated, developed, or discouraged. A person's combined intellectual capability, then, is the result of innate tendencies (the genetic contribution) and the society in which that individual develops (the environmental contribution).

Are there genes that enhance mathematical ability? Very likely. Studies of identical twins (they share the same genes) and fraternal twins (they share one-half of their genes) suggest how much a certain trait is inherited. Several studies over the past decades have found that identical twins usually exhibit similar levels of mathematical performance. In fraternal twins, however, one may be an excellent performer in mathematics while the other is just mediocre (Alarcón, Knopik, & DeFries, 2000).

Number sense, then, can be considered the innate beginnings of mathematical intelligence. But the extent to which it becomes an individual's major talent still rests with the type and strength of the genetic input and the environment in which the individual grows and learns.

We will discuss more about Gardner's theory and its application to classroom instruction in Chapters 3 and 7.

WHAT'S COMING?

Number sense provides students with a limited ability to subitize and determine the numerosity of small groups of objects. As the number of objects increases, the brain must resort to a more exact system of enumeration that we call counting. Simultaneously, the skills necessary to do exact addition and subtraction emerge. But as students need to manipulate larger and larger numbers, addition is no longer an efficient process. They must now learn to calculate through multiplication. Why is learning multiplication so difficult, even for adults? Are we teaching multiplication in the most effective way? Do we really even need to learn the multiplication tables? The answers to these and other interesting questions about how we learn to calculate are found in the next chapter.

Chapter 1 — Developing Number Sense

Reflections

Jot down on this page key points, ideas, strategies, and resources you want to consider later. This sheet is your personal journal summary and will help to jog your memory.

Chapter 2

Learning to Calculate

Mathematics possesses not only truth, but some supreme beauty—a beauty cold and austere, like that of sculpture.

—Bertrand Russell

Counting up to small quantities comes naturally to children. Either spontaneously or by imitating their peers, they begin to solve simple arithmetic problems based on counting, with or without words. Their first excursion into calculation occurs when they add two sets by counting them both on their fingers. Gradually they learn to add without using their fingers and, by the age of five, demonstrate an understanding of *commutativity* of addition (the rule that $a + b$ is always equal to $b + a$). But as calculations become more difficult, errors abound, even for adults. One thing is certain: The human brain has serious problems with calculations. Nothing in its evolution prepared it for the task of memorizing dozens of multiplication facts or for carrying out the multistep operations required for two-digit subtraction. Our ability to

> *Our ability to approximate numerical quantities may be embedded in our genes, but dealing with exact symbolic calculation can be an error-prone ordeal.*

approximate numerical quantities may be embedded in our genes, but dealing with exact symbolic calculation can be an error-prone ordeal.

DEVELOPMENT OF CONCEPTUAL STRUCTURES

Conceptual structures about numbers develop early and allow children to experiment with calculations in their preschool years. They quickly master many addition and subtraction strategies, carefully selecting those that are best suited to a particular problem. As they apply their algorithms, they mentally determine how much time it took them to make the calculation and the likelihood that the result is correct. Siegler (1989) studied children using these strategies, and he concluded that they compile detailed statistics on their success rate with each algorithm. Gradually, they revise their collection of strategies and retain those that are most appropriate for each numerical problem.

Here is a simple example. Ask a young boy to solve 9 – 3. You may hear him say, "nine . . . eight is one . . . seven is two . . . six is three . . . six!" In this instance, he counts backward starting from the larger number. Now ask him to calculate 9 – 6. Chances are that rather than counting backward as he did in the first problem, he will find a more efficient solution. He counts the number of steps it takes to go from the smaller number to the larger: "six . . . seven is one . . . eight is two . . . nine is three . . . three!" But how did the child know this? With practice, the child recognizes that if the number to be subtracted is not very close in value to the starting number, then it is more efficient to count backward from the larger number. Conversely, if the number to be subtracted is close in value to the starting number, then it is faster to count up from the smaller number. By spontaneously discovering and applying this strategy, the child realizes that it takes him the same number of steps, namely three, to calculate 9 – 3 and 9 – 6.

Exposure at home to activities involving arithmetic no doubt plays an important role in this process by offering children new algorithms and by providing them with a variety of rules for choosing the best strategy. In any case, the dynamic process of creating, refining, and selecting algorithms for basic arithmetic is established in most children before they reach kindergarten.

> *The dynamic process of creating, refining, and selecting algorithms for basic arithmetic is established in most children before they reach kindergarten.*

Exactly how number structures develop in young children is not completely understood. However, in recent years, research in cognitive neuroscience has yielded sufficient clues about brain development to the point that researchers have devised a timeline of how number structures evolve in the brain in the early years. Sharon Griffin

(2002) and her colleagues reviewed the research and developed tests that assessed large groups of children between the ages of 3 and 11 in their knowledge of numbers, units of time, and money denominations. As a result of the students' performance on these tests, they made some generalizations about the development of conceptual structures related to numbers in children within this age range. Their work is centered on several core assumptions about how the development of conceptual structures progresses. Three assumptions of particular relevance are as follows:

1. Major reorganization in children's thinking occurs around the age of five when cognitive structures that were created in earlier years are integrated into a hierarchy.
2. Important changes in cognitive structures occur about every two years during the development period. The ages of 4, 6, 8, and 10 are used in this model because they represent the midpoint of the development phases (ages 3 to 5, 5 to 7, 7 to 9, and 9 to 11).
3. This developmental progression is typical for about 60 percent of children in a modern, developed culture. Thus, about 20 percent of children will develop at a faster rate while about 20 percent will progress at a slower rate.

Structures in Four-Year-Olds

The innate capabilities of young children to subitize and do some simple finger counting enables them by the age of four to create two conceptual structures, one for *global quantity* differences and one for the *initial counting* of objects (Figure 2.1). Looking for global quantity, they can tell which of two stacks of chips is more or less, which of two time units is shorter or longer, and which of two monetary units is worth more or less. On a balance scale, they can tell which side is heavier and/or lighter and which side of the beam will go down. Children at this age are still relying more on subitizing than counting, but they do know that a set of objects will get bigger if one or more objects are added or smaller if one or more objects are removed.

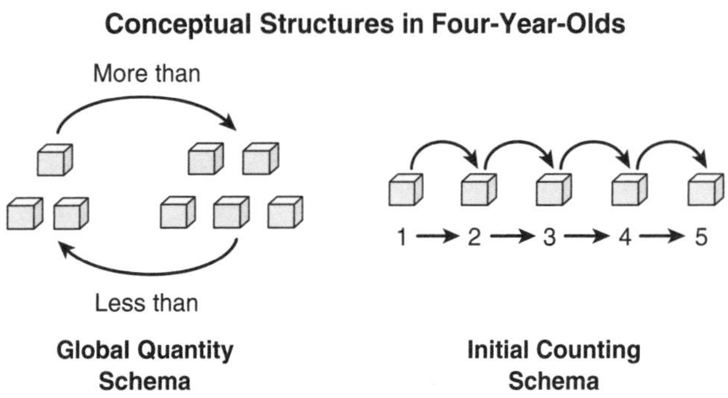

Figure 2.1 At the age of four, children have developed two major structures: one for global quantity that relies on subitizing and one for counting a small number of objects, mainly through one-to-one correspondence with fingers. (Adapted with permission from Griffin, 2002)

Counting skills are also developing. They know that each number word occurs in a fixed sequence and that each number word can be assigned to only one object in a collection.

They also know that the last number word said indicates the size of the collection. Most can count to five, and some can count to 10. Yet, despite these counting capabilities, these children still rely more on subitizing to make quantity determinations. This may be because the global quantity structure is stored in a different part of the brain from the counting structure and because these two regions have not yet made strong neural connections with each other.

Structures in Six-Year-Olds

Children around six years of age have integrated their global quantity and initial counting models into a larger structure representing the mental number line we discussed in Chapter 1. Because this advancement gives children a major tool for making sense of quantities in the real world, it is referred to as the *central conceptual structure for whole numbers.* Using this higher-order structure, children recognize that numbers higher up in the counting sequence indicate quantities that are larger than numbers lower down (Figure 2.2). Moreover, they realize that numbers themselves have magnitude, that is, that 7 is bigger than 5. The number line also allows them to do simple addition and subtraction without an actual set of objects just by counting forward or backward along the line. This developmental stage is a major turning point because children come to understand that mathematics is not just something that occurs out in the environment but can also occur inside their own heads.

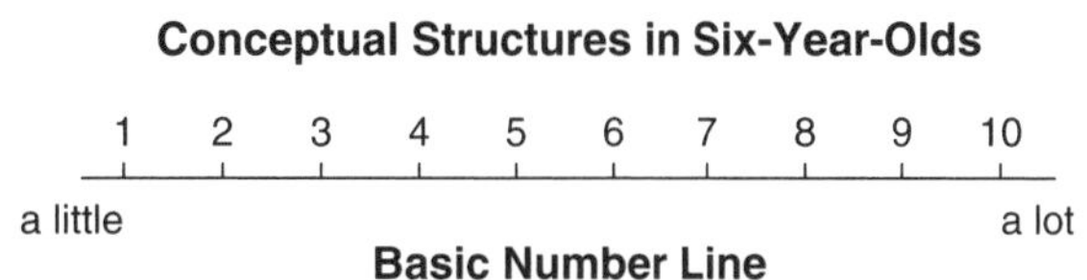

Figure 2.2 At the age of six years, children have developed a mental number line that gives them a central conceptual structure for whole numbers. (Adapted with permission from Griffin, 2002)

Now children begin using their counting skills in a broad range of new contexts. They realize that counting numbers can help them read the hour hand on a clock, determine which identical-sized money bill is worth the most, and know that a dime is worth more than a nickel even though it is smaller in size. Unlike four-year-olds, they rely more now on counting than global quantity in determining the number of objects, such as chips in a stack and weights on a balance.

Structures in Eight-Year-Olds

Children at the age of eight have differentiated their complex conceptual structure into a double mental counting line schema that allows them to represent two quantitative variables in a loosely coordinated fashion. Now they understand place value and can mentally solve double-digit addition problems and know which of two double-digit numbers is smaller or larger. The double number line structure also permits them to read the hours *and* minutes on a clock, to solve money problems that involve two monetary dimensions such as dollars *and* cents, and to solve balance-beam problems in which distance from the fulcrum as well as number of weights must be computed.

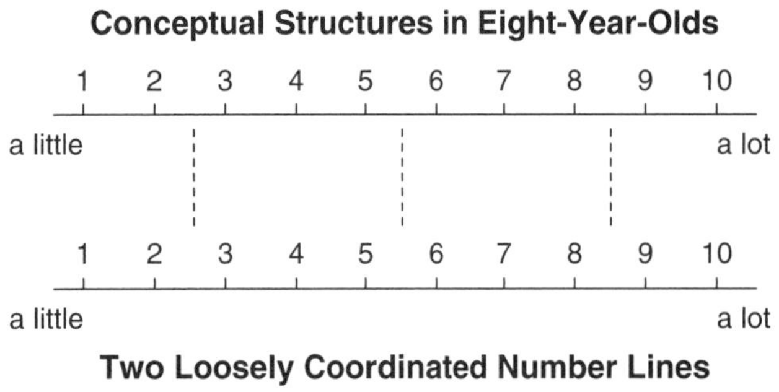

Conceptual Structures in Eight-Year-Olds
1 2 3 4 5 6 7 8 9 10
a little
a lot
1 2 3 4 5 6 7 8 9 10
a little
a lot
Two Loosely Coordinated Number Lines

Figure 2.3 By the age of eight, children can manipulate numbers along two number lines that are loosely coordinated. (Adapted with permission from Griffin, 2002)

Structures in Ten-Year-Olds

By the age of 10, children have expanded the double number line structure to handle two quantities in a well-coordinated fashion or to include a third quantitative variable. They now acquire a deeper understanding of the whole number system. Thus, they can perform mental computations with double-digit numbers that involve borrowing and carrying, and can solve problems involving triple-digit numbers. In effect, they can make compensations along one quantitative variable to allow for changes along the other variable. This new structure also allows them to translate from hours to minutes and determine which of two times, say three hours or 150 minutes, is longer. They find it easy to translate from one monetary dimension to another, such as from quarters to nickels and dimes, to determine who has more money, and also to solve balance-beam problems where the distance from the fulcrum and number of weights both vary.

Conceptual Structures in Ten-Year-Olds
1 2 3 4 5 6 7 8 9 10
a little
a lot
1 2 3 4 5 6 7 8 9 10
a little
a lot
Two Well Coordinated Number Lines

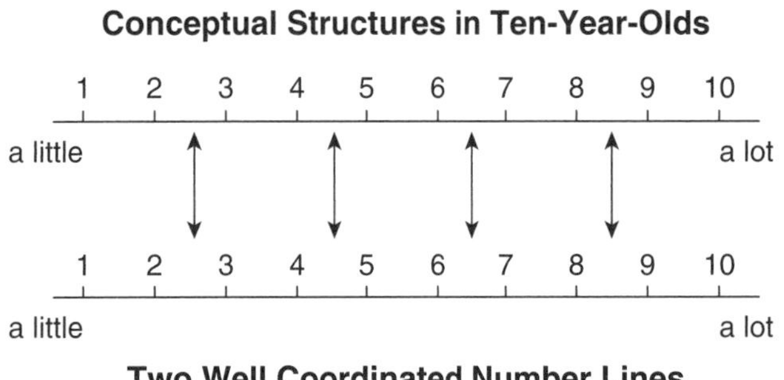

Figure 2.4 By the age of 10, children can manipulate numbers along two mental number lines that are well coordinated and thus can perform mental computations with double-digit numbers. (Adapted with permission from Griffin, 2002)

DEALING WITH MULTIPLICATION

Up to this point, we have been exploring how young children manipulate numbers using simple addition and subtraction. In school, they eventually encounter a process called multiplication, sometimes described by teachers as successive addition. However, the mental processes required to perform multiplication are more involved and somewhat different from the innate processes used for addition and subtraction. Imaging studies show that the brain recruits more neural networks during multiplication than during subtraction (Ischebeck et al., 2006). This should come as no surprise because addition and subtraction were sufficiently adequate to allow our ancestors to survive. As a result, humans need to devise learning tools to help them conquer multiplication.

Why Are Multiplication Tables Difficult to Learn?

Do you remember your first encounters with the multiplication tables as a primary student? Did you have an easy or difficult time memorizing them? How well do you know them today? Despite years of practice, most people have great difficulty with the multiplication tables. Ordinary adults of average intelligence make mistakes about 10 percent of the time. Even some of the single-digit multiplications, such as 8×7 and 9×7, can take up to two seconds, and have an error rate of 25 percent (Devlin, 2000). Why do we have such difficulty? Several factors contribute to our troubles with numbers. They include associative memory, pattern recognition, and language. Oddly enough, these are three of the most powerful and useful features of the human brain.

Multiplication and Memory

Until the late 1970s, psychologists thought that simple addition and multiplication problems were solved by a counting process carried out primarily by working memory. In 1978, Ashcraft (1995) and his colleagues began a series of experiments to test this notion with young adults. He found that most adults take about the same time to add or multiply two digits. However, it took increasingly longer to do these calculations as the digits got larger, even though the time remained the same for adding or multiplying. It took less than a second to determine the results of $2 + 3$ or 2×3, but about 1.3 seconds to solve $8 + 7$ or 8×7. If multiplication is being processed in working memory, shouldn't it take longer to multiply two digits than to add them, seeing that more counting is involved? After many experiments, Ashcraft proposed the only reasonable conclusion that was consistent with the experimental data: Solutions to the calculation problems were being retrieved from a memorized table stored in long-term memory. No counting or processing was occurring in working memory.

This effect is not that surprising for three reasons. First, we already noted in Chapter 1 that the accuracy of our mental representation of numerosity drops quickly with increasing number size. Second, the order in which we acquired arithmetic skills plays a role, because we tend to remember best that which comes first in a learning episode. When we began learning our arithmetic facts, we started with simple problems containing small digits, and the difficult problems with large digits came later. Third, because smaller digits appear more frequently in problems than larger ones, we most likely received much less practice with multiplication problems involving larger numbers.

Now, you may be saying: "So what's the big deal? We are using what we memorized in the early grades to solve arithmetic problems today. Isn't that normal?" It may be normal, but it is not natural. Preschool children use their innate but limited notions of numerosity to develop intuitive counting strategies that will help them understand and measure larger quantities. But they never get to continue following this intuitive process. When these children enter the primary grades, they encounter a sudden shift from their intuitive understanding of numerical quantities and counting strategies to the rote learning of arithmetic. Suddenly, progressing with calculations now means acquiring and storing in memory a large database of numerical knowledge, which may or may not have meaning. They also discover that some of the words they use in conversation take on different meanings when doing arithmetic. Many children persevere with this major upheaval in their mental arithmetic and language systems despite the difficulties. Unfortunately, most children also lose their intuition about arithmetic in the process.

Children in the primary grades encounter a sudden shift from their intuitive understanding of numerical quantities and counting strategies to the rote learning of arithmetic facts. Unfortunately, most children lose their intuition about arithmetic in the process.

Is the Way We Teach the Multiplication Tables Intuitive?

Not really. Through hours of practice, young children expend enormous amounts of neural energy laboring over memorizing the multiplication tables, encountering high rates of error and frustration. Yet this is happening at a same time when they can effortlessly acquire the pronunciation, meaning, and spelling of 10 new vocabulary words every day. They certainly do not have to recite their vocabulary words and their meanings over and over the way they do their multiplication tables. Furthermore, they remember the names of their friends, addresses, phone numbers, and book titles with hardly any trouble. Obviously, nothing is wrong with their memories, except when it comes to the multiplication tables. Why are they so difficult for children and adults to remember?

One answer is that the way we most often teach the multiplication tables is counterintuitive. Usually, we start with the one times table and work our way up to the ten times table. Taught step-by-step in this fashion results in 100 (10 × 10) separate facts to be memorized. But is this really the best way to teach them? Children have little difficulty remembering the one and ten times tables because they are consistent with their intuitive numbering scheme and base-10 finger manipulation strategy. Now that leaves 64 separate facts (each one of 2, 3, 4, 5, 6, 7, 8, 9, multiplied by each of 2, 3, 4, 5, 6, 7, 8, 9). But why memorize all 64 separate facts? We noted at the beginning of this chapter that children already recognize the commutativity of addition by age five. By simply showing them commutativity in multiplication (3 × 8 is the same as 8 × 3), we can cut the total number of 64 separate facts nearly in half, to just 36 (The number of four pairs of identical numbers, e.g., 2 × 2 or 5 × 5, cannot be reduced) . This is a more manageable number, but it still does not solve the problem.

Some critics say that students are just not putting in the effort to memorize their multiplication facts. Others wonder whether this endeavor is even necessary, given the prevalence of electronic calculators. But these ideas beg the question: Why do our ordinarily good memories have such difficulty with this task? There is something to be learned here about the nature of memory and the structure of the multiplication tables.

Patterns and Associations

The human brain is a five-star pattern recognizer. Human memory recall often works by association, that is, one thought triggers another in long-term memory. Someone mentions mother, and the associative areas in your brain's temporal lobes generate an image in your mind's eye. Long-term storage sites are activated, and you recall the first time she took you to the zoo. The limbic region in the brain sprinkles your memory with emotions. You were so excited then because you didn't realize that elephants were so wide or giraffes so tall. More connections are made, and you fondly remember the same excitement in your own children on their first zoo visit. The brain's ability to detect patterns and make associations is one of its greatest strengths, and is often referred to as *associative memory*. In fact, humans can recognize individuals without even looking at their faces. Through associative

> *Associative memory is a powerful and useful capability. Unfortunately, associative memory runs into problems in areas like the multiplication tables, where various pieces of information must be kept from interfering with each other.*

memory, they can quickly and accurately identify people they know from a distance by their walk, posture, voice, and body outline.

Associative memory is a powerful device that allows us to make connections between fragmented data. It permits us to take advantage of analogies and to apply knowledge learned in one situation to a new set of circumstances. Unfortunately, associative memory runs into problems in areas like the multiplication tables, where various pieces of information must be kept from interfering with each other.

Devlin (2000) points out that when it comes to the multiplication tables, associative memory can cause problems. That's because we remember the tables through language, causing different entries to interfere with each other. A computer has no problem detecting that $6 \times 9 = 54$, $7 \times 8 = 56$, and $8 \times 8 = 64$ are separate and distinct entities. On the other hand, the brain's strong pattern-seeking ability detects the rhythmic similarities of these entities when said aloud, thus making it difficult to keep these three expressions separate. As a result, the pattern 6×9 may activate a series of other patterns, including 45, 54, 56, and 58 and load them all into working memory, making it difficult to select the correct answer.

Likewise, Dehaene (1997) stresses the problems that come with memorizing addition and multiplication tables. He notes that arithmetic facts are not arbitrary and independent of each other. Rather, they are closely intertwined linguistically, resulting in misleading rhymes and confusing puns. The following example is similar to one Dehaene uses to illustrate how language can confuse rather than clarify.

Suppose you had to remember the following three names and addresses:

- Carl Dennis lives on Allen Brian Avenue
- Carl Gary lives on Brian Allen Avenue
- Gary Edward lives on Carl Edward Avenue

Learning these twisted combinations would certainly be a challenge. But these expressions are just the multiplication tables in disguise. Let the names Allen, Brian, Carl, Dennis, Edward, Frank, and Gary represent the digits 1, 2, 3, 4, 5, 6, and 7, respectively, and replace the phrase "lives on" with the equal sign. That yields three multiplications:

- $3 \times 4 = 12$
- $3 \times 7 = 21$
- $7 \times 5 = 35$

From this perspective, we can now understand why the multiplication tables present such difficulty when children first encounter them. Patterns interfere with each other and cause problems.

Pattern interference also makes it difficult for our memory to keep addition and multiplication facts separate. For example, it takes us longer to realize that $2 \times 3 = 5$ is wrong than to realize that $2 \times 3 = 7$ is false because the first result would be correct under addition. Back in 1990, studies by Miller (1990) were already revealing that learning multiplication facts interfered with addition. He discovered that students in third grade took more time to perform addition when they started learning the multiplication tables, and errors like $2 + 3 = 6$ began to appear. Subsequent studies confirm that the consolidation of addition and multiplication facts correctly into long-term memory continues to be a major challenge for most children.

Over millions of years, our brain has evolved to equip us with necessary survival skills. These include recognizing patterns, creating meaningful connections, and making rapid judgments and inferences, even with only a smattering of information. Rudimentary counting is easy because of our abilities to use language and to denote a one-to-one correspondence with finger manipulation. But our brains are not equipped to manipulate the arithmetic facts needed to do precise calculations, such as multiplication, because these operations were not essential to our species' survival. Studies of the brain using electroencephalographs (EEGs) show that simple numerical operations, such as number comparison, are localized in various regions of the brain. But multiplication tasks require the coordination of several widespread neural areas, indicating a greater number of cognitive operations are in play (Micheloyannis, Sakkalis, Vourkas, Stam, & Simos, 2005). Consequently, to do multiplication and precise calculations, we have to recruit mental circuits that developed for quite different reasons.

Our brains are not equipped to manipulate the arithmetic facts required for precise calculations. To do arithmetic, we need to recruit mental circuits that developed for different reasons.

The Impact of Language on Learning Multiplication

If memorizing arithmetic tables is so difficult, how does our brain eventually manage to do it? One of our strongest innate talents is the ability to acquire spoken language. We have specific brain regions in the frontal and temporal lobes that specialize in handling language. Faced with the challenge of memorizing arithmetic facts, our brain responds by recording them in verbal memory, a sizable and durable part of our language processing system. Most of us can still recall items in our verbal memory, such as poems and songs, that we learned many years ago.

Teachers have long recognized the power of language and verbal memory. They encourage students to memorize items such as rhymes and the multiplication tables by reciting them aloud. As a result, calculation becomes linked to the language in which it is learned. This is such a powerful connection that people who learn a second language generally continue to do arithmetic in their first language. No matter how fluent they are in the second language, switching back to their first language is much easier than relearning arithmetic from scratch in their second language.

Brain imaging studies carried out by Dehaene and his colleagues provided further proof that we use our language capabilities to do arithmetic. Their hypothesis was that exact arithmetic calculations involved the language regions of the brain because it required the verbal representations of number. Estimations requiring approximate answers, however, would not make use of the language facility (Dehaene et al., 1999).

The subjects of the experiments were adult English-Russian bilinguals who were taught two-digit addition facts in one of the two languages and were then tested. When both the teaching and the test question were in the same language, the subjects provided an exact answer in 2.5 to 4.5 seconds. If the languages were different, however, the subjects took a full second longer to provide the exact answer. Apparently, the subjects used that extra second to translate the question into the language in which the facts had been learned. When the question asked for an approximate answer, the language of the question did not affect the response time.

During the experiment, the researchers monitored the subjects' brain activity (Figure 2.6). Questions requiring exact answers primarily activated the same part of the left frontal lobe where language processing occurs. When the subjects responded to questions requiring approximate answers, the greatest activity was in the two parietal lobes, the regions that contain number sense and support spatial reasoning. Amazingly, these findings reveal that we humans are able to extend our intuitive number sense to a capacity to perform exact arithmetic by recruiting the language areas of our brain.

If you need more personal evidence of this connection between language and exact arithmetic, try multiplying a pair of two-digit numbers while reciting the alphabet aloud. You will find that this is quite difficult to do because speaking demands attention from the same language areas required for mental computation and reasoning.

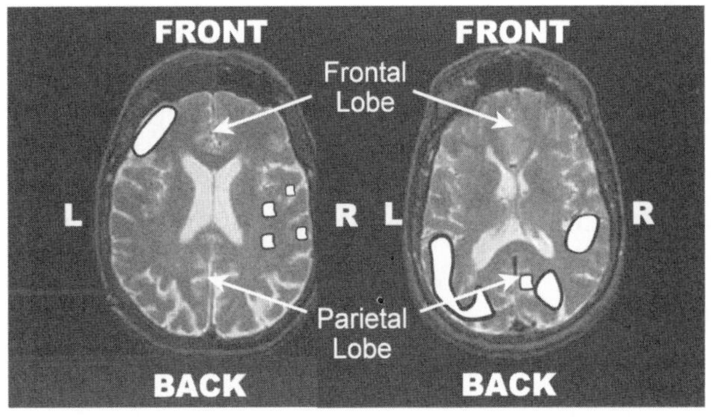

EXACT APPROXIMATE

Figure 2.6 These composite fMRI scans show that exact calculations (left image) primarily activate language areas in the left frontal lobe, where verbal representations of numbers are processed. During approximate calculations (right image), the greatest activation was in the two parietal lobes that house number sense and support spatial reasoning (Dehaene et al., 1999).

> *Because the language and number processing areas of the brain are separate, teachers should not assume that students with language problems will necessarily encounter difficulties with computation, and vice versa.*

Yet despite this seeming cooperation between the language and mathematical reasoning areas of the brain, it is still important to remember that these two cerebral areas are anatomically separate and distinct. Further proof of this separation comes from case studies showing that one area can function normally even when the other is damaged (Brannon, 2005). Teachers, then, should not assume that students who have difficulty with language processing will necessarily encounter difficulties in arithmetic computation, and vice versa.

Do the Multiplication Tables Help or Hinder?

They can do both. Remember that children come to primary school with a fairly developed, if somewhat limited, sense of number. Thanks to their brain's capacity to seek out patterns, they can already subitize, and they also have learned a pocketful of simple counting strategies through trial and error. Too often, as noted above, arithmetic instruction in the primary grades purposefully avoids recognizing these intuitive abilities and resorts immediately to practicing arithmetic facts.

If the children's introduction to arithmetic rests *primarily* on the rote memorization of the addition and multiplication tables and other arithmetic facts (e.g., step-by-step procedures for subtraction), then their intuitive understandings of number relationships are undermined and overwhelmed. In effect, they learn to shift from intuitive processing to performing automatic numerical operations without caring much about their meaning.

On the other hand, if instruction in beginning arithmetic takes advantage of the children's number sense, subitizing, and counting strategies by making connections to new mathematical operations, then the tables become tools leading to a deeper understanding of mathematics, rather than an end unto themselves.

Some students may have already practiced the multiplication tables at home. My suggestion would be to assess how well each student can already multiply single-digit numbers. Then introduce activities using dots or pictures on cards that help students practice successive addition (the underlying concept of multiplication). The idea here is to use the students' innate sense of patterning to build a multiplication network without memorizing the tables themselves. Of course, this may not work for every student, and for some, memorizing the tables may be the only successful option.

WHAT'S COMING?

People are born with a number sense that helps them to determine the numerosity of small collections of objects and to do rudimentary counting, addition, and subtraction. How can we take advantage of these intuitive skills to help them learn more complex mathematical operations? What is current research in cognitive neuroscience telling us about how the brain learns, and how should we use this information when considering effective instruction in mathematics? These are some of the questions that get answered in the next chapter.

Chapter 2 — Learning to Calculate

Reflections

Jot down on this page key points, ideas, strategies, and resources you want to consider later. This sheet is your personal journal summary and will help to jog your memory.

Chapter 3

Reviewing the Elements of Learning

A mathematician, like a painter or a poet, is a maker of patterns. If his patterns are more permanent than theirs, it is because they are made with ideas.

—Godfrey Harold Hardy

In the chapters following this one, we will look at specific ways to approach the teaching of mathematics to young children, preadolescents, and adolescents. Before doing that, however, we should review here some of the basic elements of learning. Effective teachers are continually assessing whether their choices in instructional strategies are consistent with what research is revealing about how the brain learns. This chapter will explore some recent research findings so that teachers can decide how this information compares with what they already know. Suggestions on applying this research when planning mathematics lessons are discussed in Chapter 8.

LEARNING AND REMEMBERING

I have asked teachers all over the world this question: "How long do you want your students to remember what you taught them?" Their answer is always: "Forever!" But is that what really happens? Hardly. Some critics of education have speculated that students in the United States forget over 80 percent of what they were taught in class within two years after they graduate from high school. We have no way of knowing if that figure is accurate, but most of us would agree that many of the facts presented to us in school were never permanently stored.

Because early research studies often used numbers to test the nature of memory, scientists have long known that both short-term and long-term memory can dramatically affect our mathematical capabilities. We will be discussing the effects of memory on calculations here and later in this book. If we want lessons to be remembered, this would be a good time to briefly review how the brain's memory components work.

Memory Systems

If you studied about memory a few decades ago, you were probably taught that humans have two major memories: a temporary memory called short-term memory and a permanent one called long-term memory. Neuroscientists now believe that we have two temporary memories that perform different tasks. It is a way of explaining how the brain deals briefly with some data but can continue to process other data for extended periods of time, even though that information does not get stored permanently. Short-term memory is the name used by cognitive neuroscientists to include the two stages of temporary memory: *immediate memory* and *working memory* (Squire & Kandel, 1999). Figure 3.1 illustrates the stages of our temporary and permanent memories.

Immediate Memory

Immediate memory is one of the two temporary memories and is represented in Figure 3.1 by a clipboard, a place where we put information briefly until we make a decision on how to dispose of it. Immediate memory operates subconsciously or consciously and holds data for up to about 30 seconds. (Note: The numbers used here are averages over time. There are always exceptions to these values as a result of human variations or pathologies.) The individual's experiences determine the degree of the information's importance. If the information is of little or no importance within this time frame, it drops out of the temporary memory system. For example, when you look up the telephone number of the local pizza parlor, you usually can remember it just long enough to make the call. After that, the number is of no further importance and drops out of immediate memory. The next time you call, you will have to look up the number again.

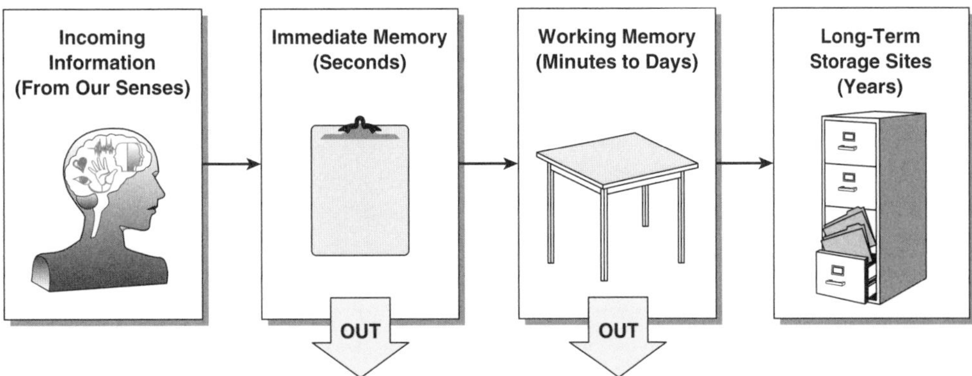

Figure 3.1 The diagram illustrates the theory of temporary and permanent memories. Information gathered from our senses lasts only a few seconds in immediate memory. Information in working memory usually endures for minutes or hours, but can be retained for days if necessary. The long-term storage sites (also called permanent memory) store information for years.

Working Memory

Suppose, on the other hand, you can't decide whether to call the pizza parlor or the Chinese take-out place, and you discuss these options with someone else in the room. Because this situation requires more of your attention, information is shifted into working memory for full conscious processing. In Figure 3.1, working memory is shown as a work table, a place of limited capacity where we can build, take apart, or rework ideas for eventual disposal or storage somewhere else. When something is in working memory, it generally captures our focus and demands our attention.

Capacity of Working Memory. Working memory can handle only a few items at one time (Table 3.1). This functional capacity changes with age. Preschool toddlers can deal with about two items of information at once. Preadolescents can handle three to seven items, with an average of five. Through adolescence, further cognitive maturation occurs, and the capacity increases to a range of five to nine, with an average of seven. For most people, that number remains constant throughout life. (You may recall from Chapter 1, however, that working memory's capacity for *digits* can vary from one culture to another, depending on that culture's linguistic and grammatical system for building number words.)

This limited capacity explains why we have to memorize a song or a poem in stages. We start with the first group of lines by repeating them frequently (a process called *rehearsal*). Then we memorize the next lines and repeat them with the first group, and so on. It is possible to increase the number of items within the functional capacity of working memory through a process called

Table 3.1 Changes in Capacity and Time Limits of Working Memory With Age

Age (in years)	Average Capacity and Range (in chunks)	Average Time Limit (in minutes)
Younger Than 5	2 ± 1	No reliable data
Between 5 and 14	5 ± 2	5 to 10
14 and Older	7 ± 2	10 to 20

chunking. In arithmetic, chunking occurs when the young child's mind quickly recognizes that both 3 + 1 + 1 and 3 + 2 equal 5.

The implication of these findings is that teachers should consider these limits when deciding on the amount of information they plan to present in a lesson. In other words, less is more.

Time Limits of Working Memory. Working memory is a temporary memory and can deal with items for only a limited time (Table 3.1). For preadolescents, that time is more likely to be 5 to 10 minutes and, for adolescents and adults, 10 to 20 minutes. These are average times, and it is important to understand what the numbers mean. An adolescent (or adult) normally can process an item in working memory intently for 10 to 20 minutes before fatigue or boredom with that item occurs and the individual's focus drifts. For focus to continue, there must be some *change* in the way the individual is dealing with the item. As an example, the person may switch from listening about a concept to physically applying it or talking to someone else about it or making connections to other learnings. If something else is not done with the item, it is likely to fade from working memory.

Of course, some items can remain in working memory for hours or even days. Sometimes, we have an item that remains unresolved—a question whose answer we seek or a troublesome family or work decision that must be made. These items can remain in working memory, continually commanding some attention and, if of sufficient importance, interfering with our accurate processing of other information. Eventually, we solve the problem, and it clears out of working memory.

> *Working memory has capacity limits and time limits that teachers should keep in mind when planning lessons. Less is more! Shorter is better!*

The implication here is that teachers should consider these working memory time limits when deciding on the flow of their lessons. In other words, shorter is better.

Rehearsal Enhances Memory

Teachers should ensure that they have included instructional strategies *purposefully* designed to increase the probability that students will retain the new learning. Any new learning is more likely to be retained if the learner has adequate time to process and reprocess it. This continuing reprocessing of information is called *rehearsal,* and it is a critical component in the transference of information from working memory to long-term storage.

Types of Rehearsal

Time for Initial and Secondary Rehearsal. Time is a critical component of rehearsal. Initial rehearsal occurs when the information first enters working memory. If the learner cannot attach sense or meaning and if there is no time for further processing, then the new information is likely to be lost. Providing sufficient time to go beyond the initial processing to secondary rehearsal allows the learner to review the information, to make sense of it, to elaborate on the details, and to assign value and relevance, thus increasing significantly the chance of retention.

Brain imaging studies indicate that the frontal lobe is very much involved during the rehearsal process and, ultimately, in long-term memory formation. This makes sense because working memory is also located in the frontal lobe (Goldberg, 2001). Several studies using fMRI scans of humans showed that during longer rehearsals the amount of activity in the frontal lobe determined whether items were stored or forgotten (Buckner, Kelley, & Petersen, 1999; Wagner et al., 1998).

Rote and Elaborative Rehearsal. *Rote rehearsal* is used when the learner needs to remember and store information exactly as it is entered into working memory. This is not a complex strategy, but it is necessary to learn information or a cognitive skill in a specific form or an exact sequence. We use rote rehearsal to remember a poem, the lyrics and melody of a song, telephone numbers, steps in a procedure, and the multiplication tables. *Elaborative rehearsal* is used when it is not necessary to store information exactly as learned but when it is more important to associate the new learnings with prior learnings to detect relationships. This is a more complex thinking process in that the learner reprocesses the information several times to make connections to previous learnings and assign meaning. Students use rote rehearsal to memorize mathematical facts, but elaborative rehearsal to probe the deeper meanings and interrelationships of mathematical concepts.

When students get very little time for, or training in, elaborative rehearsal, they resort more frequently to rote rehearsal for nearly all processing. Consequently, they fail to make the associations or discover the relationships that only elaborative rehearsal can provide.

For example, suppose a teacher presents a lesson on dividing by a fraction this way:

$$15 \div \tfrac{1}{4} = 15 \times \tfrac{4}{1} = 60$$

Instead of exploring and understanding the mathematical rationale used when dividing by a fraction, they simply remember the rote rule: "Ours is not to reason why, just invert and multiply!" Furthermore, they continue to believe that learning mathematics is merely the recalling of information as learned rather than its value for generating new ideas, concepts, and solutions. By simply adding a visual representation of a situation that is relevant to students, greater meaning can be obtained. For instance, in this lesson the teacher could say we have 15 pizzas and we cut (divide) each of them into fourths. How many pieces will we have? The visual of each pizza cut into four pieces helps students recognize the *meaning* of dividing by a fraction.

⊗ ⊗ ⊗ ⊗ ⊗ ⊗ ⊗ ⊗ ⊗ ⊗ ⊗ ⊗ ⊗ ⊗ ⊗

By cutting each of the 15 pizzas into fourths, we have 60 pieces.

Rote rehearsal is valuable for certain limited learning objectives. Nearly all of us learned the alphabet and the addition and multiplication tables through rote rehearsal. But rote rehearsal simply allows us to acquire information in a certain sequence. Too often, students use rote rehearsal to memorize important mathematical terms and facts in a lesson, but are unable to use the information to solve problems. They will probably do fine on a true-false or fill-in-the-blank test. But they will find difficulty answering higher-order questions that require them to apply their knowledge to new situations, especially those that have more than one solution. Keep in mind, too, that rehearsal only contributes to, but does not guarantee that information will transfer into, long-term storage. However, there is almost no transfer to long-term memory without rehearsal.

The Importance of Meaning

Both experimental and anecdotal evidence reveals that mathematical content often does not have meaning for students. And why is meaning so important? We noted earlier that rehearsal is one way to increase the possibility that new learning will be stored in long-term memory. Other criteria also play a crucial role. Figure 3.1 shows that information in working memory can be either encoded into long-term memory sites for future recall (from the work table to the file cabinet) or dropped out of the memory system. Which option will the brain choose? This is an important decision because we cannot later recall what we have not stored.

> *Information is most likely to get stored if it makes sense and has meaning.*

What criteria does the working memory use to make that decision? Information that has survival value is quickly stored, along with strong emotional experiences. But in classrooms, where the survival and emotional elements are minimal or absent, other factors come into play. It seems that the working memory connects with the learner's past experiences and asks just two questions to determine whether an item is saved or rejected. They are

- "Does this make sense?" This question refers to whether the learner can understand the mathematical content on the basis of experience. Does it "fit" into what the learner already knows about numbers and arithmetic operations? When a student says, "I don't understand," it means the student is having a problem making sense of the learning, usually because it doesn't connect to previous learning.
- "Does it have meaning?" This question refers to whether the item is relevant to the learner. For what purpose should the learner remember it? Meaning is a very personal thing and is greatly influenced by an individual's experiences. The same item can have great meaning for one student and none for another. Questions like "Why do I have to know this?" or "When will I ever use this?" indicate that the student has not, for whatever reason, accepted this learning as relevant.

The goal of learning is not just to acquire knowledge but to be able to use that knowledge in a variety of different settings that students see as relevant. To do this, students need a deeper understanding of the concepts involved in the learning. That's one reason mathematics teachers so often hear students asking, "Why do we need to know this?" If teachers cannot answer that question in a way that is meaningful to students, then we need to rethink why we are teaching that item at all.

> *If teachers cannot answer the question, "Why do we need to know this?" in a way that is meaningful to students, then we need to rethink why we are teaching that item at all.*

Whenever the learner's working memory decides that an item does not make sense or have meaning, the probability of its being stored is extremely low (assuming, of course, no survival or emotional component is present). If either sense or meaning is present, the probability of storage increases significantly. If both sense and meaning are present, the likelihood of long-term storage is very high. Brain scans have shown that when new learning is readily comprehensible (sense) and can be connected to past experiences (meaning), there is substantially more cerebral activity followed by dramatically improved retention (Maquire, Frith, & Morris, 1999).

Why Meaning Is So Significant

Of the two criteria, meaning has the greater impact on the probability that information will be stored. Think of all the television programs you have watched that are *not* stored, even though you spent one or two hours viewing the program. The show's content or story line made sense to you, but if meaning was absent, you just did not save it. Now think of this process when teaching mathematics. Students may diligently follow the teacher's instructions to memorize facts or perform a sequence of tasks repeatedly, and may even get the correct answers. But if they have not found meaning by the end of the learning episode, there is little likelihood of long-term storage. Mathematics teachers are often frustrated by this. They see students using a certain formula to solve problems correctly one day, but they cannot remember how to do it the next day. If the process was not stored, the brain treats the information as brand-new again!

Sometimes, when students ask why they need to know something, the teacher's response is, "Because it's going to be on the test." This response may raise the student's anxiety level but adds little meaning to the learning. Students resort to writing the learning in a notebook so that it is preserved in writing, but not in memory. Then we wonder the next day why they forgot the lesson.

Mathematics teachers get frustrated when they see students using a certain formula to solve problems correctly one day, but they cannot remember how to do it the next day. If the process was not stored, the brain treats the information as brand-new again!

Teachers spend about 90 percent of their planning time devising lessons so that students will make sense of the learning objective. But teachers need to spend more time helping students establish meaning, keeping in mind that what was meaningful for students 10 years ago may not be necessarily meaningful for students today (Sousa, 2006).

Meaning Versus Automatic Response

We have already noted that evolution did not prepare our brains for multiplication tables, complicated algorithms, fractions, or any other formal mathematical operation. So to carry out formal arithmetic, our brain has to make do with whatever networks it has, even if it means following a sequence of steps that its owner does not understand. The result is that as children spend their time memorizing arithmetic tables and facts, they become little calculators who can compute without having any idea of the underlying arithmetic principles involved.

> *Our development as a species did not prepare the brain for multiplication tables, complicated algorithms, or any other formal mathematical operations.*

When students attempt to carry out simple arithmetic computations using memorized facts, they often jump to conclusions without considering the relevant conditions of the problem. They become so skilled at the mechanics of computation that they arrive at answers that do not make sense. Furthermore, the language associated with solving a particular problem may itself interfere with the brain's understanding of what it is being asked to compute. For example, quickly answer the following questions:

- An aquarium contains 9 fish. All but 6 die. How many fish remain?
- Billy has 6 action figures, which is 3 fewer than Joey. How many action figures does Joey have?

Did you answer 3 to any of the problems? In the first problem, the presence of the numbers 9 and 6 coupled with words "all but," and "How many remain?" create a strong temptation to perform the subtraction 9 – 6 = 3, giving the answer as 3. The correct answer is 6, but to get that answer you have to think about what the problem is saying and avoid the blind manipulation of symbols. Similarly in the second problem, seeing the numbers 6 and 3, along with the words "fewer than," is sufficient to trigger the subtraction mode in your brain: 6 – 3 = 3. When you think about the problem, however, you realize that you should add 3 to 6 to get the correct answer that Joey has 9 action figures.

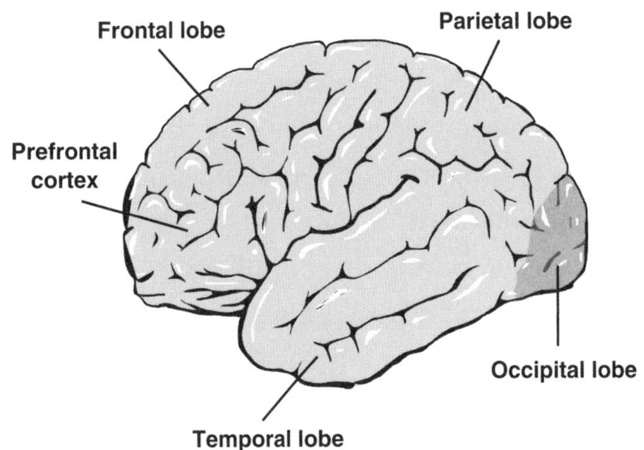

Figure 3.2 The prefrontal cortex is the part of the frontal lobe that, among other things, analyzes problems and implements and controls nonroutine strategies.

In both situations, you have to fight the automatic response and actually analyze each problem. This is the job of the front area of the brain's frontal lobe, just behind the forehead, called the *prefrontal cortex* (Figure 3.2).

However, the prefrontal cortex develops very slowly and is not fully mature until the age of 22 to 24. Thus, children and adolescents are prone to impulsive decisions while solving problems. Their prefrontal cortex areas have not had much opportunity in school to construct the nonroutine strategies needed to override the automated responses and avoid the arithmetic traps that word problems can harbor. For students to become proficient in mathematical computation, they must resist the automated and meaningless responses and proceed to thoughtfully analyze the situation and select the appropriate calculation algorithm for the problem at hand.

Teachers, then, become the means by which learners can see the links between a mechanical calculation and its meaning. While we recognize the need for learners to remember some basic arithmetic facts, memorization should not be the main component of instruction, and it should not be at the expense of exploring the underlying principles of mathematical operations. Doing so erodes the learner's intuitive understanding of approximation and counting, as discussed in Chapter 2. Students then see arithmetic solely as the memorization of mechanical recipes that have no practical applications and no obvious meaning. Such a view can be discouraging, lead to failure, and set the stage for a lifelong distaste for mathematics.

How Will the Learning Be Stored?

Information can be stored in different ways. Long-term memory can be divided into two major types, *declarative memory* and *nondeclarative memory* (Figure 3.3).

Declarative memory (also called *conscious* or *explicit* memory) describes the remembering of names, facts, music, and objects. When you think of an important event you attended with someone close to you, such as a concert, wedding, or funeral, note how easily other components of the memory come together. This is declarative memory in its most common form—a conscious and almost effortless recall. Declarative memory can be further divided into *episodic memory* and *semantic memory*.

Episodic memory refers to the conscious memory of events in our own life history, such as our sixteenth birthday party, falling off a bicycle, or what we had for breakfast this morning. It helps us identify the time and place when an event happened and gives us a sense of self. Episodic memory is the memory of personal and autobiographical *remembering*.

Semantic memory is knowledge of facts and data that may not be related to any event. It is knowing that the Eiffel Tower is in Paris, how to tell time, and the quadratic formula. Semantic memory is the memory of factual *knowing*. A student later recalling the Pythagorean theorem is using semantic memory; remembering his experiences in the classroom when he learned it is episodic memory.

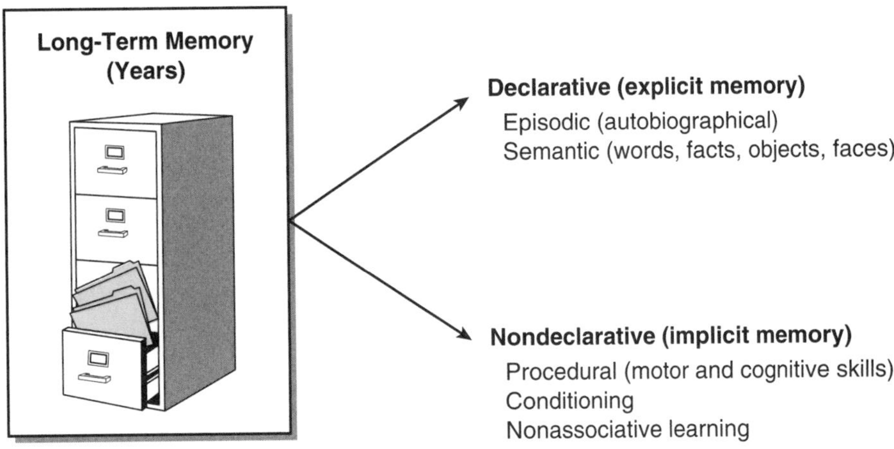

Figure 3.3 Long-term memory consists of two major types. Declarative memory is our daily recollections of people we know, our vocabulary, and related information. Nondeclarative memory is largely composed of automated procedures, such as driving a car or multiplying a pair of three-digit numbers.

Declarative memory is greatly enhanced by elaborative rehearsal because our memory of facts, people, and events is preserved best when we can make connections between and among them. This comes through elaborative discussions, new ways of looking at things, analysis of situations, and a deep understanding of why we made specific decisions and behaved in certain ways. The more connections we make through these creative and analytical processes, the stronger and longer-lasting the memory is likely to be. Could this have application for how we teach mathematics?

Nondeclarative memory. Nondeclarative memory (also called *implicit* memory) describes all memories that are *not* declarative memories, that is, they are memories that can be used for things that cannot be declared or explained in any straightforward manner. Of particular interest to teachers of mathematics is the type of nondeclarative memory called *procedural memory.*

> *Procedural memory helps us to learn things that don't require conscious attention, such as how to perform rote mathematical operations.*

Procedural memory refers to the learning of motor and cognitive skills, and remembering *how* to do something, like riding a bicycle, driving a car, and tying a shoelace. As practice of the skills continues, these memories become more efficient and can be performed with little conscious thought or recall. The brain process shifts from *reflective* to *reflexive*. Much of what we do during the course of a day—such as breakfast rituals, getting to work, and shaking the hand of a new acquaintance— involves the performance of skills. We do these tasks without being aware that we are using our memory. Although learning a new skill involves conscious attention, skill performance later becomes unconscious and relies essentially on nondeclarative memory.

The more arithmetic we can teach through declarative processes involving understanding and meaning, the more likely children will succeed and actually enjoy mathematics.

We also learn *cognitive skills*, such as reading, discriminating colors, and figuring out a *procedure* for solving a problem. Cognitive *skills*, such as performing rote mathematical operations, are different from processing cognitive *concepts* in that cognitive skills are performed automatically and rely on procedural memory rather than declarative memory. Procedural and cognitive skill acquisition involves some different brain processes and memory sites from cognitive concept learning. If they are learned differently, should they be taught differently?

Procedural memory is enhanced by the repetition of rote rehearsal. In fact, that is the only way we can retain certain information, such as remembering vocabulary words or how to add a column of numbers. Because following a step-by-step procedure usually gives us the desired outcome, we can carry out the steps without much conscious input and without having a clue as to *why* we are doing them.

Brain imaging studies indicate that procedural and declarative memories are stored in different regions of the brain, and declarative memory can be lost while procedural memory is spared (Rose, 2005). Such division of memory locations makes sense. Declarative memory requires conscious input and processing, so frontal lobe areas are actively involved. Procedural memory, on the other hand, triggers a set of automatic steps that are usually without conscious processing or frontal lobe input. This explains why you can drive your car to work (procedural memory) while your frontal lobe is simultaneously planning your day (declarative memory).

When Should New Learning Be Presented in a Lesson?

When an individual is processing new information, the amount of information retained depends, among other things, on *when* it is presented during the learning episode. At certain time intervals during the learning, we will remember more than at other intervals.

Primacy-Recency Effect

In a learning episode, we tend to remember best that which comes first, and remember second best that which comes last. We remember least that which comes just past the middle of the episode. This common phenomenon is referred to as the *primacy-recency effect* (also known as the *serial position effect*). This is not a new discovery. The first studies on this effect were published in the 1880s.

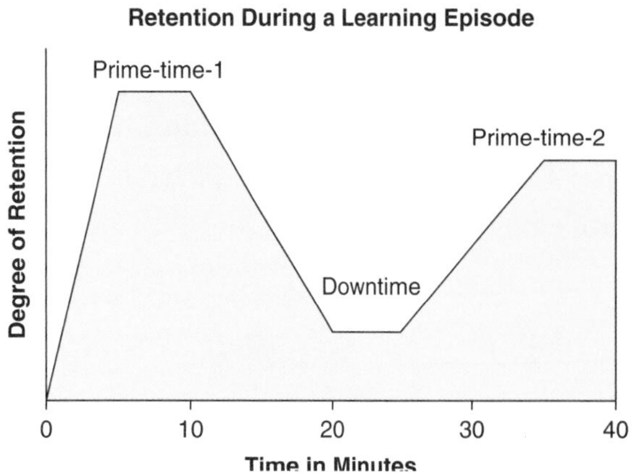

Figure 3.4 The degree of retention varies during a learning episode. We remember best that which comes first (prime-time-1) and last (prime-time-2). We remember least that which comes just past the middle.

More recent studies help to explain why this is so. The first items of new information are within the working memory's capacity limits so they command our attention and are likely to be retained in semantic memory. The later information, however, exceeds the capacity shown in Table 3.1 and is lost. As the learning episode concludes, items in working memory are sorted or chunked to allow for additional processing of the arriving final items, which are likely held in working memory and will decay unless further rehearsed (Gazzanniga, Ivry, & Mangun, 2002; Terry, 2005).

Figure 3.4 shows how the primacy-recency effect influences retention during a 40-minute learning episode. The times are averages and approximate. Note that it is a bimodal curve, each mode representing the degree of greatest retention during that time period. In my own work, I refer to the first or primacy mode as *prime-time-1,* and the second or recency mode as *prime-time-2.* Between these two modes is the time period in which retention during the lesson is least. I call that area the *downtime.* This is not a time when no retention takes place, but a time when it is more difficult for retention to occur.

During a learning episode, we remember best that which comes first, second best that which comes last, and least that which comes just past the middle.

Does Practice Make Perfect?

Practice refers to learners repeating a motor or cognitive skill over time. It begins with the rehearsal of the new skill in working memory. Later, the skill memory is recalled, and additional practice follows. The quality of the practice and the learner's knowledge base will largely determine the outcome of each practice session.

The old adage that "practice makes perfect" is rarely true. It is very possible to practice the same skill repeatedly with no increase in achievement or accuracy of application. Think of the people you know who have been driving, cooking, or even teaching for many years with no improvement in their skills. Why is this? How is it possible for one to continually practice a skill with no resulting improvement in performance?

Conditions for Successful Practice

For practice to *improve* performance, four conditions must be met (Hunter, 2004):

1. The learner must be sufficiently motivated to *want* to improve performance. If the learner has not attached meaning to the topic, then motivation is low.
2. The learner must have all the knowledge necessary to understand the different ways that the new knowledge or skill can be applied.
3. The learner must understand how to apply the new knowledge to deal with a particular situation.
4. The learner must be able to analyze the results of that application and know what needs to be changed to improve performance in the future.

Guided Practice, Independent Practice, and Feedback

Practice may not make perfect, but it does make permanent, thereby aiding in the retention of learning. Consequently, we want to ensure that students practice the new learning correctly from the beginning. This early practice that is done in the presence of the teacher (referred to as *guided practice*), who can now offer immediate and corrective feedback to help students analyze and improve their practice. When the practice is correct, the teacher can then assign *independent practice* (usually homework) in which the students can rehearse the skill on their own to enhance retention. This strategy leads to perfect practice, and, as coach Vince Lombardi once said, "Perfect practice makes perfect."

> *Practice does not make perfect.*
> *Practice makes permanent.*

Teachers should avoid giving students independent practice before guided practice. Because practice makes permanent, allowing students to rehearse a mathematical operation for the first time while away from the teacher is very

> *Giving students independent practice before guided practice can help them learn an incorrect procedure well.*

risky. If they unknowingly practice the skill or procedure incorrectly, then they will learn the incorrect method well! This will present serious problems for both the teacher and learner later on because it is very difficult to change a skill that has been practiced and remembered, even if it is not correct. Furthermore, the student gets frustrated and annoyed at having spent personal time outside of school practicing a skill incorrectly and loses the motivation to learn the process correctly. This frequent occurrence contributes to unfavorable attitudes toward mathematics.

Unlearning and Relearning a Skill or Process. If a learner practices a mathematical process incorrectly but well, unlearning and relearning that process correctly is very difficult. The degree to which the unlearning and relearning processes are successful will depend on the

- Age of the learner (i.e., the younger, the easier to relearn)
- Length of time the skill has been practiced incorrectly (i.e., the longer, the more difficult to change)
- Degree of motivation to relearn (i.e., the greater the desire for change, the more effort that will be used to bring about the change).

In any event, both teacher and student have a difficult road ahead to unlearn the incorrect method and relearn it correctly.

Massed and Distributed Practice

Hunter (2004) suggested that teachers use two different types of practice over time. (Hunter uses practice to include rehearsal.) Practicing a new learning during time periods that are very close together is called *massed practice* (Figure 3.5). This produces fast learning, as when one mentally rehearses a multiplication table. Immediate memory is involved here, and the information can fade in seconds if it is not rehearsed quickly.

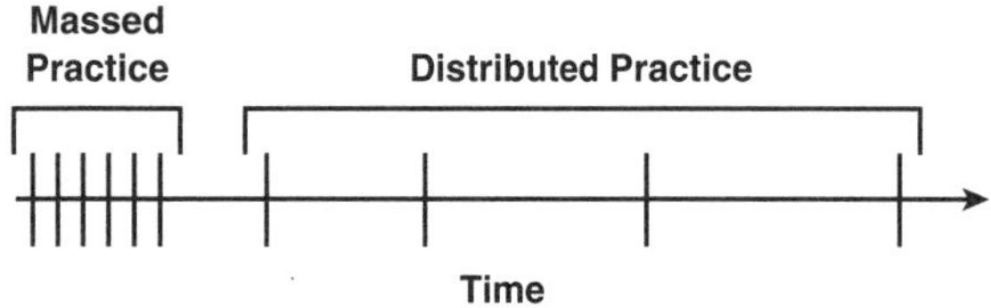

Figure 3.5 Practice repeated over a short duration of time is called massed practice. Repeating the practice over increasingly longer periods of time is distributed practice, which is more likely to lead to retention.

Teachers of mathematics provide massed practice when they allow students to try different examples of applying a new formula or concept in a short period of time, say, within one classroom period. *Cramming* for an exam is an example of massed practice. Material can be quickly chunked into working memory, but can also be quickly dropped or forgotten if more sustained practice does not follow soon. This happens because the material has no further meaning, and thus the need for long-term retention disappears.

Sustained practice over time, called *distributed practice,* is the key to retention. If you want to remember a multiplication table later on, you will need to use it repeatedly over time. Thus, practice that is distributed over longer periods of time sustains meaning and consolidates the learnings into long-term storage in a form that will ensure accurate recall and applications in the future.

Effective practice, then, starts with massed practice for fast learning and proceeds to distributed practice later for retention. As a result, the student is continually practicing previously learned skills throughout the year(s). Each test should not only test new material but also allow students to practice important older learnings. This method not only helps in retention, but it also reminds students that the learnings will be useful for the future and not just for the time when they were first learned and tested. That was the rationale behind the idea of the spiral curriculum, whereby critical mathematical facts and skills are reviewed at regular intervals within and over several grade levels. Whatever happened to it?

> *Cramming is an example of massed practice. Material is quickly chunked into working memory for a test and then forgotten unless distributed practice follows soon.*

Include Writing Activities

The *Principles and Standards for School Mathematics* (NCTM, 2000) notes, "Writing in mathematics can also help students consolidate their thinking because it requires them to reflect on their work and clarify their thoughts about the ideas developed in the lesson." Writing is an important component of communication in the classroom, and research studies have highlighted the benefits to students of writing to learn mathematics (Pugalee, 2001; Stonewater, 2002).

Benefits of Writing in Mathematics

Through writing activities, teachers help students to:

- Learn a mathematics concept more effectively and develop critical-thinking and problem-solving skills
- Have a permanent record of their thoughts where they can return to reflect on them
- Organize ideas, develop new applications for knowledge, and solve problems involving mathematical operations
- Become active participants in their own learning by engaging in an interaction with the subject or content area

- Maintain a silent dialogue with the content area in which the student internalizes knowledge and articulates it in the learning process
- Establish a personal connection to new mathematics concepts
- Get involved in an active intellectual process in which they decide what is important and what is meaningful or relevant to them
- Gain self-understanding and confidence in dealing with their concerns
- Personalize the subject matter because it gives them choices for applying their knowledge in areas that interest them

Besides helping students understand mathematical concepts, writing enhances their confidence in their writing skills for other curriculum areas. In Chapter 8, you will find specific suggestions for how to incorporate writing into mathematics lessons.

Gender Differences in Mathematics

For decades, boys have consistently scored higher than girls on standardized mathematics tests, such as the SAT and the National Assessment of Educational Progress (NAEP). High school and college mathematics classes usually contain more males than females. Those seeking to explain this gender disparity have typically put the blame on outmoded social stereotypes. Recently, however, they have added discoveries in brain science as potential explanations. They cite, for example, that male brains are about 6 to 8 percent larger than female brains. But males are on the average about 6 to 8 percent taller than females, which could also explain the similar differences in brain sizes. And brain imaging studies show that males seem to have an advantage in visual-spatial ability (the ability to rotate objects in their heads) while females are more adept at language processing. In female brains, the bundle of nerves that connects the two cerebral hemispheres, called the *corpus callosum,* is proportionally larger and thicker than in male brains. This suggests that communication between the two hemispheres is more efficient in females than in males. However, in male brains, communication appears to be more efficient within a hemisphere. But whether these differences translate into a genetic advantage for males over females in mathematical processing remains to be seen and proved.

Stereotype Threat

Although the genders have differed on test results in mathematics, researchers believe social context plays an important role. Differences in career choices, for instance, are due not to differing

> *Gender differences in mathematics performance are more likely due to cultural factors than to genetics.*

abilities in mathematics but to cultural factors, such as subtle but pervasive gender expectations that emerge in high school. One study reported that merely telling females that a mathematics test often shows gender differences was enough to hurt their performance (Spencer, 1999). This phenomenon, called *stereotype threat,* occurs when people believe they will be evaluated based on societal stereotypes about their particular group. The researchers gave a mathematics test to males and females. They told half the females that the test would show gender differences, and told the rest that it would find none. Females who expected gender differences did significantly worse on the test than males. Those females who were told there was no gender disparity performed equally to males on the test. Moreover, the experiment was conducted with females who were top performers in mathematics.

Another study of stereotype threat was designed to have people think of their strengths rather than their stereotyped weaknesses (McGlone & Aronson, 2006). Would that serve to improve their performance in areas where they were not supposed to do well, as in mathematics? Ninety college students, half male and half female, completed a questionnaire. One group was asked if they lived in a single-sex or coed dormitory, as this question in previous studies was shown to activate male and female stereotypes. A second group was asked why they chose to attend a private liberal arts college, an attempt, according to the researchers, to activate their "snob schema." The third group, used as controls, were asked to write about their experiences living in the northeastern part of the United States.

After taking a standard test of visual-spatial abilities associated with mathematics performance, the gender gap closed among those who were primed to think about their status as students in an exclusive liberal arts college. The female scores improved while the male scores were the same as the control group. There was no significant difference between the male and female scores. Simply manipulating the way female students thought of themselves improved their test performance.

Instructional Approaches Narrow the Gap

Although most neuroscientists will admit to gender differences in how the brain processes information, especially in young children, they are reluctant to support the concept that these differences offer a lifelong learning advantage for one sex over the other in any academic area. Spelke (2005) reviewed 111 studies and papers and found that most suggest that the male's and the female's abilities for mathematics and science have a genetic basis in cognitive systems that emerge in early childhood but give males and females on the whole equal aptitude for mathematics and science.

It is important for educators to know about these gender differences and how they change through various stages of human development. The danger here is that people will think that if the differences are innate and unchangeable, then nothing can be done to improve the situation. Such ideas are damaging because they leave the student feeling discouraged, and they ignore the brain's plasticity (the ability to continually change through experience) and exceptional ability to learn complex information when suitably motivated. A variety of teaching approaches and strategies may indeed make up for these gender differences.

Consider Learning Styles

As adolescents mature, their learning styles also begin to mature and consolidate. Learning style describes the ways and preferences an individual has when in a learning situation and seems to result from a combination of genetic predispositions and environmental influences. These styles are comprised of a number of variables, including

- Sensory preferences (Do I have a preference for auditory, visual, or kinesthetic-tactile input?)
- Hemispheric preference (Do I usually look at the world more analytically or more globally?)
- Intellectual preferences similar to Gardner's 10 intelligences mentioned in Chapter 1 (What are my intellectual strengths and weaknesses?)
- Participation preferences (Do I want to do something now with this learning or think about it first?)
- Sensing/intuitive preferences (Do I prefer learning facts and solve problems using established methods, or do I prefer discovering possibilities and relationships on my own?)

Remember, these are preferences, and they are not rigid. Everybody can change to another style temporarily if the situation requires it. If you consider just these five learning-style variables and their components as well as the notion that many of these variables exist along a continuum, you quickly realize that there are thousands of possible permutations. How can a teacher address all these variations in the classroom? It helps if we narrow the field of possibilities.

Addressing Multiple Intelligences

In the 20-plus years since Howard Gardner proposed his theory of multiple intelligences, educators have been developing activities to apply his ideas to classroom practice. You may be surprised to learn that there is little physical evidence from neuroscience to support Gardner's theory. About the best neuroscientists can say is that scanning studies show that different parts of the brain are used to perform certain tasks associated with Gardner's intelligences. For example, language processing is largely devoted to the left frontal lobe, while many visual-spatial operations are generally located in the right parietal lobe. Creating and processing music involve the temporal lobes, and running and dancing are controlled mainly by the motor cortex and cerebellum (Figure 3.2). Some theorists suggest that Gardner's model is simply a taxonomy of intellectual pursuits based on judgments that lack scientific support and ignore the notion and contribution of general intelligence.

Of course, there is plenty of anecdotal evidence to indicate different degrees and types of intelligences, as anyone who has been a teacher will confirm. We encounter, for example, the star athlete (high bodily/kinesthetic) who can hardly write a complete sentence (low linguistic), or the mathematics whiz (high logical/mathematical) who rarely communicates with classmates (low interpersonal). Classroom observations and studies have shown that more students are likely to be motivated and succeed in classes where teachers use a variety of activities designed to appeal to students whose strengths lie in one or more of the intelligences described by Gardner (Shearer, 2004). However, it is important to remember that these intelligences describe the different types of competencies that we all possess in varying degrees and that we use in our daily lives.

Studies show that more students are motivated and succeed in classes where teachers use activities that address the various intelligences.

Whether scientists will eventually discover the underlying neurological networks that comprise different intelligences remains to be seen. In the meantime, I think Gardner's theory can still be beneficial for two reasons. First, it reminds teachers that students have different strengths and weaknesses, and different interests, and that they learn in different ways. By using Gardner's ideas, teachers are likely to address the needs of a wider range of students. Second, teaching the mathematics curriculum through a variety of approaches will probably be more interesting; and this in itself often motivates students to learn.

Figure 3.6 takes a closer look at eight of the intelligences and some of their relevant behaviors as described and revised by Gardner (1993). I am not including in this discussion the most recent intelligences proposed by Gardner, *spiritualist* and *emotionalist,* because there has not been sufficient time to study and explore their characteristics and educational implications. Specific suggestions for activities to consider in mathematics lessons that address these intelligences are found in Chapter 7.

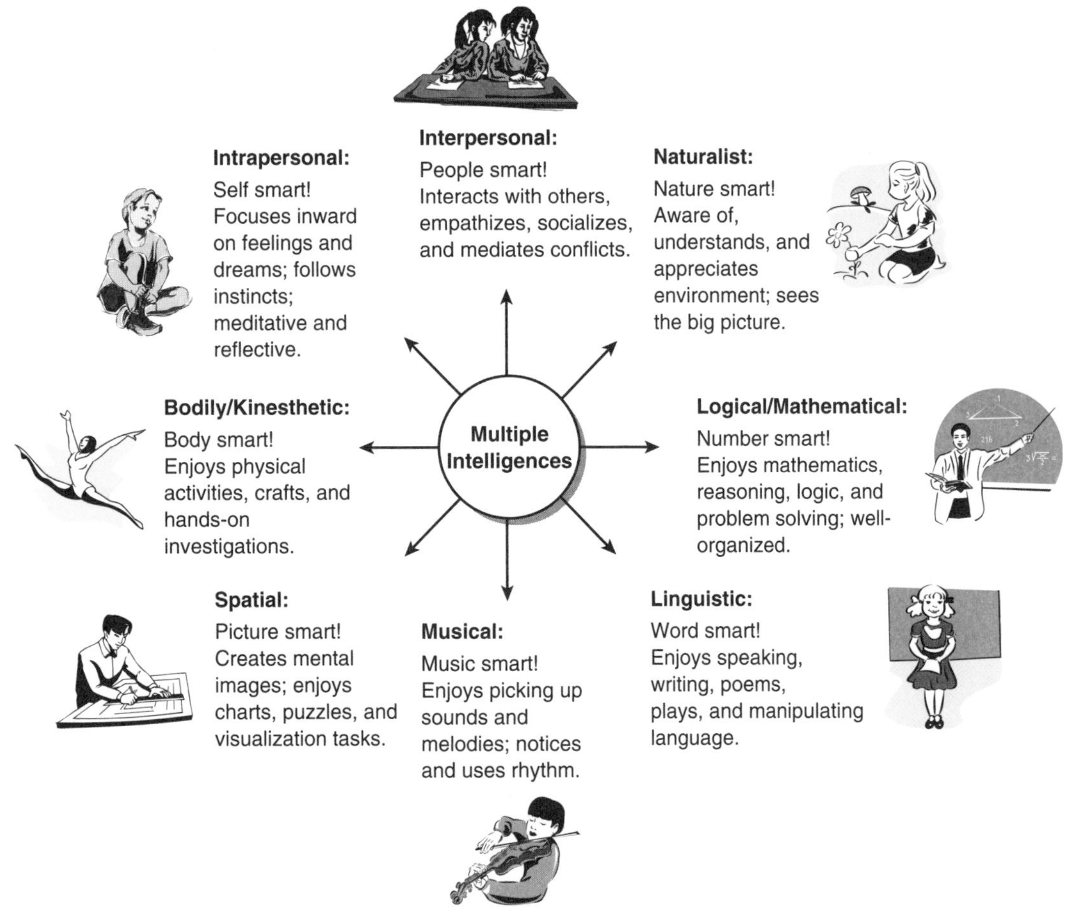

Figure 3.6 The eight intelligences describe the different types of competencies that we all possess in varying degrees and that we use in our daily lives (Gardner, 1993).

Consider Teaching Styles

Quick, finish this statement: "Teachers tend to teach the way they ______." Did you say, "were taught"? That is a common response but not truly accurate. Observational data and research on learning styles show that teachers really tend to teach the way they *learn.* Thus, our learning style drives our teaching style. Teachers who are predominately auditory learners will do lots of talking in their classes and personally enjoy going to lectures and hearing others recount their vacation trips and other stories. But teachers who are predominantly visual learners will use lots of charts and visual aids in their classes and personally prefer movies, television, museums, and the like for entertainment. Actually, the alternative response that teachers teach the way they were taught is indirectly related to learning style. If a student (prospective teacher) is in a class where the teacher's teaching style closely matches the student's learning style, then the student is more likely to achieve successfully. Later, the student will feel comfortable emulating that teacher's teaching style because it was so compatible with the student's learning style. As a result, that student is now teaching as the student was taught.

I could go into lots of other combinations of learning styles and discuss their characteristics, but that would take up many pages, and it is really not my purpose here. Rather, my discussion turns to the thinking and learning style of mathematicians. Many high school mathematics teachers majored in mathematics in college and perhaps in graduate school as well. It is fair to say, then, that many of these teachers think and learn like mathematicians.

How Do You Think About Mathematics?

If you are a mathematics educator, how do you think about mathematics? Do you see mathematics as mainly an abstract construct of the human mind and mathematical objects as having no relation to reality? Perhaps you see mathematical objects as real and necessary for our daily experiences. Dehaene (1997), himself a mathematician and researcher in cognitive neuroscience, suggests that mathematicians view their subject from any one of the following three perspectives (Figure 3.7):

- **Platonist.** For these individuals, mathematics exists in an abstract plane, but the objects of mathematics that they study are as real as everyday life. Mathematic reality exists outside the human mind, and the function of the mathematician is to discover or observe mathematical objects.
- **Formalist.** For them, mathematics is only a game in which one manipulates symbols in accordance with precise formal rules. Mathematical objects such as numbers have no relation to reality. Rather, they are defined solely as a set of symbols that satisfy certain axioms and the theorems of geometry.
- **Intuitionist.** These people believe that mathematical objects are merely constructions of the human mind. Mathematics does not exist in the real world, but only in the brain of the mathematician who invents it. After all, neither arithmetic, nor geometry, nor logic existed before human beings appeared on earth.

After reading the descriptions of these three perspectives, where would you classify yourself? Keep in mind that just as your learning style directs your teaching style, so will your perspective

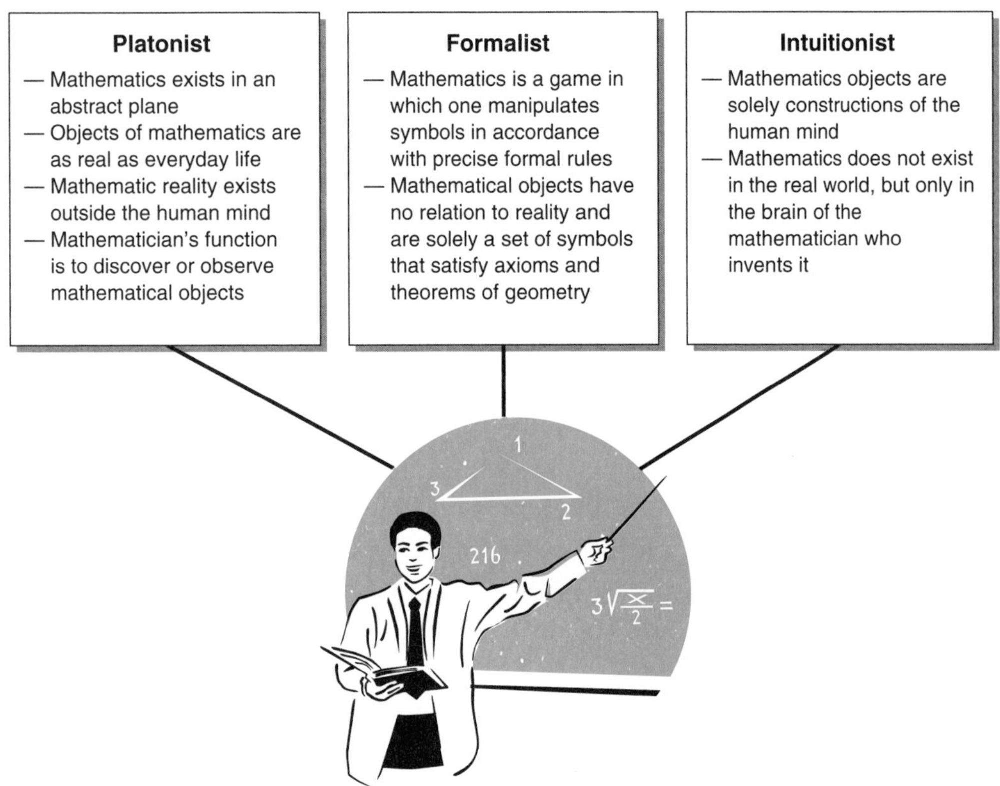

Figure 3.7 Dehaene (1997) suggests that mathematicians view their subject from any one of three different perspectives: Platonist, Formalist, or Intuitionist. This diagram gives a brief description of each perspective. Whichever perspective a teacher has likely will affect that individual's approach to presenting mathematics in the classroom.

on the subject close to your heart affect your approach to designing and presenting lessons in mathematics.

From the information presented in Chapters 1 and 2, it would seem that the intuitionist perspective provides the best account of the relationship between arithmetic and the human brain. We noted in those chapters that

- Human beings are born with the innate mechanisms separating objects and for determining the numerosity of small sets of objects.
- Number sense is present in animals as well, and thus is independent of language and has a long history in the development of our species.
- In children, the capability to do numerical estimation, comparison, finger counting, simple addition and subtraction arises spontaneously without much direct instruction.

- Mental manipulation of numerical quantities is carried out by neural networks located in the parietal areas of both brain hemispheres.

Thus intuition about numbers is deeply rooted in our brain. It is one of the ways in which we search for structure in our environment. Just as specialized brain circuits allow us to locate objects in space, so do circuits in our parietal lobes allow us to effortlessly determine numerical quantities.

WHAT'S COMING?

Now that we have looked at the major components of learning, the next step is to decide how these components need to be adapted to serve the needs of preschool, preadolescent, and adolescent learners. Are there limits to what mathematics concepts we can teach at each developmental level? Are preschoolers even ready for mathematics? Is the preadolescent brain really mature enough to learn algebra? Are we sufficiently challenging adolescents in mathematics classes or just scaring them off? The answers to these questions will emerge in the next three chapters. First, we start with preschoolers and kindergartners.

Chapter 3 — Reviewing the Elements of Learning

Reflections

Jot down on this page key points, ideas, strategies, and resources you want to consider later. This sheet is your personal journal summary and will help to jog your memory.

Chapter 4

Teaching Mathematics to the Preschool and Kindergarten Brain

I recommend you to question all your beliefs, except that two and two make four.

—Voltaire

Chapters 1 and 2 provided detailed discussions about the development of a child's innate capabilities for subitizing, estimating, counting, and doing simple arithmetic processing. By the time most children reach the age of four, their interactions with the environment have offered them opportunities to practice these basic numerical operations. The purpose of preschool is to provide children a wide variety of learning experiences that they might not otherwise get. But should these experiences include mathematics? Is the brain of a four-year-old sufficiently prepared to tackle numerical operations beyond their limited inborn talents? Let's see.

SHOULD PRESCHOOLERS LEARN MATHEMATICS AT ALL?

Should there even be mathematics in preschool? Some people think that the preschool brain is not sufficiently mature to deal with number manipulation. But as we have already explained in earlier chapters, humans are born with intuitive capabilities for handling simple numerical quantities. Mathematics at the preschool level, then, should take advantage of a young child's innate number sense. This means that instructional activities should be deeper and broader than mere practice in counting and adding.

Clements (2001) suggests four reasons that mathematics should be taught in preschool:

- Preschoolers already encounter curricular areas that include only a small amount of mathematics. Supplemental instruction would help make these areas more understandable.
- Many preschoolers, especially those from low-income and minority groups, have often experienced difficulties with mathematics in their later years. This potential gap can be narrowed by including more mathematics at the preschool level.
- Preschoolers already possess number and geometry abilities ranging from counting objects to making shapes. Children use mathematical ideas in their everyday life and can develop surprisingly sophisticated mathematical knowledge. Preschool activities should extend these abilities.
- Recent brain research affirms that preschoolers' brains undergo significant development, that their learning and experiences affect the structure and organization of their brains, and that their brains develop most when challenged with complex activities and not with rote skill learning.

Because the human brain is such a powerful pattern seeker, preschoolers are self-motivated to investigate shapes, measurements, the meaning of numbers, and how numbers work. Activities in preschool mathematics, therefore, should be designed to raise their intuitive number sense and pattern-recognition abilities to an explicit level of awareness. Teachers should not assume that preschoolers perceive situations, problems, or solutions the same way adults do. Clements (2001) reports how one researcher asked a student to count six marbles. Then the researcher covered the marbles, showed the student one more, and asked how many there were in total. The student responded that there was just one marble. When the researcher pointed out that he had six marbles hidden, the preschooler replied adamantly that she didn't see six. For her, no number could exist unless there were objects to count.

Mathematics activities in preschool should raise children's intuitive number sense and pattern-recognition abilities to an explicit level of awareness.

Preschool teachers need to interpret what the student is thinking and doing and use these interpretations to assess what concepts the student is learning and how they can be linked to the student's own experiences. Young students do not see the world as separate subject areas. They try to link everything together. Their play is usually their first encounter with mathematics, be it counting objects or drawing geometric designs.

Assessing Students' Number Sense

One of the first tasks of a preschool and kindergarten teacher is to determine the level of number sense that each student has already reached. Designing a number knowledge test is no easy task. Researchers Sharon Griffin and Robbie Case tackled this problem. Starting in the 1980s, they refined their assessments over the years on the basis of their research to ensure that the items reflected the capabilities possessed by a majority of students at ages 4, 6, 8, and 10 (Griffin & Case, 1997; Griffin, 2002).

By administering this test, a teacher can determine how far an individual student's number sense has progressed. The teacher can then use differentiated activities to develop the number sense for students of the same age who may be at different levels of competence. Table 4.1 shows the current version of the test for four-year-olds, which is reprinted here with permission (Griffin, 2002). Tests for the other grade levels are found in Chapter 5.

Preschoolers' Social and Emotional Behavior

A young child's social and emotional functioning will have an impact on practically any content the child studies, including the development of mathematical competence. Not surprisingly, recent studies done with preschoolers show that those students who had initiative, self-control, and attachment, regardless of gender, were better at acquiring mathematics skills than students with behavior, social, and attention problems. Moreover, students who received interventions designed to address their social and emotional problems improved their mathematics skills as compared to the students who did not receive the interventions (Dobbs, Doctoroff, Fisher, & Arnold,

> *Preschoolers with social and emotional problems will need to have those problems addressed before they can successfully develop their mathematical skills.*

2006). The obvious implication here is that young students who consistently display social and emotional problems will need to have those problems addressed before we can expect them to successfully acquire and develop their mathematics skills.

Table 4.1 Number Knowledge Test for 4-Year-Olds

Level 0 (4-year-old level): Go to Level 1 if 3 or more correct (See Chapter 5).	
1	Can you count these chips and tell me how many there are? (Place 3 counting chips in front of the child in a row.)
2a	(Show stacks of chips, 5 versus 2, same color.) Which pile has more?
2b	(Show stacks of chips, 3 versus 7, same color.) Which pile has more?
3a	This time I'm going to ask you which pile has less. (Show stacks of chips, 2 versus 6, same color.) Which pile has less?
3b	(Show stacks of chips, 8 versus 3, same color.) Which pile has less?
4	I'm going to show you some counting chips. (Show a line of 3 red and 4 yellow chips in a row, as follows: R Y R Y R Y Y). Count just the yellow chips and tell me how many there are.
5	Pick up all chips from the previous question. Then say: Here are some more counting chips (Show mixed array, not in a row, of 7 yellow and 8 red chips). Count just the red chips and tell me how many there are.

Source: Griffin, 2002. Reprinted with permission of the author.

WHAT MATHEMATICS SHOULD PRESCHOOLERS LEARN?

NCTM's *Curriculum Focal Points* (2006) suggest that prekindergarten children should be

- Developing an understanding of whole numbers, including concepts of correspondence, counting, cardinality, and comparison
- Identifying shapes and describing spatial relationships
- Identifying measurable attributes and comparing objects by using these attributes

NCTM's *Curriculum Focal Points* (2006) suggest that kindergarten children should be

- Representing, comparing, and ordering whole numbers and joining and separating sets
- Describing shapes and space
- Ordering objects by measurable attributes

More specifically, early childhood researchers and mathematics educators agree that preschoolers and kindergartners should be exposed to the following areas and skills:

- **Numbers.** Children learn about numbers by counting objects and talking about their results. "You gave Billy five cards. How many does Mary need?" Children count spaces on board games. "You are now on space three. How many more spaces do you need to go to get to space seven?" They count the days until their birthdays. The teacher might say, "Yesterday there were nine days until your birthday. How many days are there now?" Children read counting books and recite nursery rhymes with numbers.
- **Geometry and spatial relations.** Children practice constructing various shapes and discussing their properties. They can see thin triangles, fat triangles, and upside-down triangles and gradually realize that they are all still triangles.
- **Measurement.** Children compare the height of a block tower with the height of a chair or table. They measure each other's height and the distance from the desk to a wall. They learn that a block is too short or too long to complete a project.
- **Patterns/geometry.** Children become aware of patterns in their environment. They learn to recognize patterns of different colors and sizes in beads, blocks, and their clothes. They practice reproducing simple patterns by stringing beads and copying designs with colored blocks.
- **Analyzing data.** Children sort objects by color, size, and shape, count them, and record the data on graphs and charts. These charts might reflect how many bean plants have sprouted, the class pet's growth, the number of rainy days in March, or the number of children with a birthday in January.

PRESCHOOL AND KINDERGARTEN INSTRUCTIONAL SUGGESTIONS

General Guidelines

Researchers in mathematics education offer some suggestions that should guide preschool and kindergarten instruction (Clements, 2001).

✓ Plan a learning environment conducive to mathematical explorations, including unit blocks and manipulatives. This includes building on the students' languages and cultural backgrounds as well as their current mathematical ideas and counting strategies.

- ✓ Recognize whether a student's mathematical thinking is developing or stalled. When thinking is developing, you can observe and take notes, leave the students alone, and later talk with the students or the entire class to explain the mathematics involved. If the thinking is stalled, then intervene in order to clarify and discuss the ideas. For example, two students might be arguing about whose block set is bigger. It might be that one child is talking about height, while the other is looking at width or volume. Use this opportunity to discuss how size can be measured in different ways.

- ✓ Introduce activities that specifically rely on mathematics. For example, card games that use numbered cards and board games with number cubes offer students experiences with counting and comparison. Many students' books have mathematical themes that develop classifying and ordering, and strengthen students' number and geometric knowledge.

- ✓ Use a variety of instructional strategies that create meaningful age-appropriate contexts and require students to be active participants in their learning.

- ✓ Continue to enhance the students' thinking about mathematics by posing higher-order questions, such as "Have you tried this way?" or "What do you think would happen if . . .?" and "Is there another way we could . . . ?"

Suggestions for Teaching Subitizing

In Chapter 1 we discussed the innate skill of subitizing, which is the ability to know the number of objects in a small collection without counting. If, as it seems, conceptual subitizing is the prerequisite skill for learning counting, then strengthening this skill should make learning to count easier for young students.

It may seem odd to suggest that it is possible to strengthen an innate ability. But we do this continually as we grow. Humans are born with the innate abilities to move and to speak, abilities that are strengthened through developmental learning experiences. The ability to subitize can be developed as well. Thus, preschool and kindergarten teachers should consider incorporating activities that strengthen this capability in their young students.

In searching for activities that strengthen subitizing, teachers should use cards or objects with dot patterns and avoid using manipulatives. Why? The brain is a superb pattern seeker, and we want to take advantage of this capability by getting students to form mental images of number patterns. If students use manipulatives, they are more likely to rely on counting by ones rather than on mental imagery (Kline, 1998).

> *Subitizing is best practiced with dot card patterns, rather than with manipulatives, to enhance imagery and eliminate counting by ones.*

Clements (1999) suggests four guidelines that should be followed when designing activities that encourage conceptual subitizing in young students. The groups to be subitized should (1) stand alone and not be embedded in pictures; (2) be simple forms, such as groups of circles or squares rather than pictures of animals (which could be distracting); (3) emphasize regular arrangements that include symmetry; and (4) have strong contrast with the background. Here are some examples of activities for preschool and Kindergarten students:

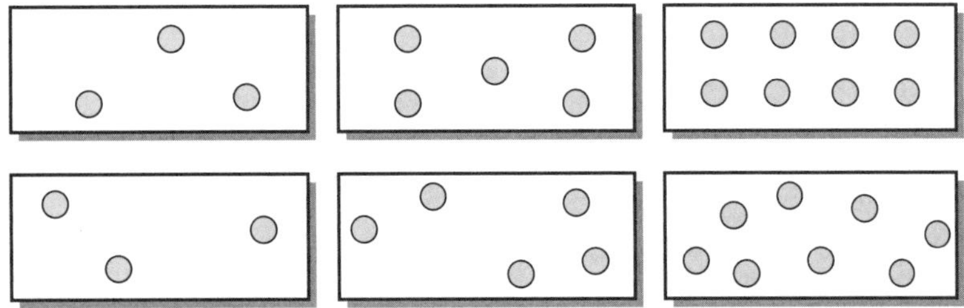

Figure 4.1 Cards like these, which have dots placed randomly and in patterns, help young children enhance their ability to subitize, which is determining the number of a collection without counting.

✓ **Dot patterns on cards.** Draw circles on cards (or punch holes in cards for use with an overhead projector). The circles (or holes) should be arranged in geometric patterns on some cards and randomly on others. Some examples are shown in Figure 4.1 (Clements, 1999).

- One activity uses cards with randomly placed dots and asks the students to say how many dots are on a card without counting them.
- Another activity is to play a matching game. Display several cards which have the same number of dots, except one. Ask the students to say which card does not belong with the others without counting the dots.
- Select decks of cards that have zero to ten dots arranged randomly and in patterns. Give a deck to each student. Ask the students to spread the cards out in front of them. Say a number and ask students to find the matching card as fast as they can and to hold it up. On other days, use different sets of cards with different arrangements.
- Display a card and ask students to say the number that is one more than the number of dots on the card. You can have them respond aloud, by writing down the numeral, or by holding up a numeral card. Remind them to try to avoid counting the dots.

- Place dots on a large sheet of paper or poster board in various arrangements. Point to an arrangement and ask the students to say its number as fast as possible. Each time you play this game, rotate the paper or board so that it is in a different orientation.
- Another variation is to flash one particular pattern on the overhead projector for just three seconds. The goal here is to encourage the students to think about the parts of the image. Ask them to tell how many dots were shown and to describe what they saw. You may want to flash it a second time for three seconds to give them a chance to organize their images. That second look will be unnecessary once the students get better at recognizing patterns instantaneously. Timing is important. If you show the pattern for too long, the students will work from the picture rather than from their mental image. Showing it too briefly will not give them sufficient time to form the mental image (Kline, 1998).

✓ **Visualization.** Subitizing relies heavily on visualization because the goal is to determine the number of a small group of objects with a quick visual glance and without counting. Visualization abilities develop rapidly in young children. Thus activities that rely on visual cues enhance this development and allow students to make mental connections between patterns of objects and their numerosity.

For instance, cards displaying dot patterns in specific geometric shapes (Figure 4.2) help students to associate number and geometry by purposefully combining the two.

- Visuals also help young students see that different patterns can show the various ways a number can be partitioned, or decomposed (Figure 4.3). Through partitioning, students come to understand the idea that numbers can be broken down into other numbers. They also begin to recognize the relationship of parts to the whole. When students interpret numbers in terms of part-whole relationships, they think about numbers as made up of other numbers, and this way of thinking is the major conceptual achievement of the early school years.

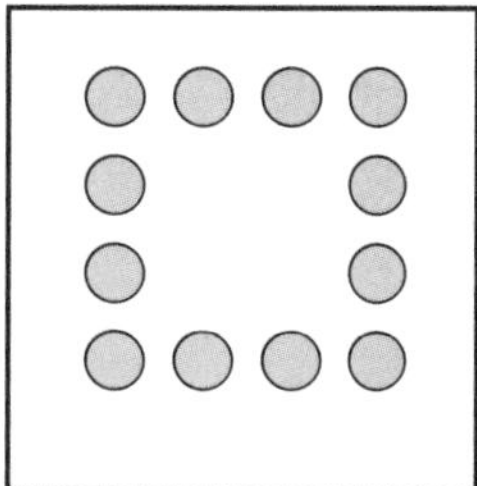
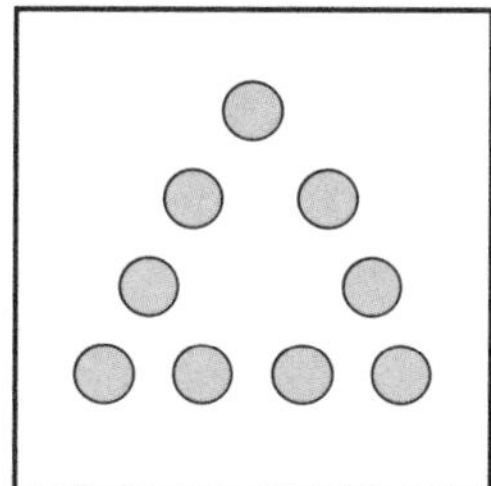
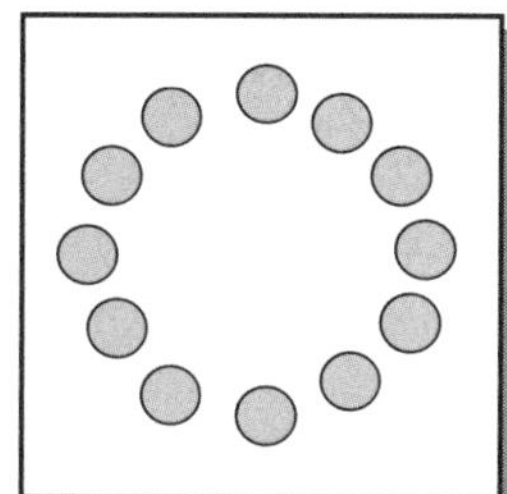

Figure 4.2 These types of cards combine number with geometry and are useful in developing conceptual subitizing in young students.

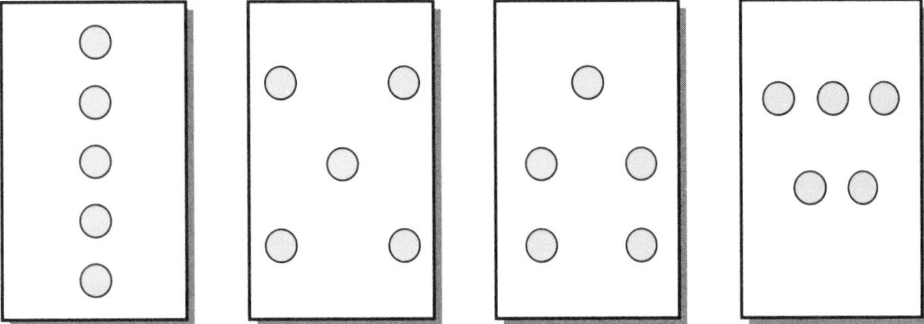

Figure 4.3 Showing different arrangements of the same number of objects helps students recognize different decompositions or partitioning of a number (Clements, 1999).

Subitizing and Understanding Part-Whole Relationships

Enhancing subitizing helps students as young as four to understand part-whole relationships. Thus preschool and kindergarten students should be investigating different ways of splitting up numbers in a variety of contexts. If the quantities are small and the activities meaningful, the idea of the parts and the whole can be introduced successfully in the early childhood years. As students become better able to take numbers apart and put them back together without even thinking, they develop a fluency with small numbers that will help them later when working with larger numbers.

Two other ideas that are central to the notion of quantifying without counting (that is, subitizing) are *covariation* (the idea that the whole quantity increases/decreases if one of the parts is increased/decreased), and *compensation* (the idea that removing some items from one part and adding them to the other part leaves the whole quantity unchanged). Studies have shown that children as young as four were able to give the correct answer on problems involving covariation and compensation. Furthermore, they were able to justify their answers by giving appropriate reasons for their responses. These results support the idea that children need experiences that draw their attention to the dynamic relationship between the parts and the whole, and the effect on the whole when there are changes to one of the parts. Having an understanding of part-whole relationships is important for learning numeracy. Counting is a valuable tool, but it need not be the first step toward the development of part-whole understanding. Early childhood teachers have an important role in helping students appreciate the ways that numbers are composed of other numbers and how these part-whole relationships can be used to solve arithmetic problems (Young-Loveridge, 2002).

Using visualization to enhance conceptual subitizing eventually will help young students develop ideas about addition and subtraction. Visuals provide a basis for students to see addends and the sum by recognizing that two apples and two apples make four apples. Some students may advance to counting on one or two, solving 3 + 2 by saying "3, 4, 5. Counting on one or two gives students an idea of how counting on works. Later they can learn to count on using larger numbers by developing their conceptual subitizing.

Studies indicate that the maximum size for objects to be subitized is about five, even for adults (Dehaene, 1997). Eventually, we have to deal with quantities that exceed our ability to subitize, and counting becomes necessary. But remember that persistent practice with activities that enhance subitzing will make it much easier for young students to count and to manipulate numbers for basic arithmetic.

Subitizing With Audio Input

Would adding audio input improve a child's ability to perform simple arithmetic by subitizing? The answer to this question is yes, and it came from a study conducted by Hilary Barth and her colleagues at Harvard University (Barth, La Mont, Lipton, & Spelke, 2005). In these experiments, 5-year-olds, who had no real experience using number symbols, were able to add two arrays of dots and compare them to a third array. When researchers replaced the third array of dots with beeps, the children integrated the sight and sound quantities easily. The children performed all these tasks successfully, without actual counting or having any knowledge of number symbols.

To study this ability further, the Harvard researchers investigated the responses of preschoolers to both visual and audio inputs. On the first test, the children were shown some blue dots. After these were covered, they saw red dots. They were asked if there were more red or blue dots. The preschoolers had no trouble answering correctly even when the difference was only a matter of a few dots. On another test, the children had to visually add two arrays of blue dots and compare them with the number of red dots in a third array. This they did without problems. Then sound was added. First, they compared numbers of dots to numbers of beeps. After that they added two arrays of dots and compared them to a sequence of beeps. Surprisingly, the children added and compared dots and beeps as easily as they had dots alone.

At the conclusion of this study, the researchers reflected on how their findings could be used to help the many young children who experience trouble learning basic arithmetic. Perhaps devising new teaching strategies in elementary education that harness children's preexisting arithmetic intuitions can foster the acquisition of knowledge about symbolic numbers and operations. They came up with two suggestions.

- ✓ First, youngsters who struggle with symbols for numbers might be encouraged and reassured if they discover that they can successfully play the kinds of games mastered by the children in the Harvard experiments. This play could show them that they already have the abilities they need to do the operations that their mathematics teachers are presenting in the classroom.

✓ Second, joining nonsymbolic play with symbolic arithmetic problems could help children master the symbol system. Numerical symbols and operations may be less confusing to children if they are coupled with examples of sets of dots that are added, subtracted, multiplied, or divided—events they may already intuitively understand.

Learning to Count

There are several activities that can be used to help young children learn the principles of counting.

✓ Reinforce the cardinal principle with number line activities, using, for instance, chips that have different-colored sides. Lay the chips out with the same color facing up. Turn each chip as it is counted (Figure 4.4). Cover up a group that has just been counted and ask the students "How many did you count?" Keep extending the wait time before asking the question. You can also ask the students to count the items in their hands and to put their hands behind their backs. The ask them the "how many" question. Vary the activity by having students do counting without the number line and in various pattern arrangements (Solomon, 2006).

Figure 4.4 Using chips with different-colored sides can enhance students understanding of the cardinal principle. Turn each chip over as it is counted, cover up the counted group, and then ask the students to say how many have been counted. The idea is to get students to recognize that the last number said indicates the number of total items in a group.

✓ Students also need to realize that number words describe "how many" objects and not their arrangement or size. This concept is reinforced when students have practice in counting objects that are arranged in different patterns (Figure 4.5) or a collection of objects of different size.

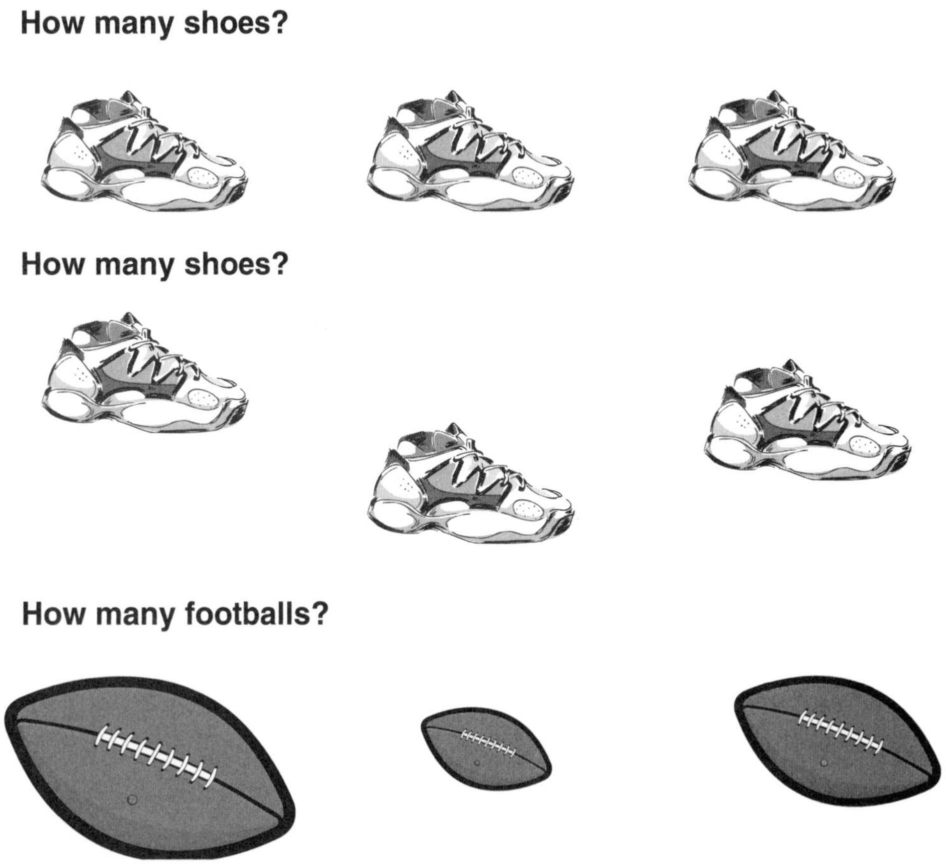

How many shoes?

How many shoes?

How many footballs?

Figure 4.5 Activities that allow young students to practice counting objects in different arrangements and sizes help to reinforce the notion that number is independent of other physical qualities.

By the age of four, most children have mastered basic counting and can apply counting to new situations. Exactly how this competence emerges is not fully understood. It most likely starts with the genetic predisposition to understanding the numerosity of a small group of objects in the environment. Reciting number words in a fixed sequence is a natural outcome of our facility with language. And the principle of one-to-one correspondence is actually widespread in the animal kingdom.

Once children learn to count using objects, the next challenge is to learn to count mentally without objects. Children who have been practicing activities that enhance visualization are likely to learn mental counting more easily because it is so heavily dependent on imagery. The next step is the realization that when two quantities are joined, counting can begin from the last number of one quantity rather than starting all over from one. This is called *counting on* and is an advanced strategy used by children to solve problems in addition.

An Easier Counting System

We discussed in Chapter 1 that young Asian children have a much easier time learning how to count because their language logically describes the counting sequence. Some early childhood researchers suggest trying out this approach with English-speaking children, using English counting words in a pattern similar to that used in some Asian languages. This method requires just 10 different words to count from 1 to 100 instead of the 28 English words needed for the traditional counting method.

> *Teaching how to count might be easier using a method modeled after some Asian languages, such as Japanese and Chinese. The system is easier and more logical, and gives students a deeper understanding of our base-10 system.*

The numbers in this approach are not shorter or faster to say, but they make a lot more sense and help children get a deeper understanding of our base-10 system. Some people fear that adding this approach may be confusing, but schools in North America where this has been used have not reported any significant confusion. Children will learn the traditional counting words without any instruction through their exposure to adults, television, and other media. No one believes it is practical to suggest that this method replace the traditional one, but its use may help those students who struggle to understand our numbering system. Table 4.2 shows what the easier counting system from 1 to 100 would look and sound like.

Teacher Talk Improves Number Knowledge

✓ A research study showed that preschool teachers who use numbers in their everyday speech aid the growth of their students' conventional mathematical knowledge over the school year. Klibanoff and her colleagues recorded the speech of 26 preschool teachers during a randomly selected hour of class instruction, including the times when the teacher gathered the class for a story or games. Although the teachers did not present planned mathematics activities during the recorded hour, many incorporated counting and even calculation into their speech.

The researchers assessed the students' skills in mathematics at the beginning and the end of the school year. Students who were in classrooms where the teachers talked a lot about numbers tended to improve more over the course of the school year than students who were less exposed to mathematics vocabulary. Furthermore, the improvements were unrelated to general teacher quality, the complexity of the teachers' sentence structure, or the students' socioeconomic status (Klibanoff, Levine, Huttenlocher, Vasilyeva, & Hedges, 2006).

Table 4.2 A More Logical Counting System for Numbers 1 to 100

1 one	2 two	3 three	4 four	5 five	6 six	7 seven	8 eight	9 nine	10 ten
11 ten-one	12 ten-two	13 ten-three	14 ten-four	15 ten-five	16 ten-six	17 ten-seven	18 ten-eight	19 ten-nine	20 two-ten
21 two-ten one	22 two-ten two	23 two-ten three	24 two-ten four	25 two-ten five	26 two-ten six	27 two-ten seven	28 two-ten eight	29 two-ten nine	30 three-ten
31 three-ten one	32 three-ten two	33 three-ten three	34 three-ten four	35 three-ten five	36 three-ten six	37 three-ten seven	38 three-ten eight	39 three-ten nine	40 four-ten
41 four-ten one	42 four-ten two	43 four-ten three	44 four-ten four	45 four-ten five	46 four-ten six	47 four-ten seven	48 four-ten eight	49 four-ten nine	50 five-ten
51 five-ten one	52 five-ten two	53 five-ten three	54 five-ten four	55 five-ten five	56 five-ten six	57 five-ten seven	58 five-ten eight	59 five-ten nine	60 six-ten
61 six-ten one	62 six-ten two	63 six-ten three	64 six-ten four	65 six-ten five	66 six-ten six	67 six-ten seven	68 six-ten eight	69 six-ten nine	70 seven-ten
71 seven-ten one	72 seven-ten two	73 seven-ten three	74 seven-ten four	75 seven-ten five	76 seven-ten six	77 seven-ten seven	78 seven-ten eight	79 seven-ten nine	80 eight-ten
81 eight-ten one	82 eight-ten two	83 eight-ten three	84 eight-ten four	85 eight-ten five	86 eight-ten six	87 eight-ten seven	88 eight-ten eight	89 eight-ten nine	90 nine-ten
91 nine-ten one	92 nine-ten two	93 nine-ten three	94 nine-ten four	95 nine-ten five	96 nine-ten six	97 nine-ten seven	98 nine-ten eight	99 nine-ten nine	100 ten-ten

Questioning

✓ Help young students to think mathematically by asking questions about numbers and following up with an appropriate activity. Some examples are (Burns, 1998):

- **"How many are there?"** Young students love to count but need practice learning the correct sequence of numbers. To develop an understanding of the *meaning* of numbers, they must learn about one-to-one correspondence—counting objects one by one, pointing to them as they say the numbers in the sequence. Students must also grasp the concept of cardinality—that the last number in the sequence tells how many objects there are. **Activity idea:** Play "How Many Buttons?" Ask the students to come to the front of the classroom one by one and to count how many buttons are on each student's shirt. This is a good way to introduce the idea that zero means none at all.
- **"How many of each kind?"** Students develop classification and counting skills as they think about this question. "How many?" asks them to count the number of items, but they must first sort the items to determine "each kind." Students learn that different types of things belong to different groups.

  Activity idea: Provide collections of almost anything in your classroom, such as buttons, crayons, blocks, markers, and beads, for students to sort and count.
- **"How are these items the same or different?"** To answer this question, the students look at two items and identify how they are alike or different. Answering the question requires students to observe, compare, analyze, and then reach a conclusion, the basic skills of mathematical and scientific exploration.

  Activity idea: Gather students in a circle and ask each child to remove one shoe. Pick up two shoes and ask, "How are these the same?" Allow the students to share their ideas. Then ask, "How are they different?"
- **"Which has more or fewer?"** Comparing quantities is key to setting the stage for students' later thinking about subtraction.

  Activity idea: Play "Coin Toss." Give a student an odd number of pennies to toss, such as five or seven, to start. Ask, "Which are there more of, heads or tails?" This activity also helps students become familiar with coins.
- **"Which is taller, longer, or shorter?"** Young students are most comfortable comparing lengths by using direct comparison and matching up objects to see which is taller, longer, or shorter. If this is not possible, such as figuring out which table is longer when they are on different sides of the room, students can use a variety of nonstandard measures (paper clips, pencils, baby steps). Making direct comparisons and using nonstandard measures help prepare students for learning standard units such as inches, centimeters, and feet.

Activity idea: Choose one length of ribbon from a basket of ribbons, and ask students to sort the rest according to whether they're longer or shorter.

Developing Sorting and Classifying Skills

Young children use sorting and classifying skills to help them organize the world around them. Both of these skills, which emerge around the age of three, are essential in developing a child's understanding of the real world. As these skills develop, children begin to recognize the differences between plants and animals, day and night, and different geometric shapes. They enhance their number sense and their intuitive understandings about how to manipulate numbers during mathematical operations. As a result, they begin to apply logical thinking to the mathematical concepts they encounter. Platz (2004) offers the following suggestions on how to teach young children sorting and classifying skills.

> *Teaching young students sorting and classifying skills enhances their number sense and their intuitive understandings about how to manipulate numbers.*

Sorting versus classifying. Sorting and classifying are terms that are often used synonymously, but they really represent two separate levels of logical thinking. Sorting is a beginning type of grouping task in which the student is told how the objects will be sorted: "Give me all the green blocks." Classifying, however, requires students to discover how a given set of objects might be grouped: "Look at these different blocks and show me how you could put them into groups." Unlike sorting tasks, the students are not told to put objects into groups based on a particular attribute. With classifying tasks students must decide how the objects in each group might be alike.

✓ Keep the following key developmental factors in mind when selecting activities for young students on sorting and classification tasks.

- *Age.* Tasks that challenge a three-year-old student may not be challenging to a four-year-old student. Younger students may be assigned simple sorting tasks in which real objects, such as fruit, are shown, and their task is to find all the objects in a group that are like the one shown. Older students may work with a set of attribute blocks and be asked to place the attribute blocks into different groups so that the blocks in each group are alike in some way.
- *Perceptions.* How things look to students becomes the foundation for understanding their environment. As they engage in sorting and classifying, things that look more similar

may be considered the same. Thus, for younger students it is more helpful to use objects that are more dissimilar at first in their appearance.

- *Constructing information.* Because of their limited experience, young students construct information differently than adults. Adults may expect that a young student will sort or classify a group of objects by triangles and circles when the student actually groups the objects by things that roll or do not roll. Students often see categories or groupings that adults do not anticipate.
- *Tactile and kinesthetic tasks.* Even before young students learn numbers, using tactile or kinesthetic tasks with real objects permits signals to be sent directly to the brain about the numerosity of items. This has great value for learning mathematical concepts that include sorting and classifying.
- *Quantity of objects.* Three-year-old students are less likely to attend to sorting and classifying tasks if there are too many objects involved. Starting with four to five objects and increasing to six to eight objects should be sufficient when starting with sorting and classifying tasks.
- *Mathematical talking.* As students sort and classify objects, they should communicate their thinking aloud as to how they sorted or classified them. We know that task-related talking is important for learning the vocabulary of mathematics. Providing students the opportunity to communicate their actions can clarify mathematical terms and phrases.
- *Make it fun and offer choices.* Providing students with various opportunities to sort and classify in fun ways through individual play and group time activities will promote healthy learning as they engage in these activities.

Levels of sorting. Sorting tasks are excellent beginning activities for promoting understandings relating to grouping. The teacher's responsibility here is to provide a set of objects to students and identify how the set is to be grouped. For example, the teacher may show students five different fruits and ask the students to pick out all the red apples. In sorting, the tasks can become more challenging by increasing the number of objects to be sorted, by having students consider more attributes, and by giving verbal instead of visual clues. Platz (2004) suggests the following four levels for moving from simple to complex sorting tasks (Figure 4.6).

✓ *Level 1: One different attribute.* To start, the students complete a number of tasks with four or five objects that contain only one different attribute. For example, the student may be given all different shapes with the same color or size and be asked to indicate all the shapes that are like the one shown, perhaps a square. Students need to sort by shape only. At this level, show the object and ask the students to place all like objects in a container (or similar space). After the students learn shapes, ask them to give the squares—a verbal cue instead of a visual cue. The students should also explain why they picked out the objects they did. This communication component helps teachers gain insight into the students' rationale for picking the objects they did while helping students clarify their own understanding of the task. Increase the number of objects to five through eight as they work through Level 1.

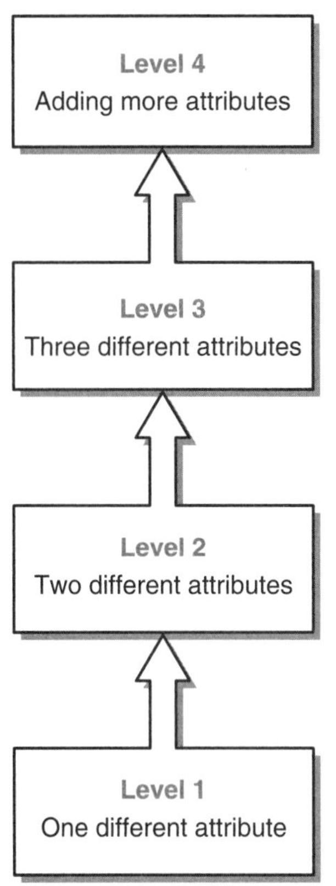

Figure 4.6 These are four levels of sorting tasks for children in preschool (Platz, 2004).

- ✓ *Level 2: Two different attributes.* Provide students with six to eight objects that have different colors as well as different shapes. Show the students an object with two attributes, such as a red circle, and ask them to give you all objects like the one shown. Include several different shapes and colors in the pile of objects used. Students who select all the red circles are classifying based on two different attributes. Again, provide students with the opportunity to talk about how they are sorting into groups. You can add more objects as the student becomes successful.
- ✓ *Level 3: Three different attributes.* The next step is to sort objects with three different attributes: color, size, and shape. Show a large green square and ask the students to give you all objects like this one. Make sure that the pile contains a variety of shapes that represent the three different attributes.
- ✓ *Level 4: Adding more attributes.* Another attribute, such as thickness, is added as the students become more successful in their sorting. A different task might include sorting based on a function, such as a spoon, fork, and knife. Have a group of objects containing objects used for eating and not eating, and ask students to give you things they would use to eat with. When sorting by function, ask the students to explain why they selected the objects for each grouping.

Levels of classifying. As students become proficient in sorting tasks, teachers can introduce classification tasks. When using classification tasks, the students are not told how to classify. When asking students to classify sets of objects based on their thinking, teachers should also ask them to explain their reasoning behind the classifications they have made. Basic attribute blocks of different colors, sizes, and shapes are useful for the four levels of strategies for developing classification tasks (Figure 4.7) (Platz, 2004).

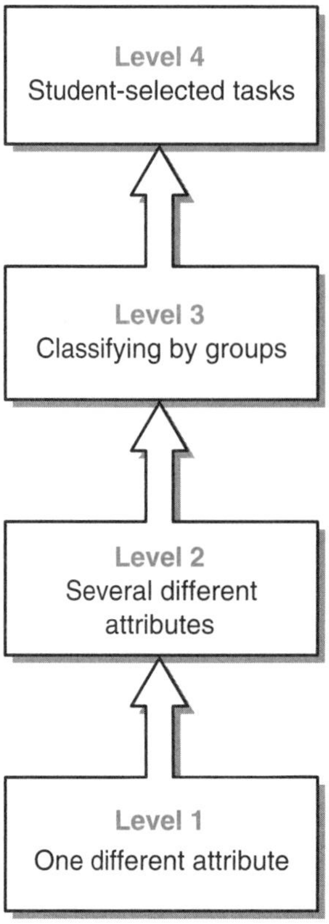

Level 4
Student-selected tasks

Level 3
Classifying by groups

Level 2
Several different attributes

Level 1
One different attribute

Figure 4.7 These are the four levels of classifying tasks for children in preschool (Platz, 2004).

- ✓ *Level 1: One different attribute.* Initial classification tasks follow similar strategies used in sorting tasks. Start with four to five objects that have only one different attribute. For example, the objects may have the same color and size but have different shapes. Ask the student to put objects into different piles that are alike in some way. If the students do not classify them by shapes, the teacher puts the objects back into a pile and ask them to show another way they can be classified. Any reasonable explanation by students as to how objects were classified is acceptable. As students work through level 1, add more objects.
- ✓ *Level 2: Several different attributes.* The next stage is to give students a group of objects that have several different attributes and ask them to show several ways in which they could be classified into groups. For example, if given attribute blocks with different colors, sizes, and shapes, the students could first classify them by color, and then the objects could be put into groups of the same size or shape. Normally, young students will look first for the attributes of color and shape before the attribute of size. Here again, the students should explain why particular objects were placed into certain groups, giving you an insight into the students' thinking and an opportunity to ask for clarification, if needed.
- ✓ *Level 3: Classifying by groups.* This level challenges students to classify objects in such a way that the objects fit into a specific number of groups. For example, a collection may include objects with three different colors, two different shapes and two different sizes. Ask the students to put the objects into three different groups so that the objects in each group are alike in some way. Some students of four and five years of age who can complete classification tasks for level 2 may struggle at first with level 3 tasks. The intent of this level is to have students think logically about the possible ways a set of objects could be classified and deduce the one way that best fits the specific number of groups being sought.

✓ *Level 4: Student-selected tasks.* Beyond the teacher-directed tasks in levels 1 through 3, provide opportunities for student-to-teacher and student-to-student classification tasks. A student can select a group of objects for you or other students to classify based on a system the student has in mind. This reversal of roles provides students the opportunity to develop another level of understanding with regard to classification. By setting up tasks for others to solve, students perform classification thinking in new ways that add to, and clarify, their understandings.

By using sorting and classification tasks, teachers help develop students' thinking in terms of grouping and regrouping, which is important to learning mathematical operations. By selecting and developing tasks organized in some sequential manner, students will have the opportunity to expand the ways they think about new situations and assist them in organizing new information.

WHAT'S COMING?

We have looked here at some basic activities in mathematics for students in preschool and kindergarten. The focus has been on assessing number sense, helping students to learn to count, and developing sorting and classifying skills. With brain growth and development proceeding at a break-neck pace, students moving into the elementary and middle school grades are ready for more difficult and complex challenges. The next chapter examines the components and strategies that teachers of elementary and middle school students should consider when constructing lessons in mathematics.

Chapter 4 — Teaching Mathematics to the Preschool and Kindergarten Brain

Reflections

Jot down on this page key points, ideas, strategies, and resources you want to consider later. This sheet is your personal journal summary and will help to jog your memory.

Chapter 5

Teaching Mathematics to the Preadolescent Brain

The different branches of arithmetic:
Ambition, Distraction, Uglification, and Derision

—Lewis Carroll
Alice in Wonderland

WHAT IS THE PREADOLESCENT BRAIN?

Exactly what is the preadolescent brain? Teachers and parents have been struggling with the answer to this question for a long time. Many ideas have emerged about the internal and external forces acting on the young brain as it develops through the preadolescent years. Now neuroscience weighs in with evidence from brain imaging technologies that may shed more light on the mysteries of the preteen brain. Let's take a look at how nature (genetic contribution) and nurture (environmental influence) interact to sculpt the preadolescent mind. For our purposes, we will define preadolescence as the growth period between the ages of 6 and 12.

How Nature Influences the Growing Brain

Humans are born with certain innate abilities to help them survive during their long trek from infancy to adulthood. Our genetic predispositions for spoken language, numerosity, and social

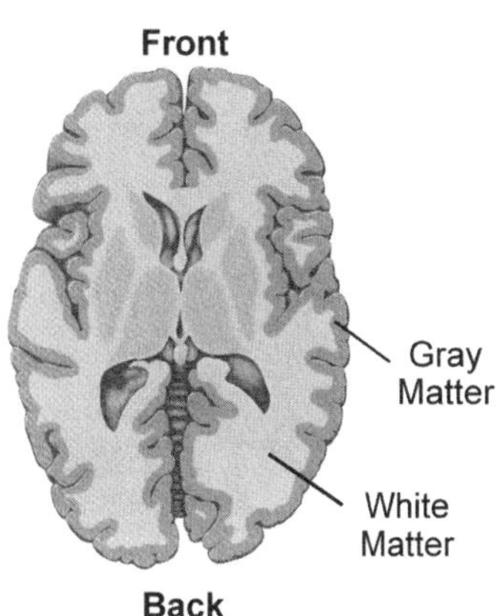

Figure 5.1 A horizontal cross section of the brain. The gray matter is composed primarily of neurons, and the white matter below is composed of myelinated axons.

bonding, among others, allow us to develop the skills needed to remain alive and become a contributing part of a family unit. The brain guides these actions, and while it grows and develops, new capabilities emerge. But brain growth is not linear. It is sporadic, and different regions of the brain develop at different rates. At any given moment, some parts of the brain are already sufficiently developed to carry out their functions while others are just beginning to get their neural networks organized. Early learning, therefore, depends largely on the maturity level of those brain regions responsible for acquiring cognitive, motor, and emotional skills.

Gray Matter and White Matter

No doubt you have come across references to the brain's gray and white matter. But what are they, exactly? *Gray matter* (Figure 5.1) is the one-tenth of an inch thick, six-layered covering of the brain (also called the *cerebral cortex*) that contains mainly the cell bodies of neurons and their support cells. It is so named because it appears gray in preserved brains. The gray matter includes areas of the brain responsible for sensory perception, such as seeing and hearing, muscle control, speech, numerosity, and emotions. This cortex is where most conscious thinking, creating, and problem solving occur.

The *white matter* is below the gray matter. It looks lighter than the gray matter in preserved tissues, due to *myelin,* the milky and fatty substance that surrounds the transmitting arm of each neuron, called the *axon.* Nerve axons are connected in a complex array of neural networks that relay information back and forth between the rest of the body and the cerebral cortex. These networks also interact with systems that regulate the body's autonomic (unconscious) functions, such as blood pressure, heart rate, and body temperature. Certain nuclei in the limbic system (Figure 5.2) are responsible for the expression of emotions, the release of hormones, and the regulation of food and water intake.

What brain scans show. Longitudinal brain imaging studies of individuals between the ages of 4 and 21 have revealed some interesting clues about how parts of the young brain develop. There may not be many surprises here for people who work with preadolescents, but it is interesting to see how examining brain development can explain the learning and behavior of these children. Table 5.1 has the major imaging findings related to preadolescents along with my own thoughts on some possible implications for learning and teaching (Gogtay et al., 2004). Findings related to the adolescent brain are discussed in the next chapter.

Table 5.1 Preadolescent Brain Development and Some Implications

Research Finding	Possible Implications for Learning Mathematics
The volume of gray matter and white matter continues to increase from childhood until puberty as the brain grows in size.	Children can tackle problems of increasing difficulty as they move through the intermediate grades. There is no "learning pause" in the intermediate grades as some people still believe.
At puberty, when the brain is nearly at its full adult size, gray matter volume begins to decrease because unneeded and unhealthy neurons are pruned away.	By sixth grade, creative problem solving should start becoming easier, include more options, and show greater sophistication of thought.
Parts of the brain associated with basic functions mature early. Motor and sensory functions (taste, smell, and vision) mature first, followed by areas involved in spatial orientation, speech and language development, and attention (upper and lower parietal lobes).	Primary grade children may have some difficulty solving complex visual-spatial problems. Boys may do better than girls at these types of challenges in the early grades, but the gap narrows in the intermediate grades. Multimodality approach likely to be successful.
Later to mature are those areas involved in executive functions (creativity, problem solving, reflection, analysis), attention, and motor coordination (frontal lobes).	These skills are just emerging in the intermediate grades, so problems with multiple approaches and answers are a challenge, but doable.
Most areas of the temporal lobes mature early. These areas are involved mainly in auditory processing. Maturing last is a small section of the temporal lobe involved in the integration of memory, audiovisual association, and recognitions of objects.	Because the auditory areas are rapidly maturing, reading problems aloud is helpful. Three-dimensional object rotation and manipulation would be difficult for intermediate grade students.

Source: Gogtay et al., 2004.

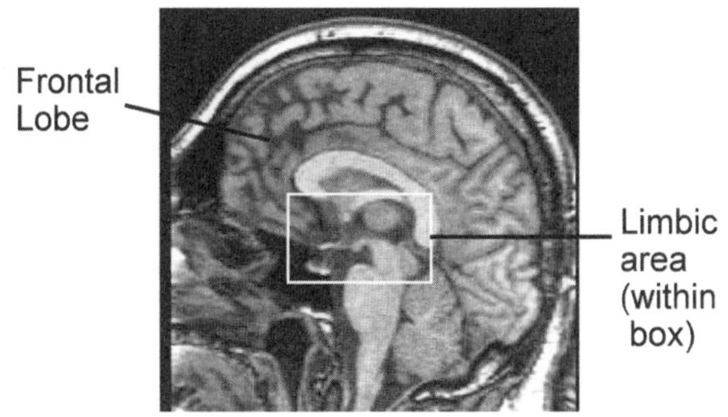

Figure 5.2 Emotional responses are generated in the limbic area. Moderating the intensity of those responses is one function of the frontal lobe.

Emotional and Rational Behavior

Deep within the brain lies the limbic area, which is largely involved in generating emotional responses. Because these emotions can get out of hand, one of the functions of the frontal lobe is to assess and control the types and intensity of emotions emanating from the limbic area (Figure 5.2). But this is hardly a balanced system in preadolescents. Among other things, human survival depends on the family unit, where emotional bonds increase the chances of producing children and raising them to be productive adults. The human brain has learned over thousands of years that survival and emotional messages must have high priority as it filters through all the incoming signals from the body's senses. So it is no surprise that studies of human brain growth show that the emotional (and biologically older) system develops faster and matures much earlier than the frontal lobes (Paus, 2005; Steinberg, 2005). Figure 5.3 shows the percent development of the brain's limbic area and frontal lobes from birth through the age of 24 years. The limbic area is fully mature around the age of 10 to 12, but the frontal lobes mature closer to 22 to 24 years of age. Consequently, the emotional system is more likely to win the tug-of-war for control of behavior during the preadolescent years.

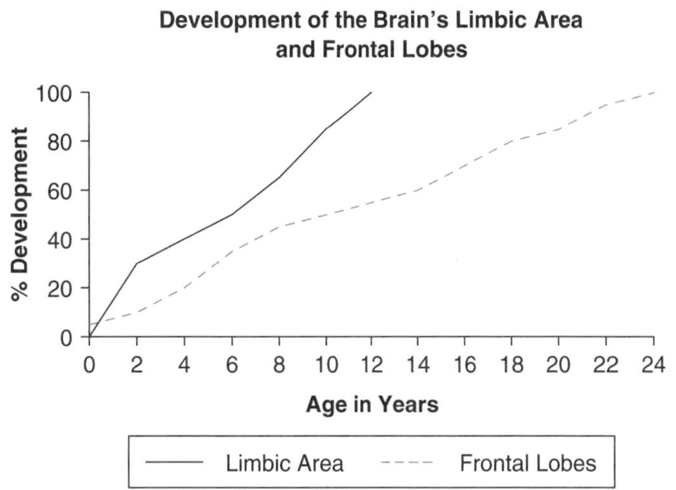

Figure 5.3 Based on recent studies, this chart suggests the possible degree of development of the brain's limbic area and frontal lobes (Paus, 2005; Steinberg, 2005).

What does this mean in a classroom of preadolescents? Emotional messages guide the individual's behavior, including directing its attention to a learning situation. Specifically, emotion drives attention, and attention drives learning. But even more important to understand is that emotional attention comes *before* cognitive recognition. For instance, you see a snake in the garden, and within a few seconds your palms are sweating, your breathing is labored, and your blood pressure is rising—all this before you know whether the snake is even alive. That's your limbic system acting without input from the cognitive parts of the brain (frontal lobe). Thus the brain is responding emotionally to a situation that could be potentially life-threatening without the benefit of cognitive functions, such as thinking, reasoning, and consciousness (Damasio, 2003).

Preadolescents are likely to respond emotionally to a learning situation much faster than rationally. Getting their attention for a lesson in mathematics means trying to find an emotional link to the day's learning objective. Starting a lesson with, "Today we are going to study fractions" will not capture their focus anywhere near as fast as asking whether they would rather have one-third, one-fourth, or one-sixth of a pie. Whenever a teacher attaches a positive emotion to the mathematics lesson, it not only gets attention, but it also helps the students to see mathematics as having real-life applications.

Environmental Influences on the Young Brain

Part of our success as a species can be attributed to the brain's persistent interest in novelty, that is, changes occurring in the environment. The brain is constantly scanning its environment for stimuli. When an unexpected stimulus arises—such as a loud noise from an empty room—a rush of adrenaline closes down all unnecessary activity and focuses the brain's attention so it can spring into action. Conversely, an environment that contains mainly predictable or repeated stimuli (like some classrooms?) lowers the brain's interest in the outside world and tempts it to search within for novel sensations.

We often hear teachers remark that students are more different today in the way they learn than ever before. They seem to have shorter attention spans and bore easily. Why is that? Is there something happening in the environment of learners that alters the way they approach the learning process? Let's look at Table 5.2 and review the kind of environment the brain of today's preadolescent is facing, along with some of my thoughts on implications for learning. Note how students today are immersed in multimedia experiences and are acclimated to multitasking. They want to participate in their learning experiences. When students appear uninterested in a topic, it may be because the lesson is almost entirely teacher directed and there is little opportunity for active student participation. Furthermore, they may not see meaning in what is being presented.

Students today are immersed in multimedia, are acclimated to multitasking, and want to participate in their learning experiences.

Table 5.2 The Preadolescent Environment and Some Implications

Environmental Factor	**Possible Implications for Learning**
Family units are not as stable as they once were. Single-parent families are more common, and children have fewer opportunities to talk with the adults who care for them. Their dietary habits are changing as home cooking is becoming a lost art.	More preadolescents come to school looking to have their emotional needs met *before* they can focus on course content. Also, many have low blood sugar because they do not eat breakfast. Make sure they are fed and make them feel that you really care about their success.
They are surrounded by media: cell phones, movies, computers, video games, e-mail, and the Internet, where they spend 17 hours a week and another 14 hours a week watching television.	Media is part of their learning experience. Because it is so interactive, students today want to participate in their learning experiences. Use all the technology and active participation that you can in your lessons.
They get information from many different sources besides school.	Students are exposed to so much information outside of school that they come with many preconceived notions about numbers, geometry, and problem solving. Find out what they know and what their interests are, and use that information for motivation.
Children have become accustomed to their information-rich and rapidly changing messages in their environment. It divides their attention so they try to pay attention to several things at once, but they seldom go into any one thing in depth.	Multitasking has not shortened children's attention span. But it has made it more difficult to get them to focus on *one* concept long enough to probe it in depth. That is one reason that they are in a hurry to get the answer. By offering problems that can be solved in different ways, we force them to spend more time analyzing the situation as they look for various solutions.
They spend much more time indoors with their technology, thereby missing outdoor opportunities to develop the gross motor skills and socialization skills necessary to communicate and interact personally with others.	Look for opportunities to present and solve problems outdoors or in a large indoor area like the gymnasium. Movement and greater social interaction stimulate long-term memory and create interest in the lesson.
Young brains have responded to technology by changing their functioning and organization to accommodate the large amount of stimulation occurring in the environment. By acclimating themselves to these changes, brains respond more than ever to the unique and different—or *novelty.*	Doing the unexpected is a form of novelty. Every day students have a fairly accurate expectation of how their teachers will present lessons. Anytime you violate that expectation, you create novelty. How many ways can you think of to introduce different types of polygons?

In Chapters 1 and 2, we saw evidence that humans are born with an innate number sense that enables them to estimate small numbers of objects without counting (subitizing) and to understand some basic rules of numbers in base 10, using one-to-one correspondence with finger manipulation. Their brains are excellent pattern recognizers that seek meaning in whatever they encounter. Will the learning environment support or hinder the development of these innate capabilities? As children begin their formal schooling, they will find out there is a lot more to learn about manipulating numbers. How teachers introduce numbers in the primary grades will affect how children view mathematics later. Will we insist that they focus on memorizing symbols, while not understanding the numbers those symbols represent? Will we show them how to perform symbolic procedures, such as how to add fractions, in an essentially mindless fashion?

Because the human brain has superb adaptive capabilities, it can be coaxed to learn the procedures for manipulating symbols during the addition of fractions. After all, lots of school children get good grades in mathematics because they mastered a sequence of actions without any understanding of what they were doing. Many intelligent adults cannot add fractions, even though they could do it as children in school. What happened? If only they had really understood what was going on in their lessons on the addition process, they would never forget how to do it. Instead, they carried the rote procedures in working memory long enough to take the test. After that, the information was dropped out of working memory because it had no meaning.

Teaching for Meaning

We already explained in Chapter 3 the importance of teaching mathematics in a way that makes it meaningful for students. Recognizing that meaning is a criterion for long-term storage, teachers at all grade levels should *purposefully* plan for meaning in their lessons. We also noted that closure was a valuable strategy for helping students attach meaning to their new learning. Here are two basic ideas, with examples, about how to teach arithmetic for meaning using models (Dehaene, 1997) and closure (Sousa, 2006).

Using Models

✓ **Use multiple models.** Arithmetic and mathematical knowledge should be based first on concrete situations rather than abstract concepts. Numerical representations help students develop mental models of arithmetic that connect to their intuitive number sense. For instance, a simple subtraction problem such as $8 - 3 = 5$ can be presented in different ways using concrete situations. It can be shown using a set of objects model: A box has eight toys.

Take away three, and there are five toys left. It can also be applied to a temperature model: If it is only 8 degrees outside and the temperature drops 3 degrees, then it will be 5 degrees. A distance model is another option: In a board game, a chip moving from space 3 to space 8 requires 5 moves. While these examples may seem the same to an adult, they are new for a young student who must discover that subtraction is the arithmetic process applied to them all.

The use of various models is important because relying on just one model may not be sufficient. Suppose you introduce negative numbers, for example, and you ask the class to compute 3 – 8. A student who relies solely on the set of objects model will say that this operation is illogical and impossible because you cannot take eight toys away from three. But this problem would be logical using the temperature model because most young students can comprehend the concept of negative degrees.

✓ **Select the correct model**. Children encounter fractions in real life long before they meet them in school. They have a few concrete examples, such as portions of pie or cake. When first confronted with the problem of adding the fractions 1/2 and 1/3, they can relate these numbers to their intuitive notions of sections of a pie. They may soon realize that these two portions will add up to just less than 1. However, children who have no intuitive understanding of fractions are very likely to simply add the numerators and denominators and get the incorrect result, 1/2 + 1/3 = 2/5.

This result is not as far-fetched as it seems because it does have a concrete representation in the real world. If a baseball player gets one hit out of two times at bat, his average is 1/2. In his next game, if he gets one hit out of three times at bat, his average is 1/3. For both games, his total performance is 2 hits for 5 times at bat, or 2/5. Here is a situation where 1/2 "plus" 1/3 equals 2/5. How do you explain this seeming conflict? When teaching fractions, it is important to make clear to students that they should have the "portion of pie" model in their head, not the "scoring average" model.

Using Cognitive Closure to Remember Meaning

Closure in a lesson does not mean to pack up and move on. Rather, it is a cognitive activity that helps students focus on what was learned and whether it made sense and had meaning. Attaching meaning greatly increases the probability that the learning will be remembered. Remembering the meaning increases the likelihood that the learning will be used again in a new future situation.

✓ One way to assist students in remembering the meaning of what was learned is to have them write it down in a journal after each lesson where something new is presented. It is important that they write down the answers to these three questions:

- **What did we learn today?** This question ensures that the students have made sense of what they learned.
- **How does what we learned today connect or add to something we already have learned?** This question increases the likelihood that the new learning will be associated in memory with similar or related concepts, making future recall easier.
- **How can what we learned today help us in the future?** This question goes to the heart of meaning. The human brain is apt to save information that can be useful to its owner in the future.

Today's Lesson: *Commutative property in multiplication*

1. **Today I learned:** *That I can multiply numbers in any order and get the same answer, so $3 \times 6 \times 7$ is the same as $7 \times 3 \times 6$. This is known as the commutative property.*
2. **This connects/adds to what I know about:** *The same rule worked when learned in addition that $3 + 6 + 7$ was the same as $7 + 3 + 6$.*
3. **What I learned today can help me later when:** *I will be able to rearrange longer lists of numbers to add or multiply faster.*

Figure 5.4 Sample journal entry sheet to help students remember meaning in a lesson.

This writing task should not take more than a few minutes (depending on the age of the students). Preprinted journal pages can make this go faster with younger students. Figure 5.4 suggests one way this preprinted page could be organized, and shows a sample student entry.

Mathematics becomes much easier when students understand what it is about, and when the symbols have meaning for them and become a means to an arithmetic end rather than an end unto themselves. People who do not see meaning in arithmetic computations are often the ones who say they are not good at mathematics.

WHAT CONTENT SHOULD WE BE TEACHING?

Elementary and middle school teachers have expressed to me their concern that there are too many elements in the mathematics curriculum at each grade level and not enough time to cover them. In some cases, important concepts are not given enough time while less important topics are repeated in different grade levels. We have all heard of the "mile-wide and inch-deep curriculum." Despite the widespread standards movement, there still seems to be a lack of focus for specific topics at each grade level that will provide for the progressive development of mathematical competence and be consistent with the student's cognitive growth.

One suggestion for dealing with this situation was proposed by Ainsworth and Christinson (2000). Working with teachers in California, they agreed that each grade level, from kindergarten through grade seven, should focus on one big idea that would be taught in depth. Their rationale was that if students developed a deep understanding of the big idea in their grade, they would not have to be retaught it repeatedly in subsequent grades, but would build on that understanding. As we have previously discussed, their approach is consistent with the notions from cognitive neuroscience that deep understanding leads to meaning, increases the probability that concepts will be remembered, and builds the framework for solid mathematical competence.

Their recommendations for the big idea at each grade level are

- Kindergarten — Number sense
- First grade — Number sense and addition
- Second grade — Subtraction
- Third grade — Multiplication
- Fourth grade — Division
- Fifth grade — Fractions
- Sixth grade — Fractions, decimals, and percentages
- Seventh grade — Ratio and proportions

Of course, the big idea would not be the only concept taught at the grade level, but it would represent the main focus of instruction. Grade 8 was not included in this list because it was assumed that algebra would be the main area of focus. This seems like a commonsense approach consistent with the NCTM *Practices and Standards for Mathematics* (2000) and many state curriculum frameworks in mathematics.

TEACHING PROCESS SKILLS

Understanding how to manipulate numbers, detect and analyze patterns, solve problems, and apply mathematical knowledge to the real world requires the acquisition of certain process skills. NCTM's *Principles and Standards for Mathematics* (NCTM, 2000) contains 10 standards, of which five are content standards and five are process standards. The process standards are (1) problem solving, (2) reasoning and proof, (3) communication, (4) connections, and (5) representation.

Three areas related to the process standards that cognitive neuroscience has explored to some extent are number sense, estimation (a by-product of subitizing), and reasoning. When planning and presenting lessons for preadolescents, here are some questions to ask about these skills.

Does the Lesson Enhance Number Sense?

Chapter 1 provides an in-depth look at that innate quantifying capability that we call number sense, particularly as it applies to cognitive development in a child's early years. We have already noted that cognitive neuroscientists view number sense as a biologically based innate quality that is limited to simple intuitions about quantity, including the rapid and accurate perception of small numerosities (subitizing), the ability to count, to compare numerical magnitudes, and to comprehend simple arithmetic operations.

As we discussed in Chapter 2, mathematics educators have a much broader view of number sense than cognitive neuroscientists. Because the development of number sense is not limited to the primary grades, teachers of mathematics at all grade levels should be determining which of the number sense abilities are being addressed in each lesson.

Assessing Students' Number Sense

As teachers prepare lessons to develop number sense in their students, it is important for them to know the level of number sense that each student has already reached. We noted in Chapter 4 that designing a number knowledge test is no easy task but that researchers Sharon Griffin and Robbie Case started addressing this problem in the 1980s. While using their assessments for over 20 years, they made refinements based on their research to ensure that the items reflected the capabilities possessed by a majority of students at each age level (Griffin & Case, 1997; Griffin, 2002).

> *As teachers prepare lessons to develop number sense, they should determine what level of number sense each student has already reached.*

By administering these tests, a teacher can determine how far an individual student's number sense has progressed at ages 4, 6, 8, and 10. The teacher can then use differentiated activities to develop the number sense for students of the same age who may be at different levels of competence. Table 5.3 shows the current version of the test for ages 6, 8, and 10, which is reprinted here with permission (Griffin, 2002). The test for age 4 is found in Chapter 4.

Table 5.3 Number Knowledge Test for 6-, 8-, and 10-Year-Olds	
Level 1 (6-year-old level): Go to Level 3 if 5 or more correct.	
1	If you had 4 chocolates and someone gave you 3 more, how many chocolates would you have altogether?
2	What number comes right after 7?
3	What number comes two numbers after 7?
4a	Which is bigger: 5 or 4?
4b	Which is bigger: 7 or 9?
5a	This time, I'm going to ask you about smaller numbers. Which is smaller: 8 or 6?
5b	Which is smaller: 5 or 7?
6a	Which number is closer to 5: 6 or 2? (Show visual array after asking question)
6b	Which number is closer to 7: 4 or 9? (Show visual array after asking question)
7	How much is 2 + 4? (OK to use fingers for counting)
8	How much is 8 take away 6? (OK to use fingers for counting)
9a	(Show visual array of 8 5 2 6 and ask child to point to and name each numeral). When you are counting, which of these numbers do you say first?
9b	When you are counting, which of these numbers do you say last?
Level 2 (8-year-old level): Go to Level 3 if 5 or more correct.	
1	What number comes 5 numbers after 49?
2	What number comes 4 numbers before 60?
3a	Which is bigger: 69 or 71?
3b	Which is bigger: 32 or 28?
4a	This time I'm going to ask you about smaller numbers. Which is smaller: 27 or 32?
4b	Which is smaller: 51 or 39?
5a	Which number is closer to 21: 25 or 18? (Show visual array after asking question)
5b	Which number is closer to 28: 31 or 24? (Show visual array after asking question)
6	How many numbers are there in between 2 and 6? (Accept either 3 or 4)
7	How many numbers are there in between 7 and 9? (Accept either 1 or 2)
8	(Show card: 12 54) How much is 12 + 54?
9	(Show card: 47 21) How much is 47 take away 21?

Table 5.3 Number Knowledge Test for 6-, 8-, and 10-Year-Olds

Level 3 (10-year-old level):	
1	What number comes 10 numbers after 99?
2	What number comes 9 numbers after 999?
3a	Which difference is bigger: the difference between 9 and 6 or the difference between 8 and 3?
3b	Which difference is bigger: the difference between 6 and 2 or the difference between 8 and 5?
4a	Which difference is smaller: the difference between 99 and 92 or the difference between 25 and 11?
4b	Which difference is smaller: the difference between 48 and 36 or the difference between 84 and 73?
5	(Show card: 13 39) How much is 13 + 39?
6	(Show card: 36 18) How much is 36 – 18?
7	How much is 301 take away 7?

Source: Griffin, 2002. Reprinted with permission of the author.

Developing Multidigit Number Sense

Students in primary grades have developed a notion of counting but have a difficult time studying subject matter that contains large numbers, such as the population of a country, distances to the planets and stars, and the cost of running a space mission. Although they are fascinated by large quantities, they have a limited understanding of them and often express exaggerated amounts in their conversation as in, "There were thousands of people at my birthday party." When students lack an understanding of large numbers, they cannot reason effectively with the information they are given. In this situation, teachers need to develop the students' ability to process large numbers, that is, develop their multidigit number sense.

> *Multidigit number sense allows students to acquire an understanding of large numbers and to make judgments about their reasonableness in different problem situations.*

The concept of multidigit number sense refers to the students' understanding of, and flexibility in, using numbers of more than one digit. It includes intuitive feelings for large numbers and their uses as well as the ability to make judgments about the reasonableness of multidigit numbers in different problem situations (Jones, Thornton, & Putt, 1994). Because of the complexity of this topic, teachers should select meaningful activities that help students make sense of how large numbers are used in context.

Diezmann and English (2001) have found success working with students in the primary grades by selecting activities that help the students read large numbers, develop meaningful examples for large numbers, and understand large numbers that represent quantity, distance, and money.

✓ **Reading large numbers.** In this activity, students are introduced to the pattern in reading large numbers. Numbers of increasing magnitude are displayed for the students, starting with the ones column, progressing to the thousands column, and finally, the millions column. The name of each column is added to facilitate students' reading.

✓ **Developing physical examples of large numbers.** Concrete examples help students understand the nature of ever-increasing numbers. One activity to show visually the quantities 1, 10, 100 and 1,000 is to use colored sprinkles (confectionery decoration) on buttered bread that is cut into four pieces. The students add 1 sprinkle on the first piece of bread, 10 sprinkles on the second piece, approximately 100 sprinkles on the third piece (by estimating groups of 10), and approximately 1,000 sprinkles on the final piece (by estimating groups of 100).

The sprinkles activity provides a meaningful example for the students' understanding of the relative magnitude of numbers to a thousand. Some students may extrapolate beyond the physical examples, and observe that you probably cannot fit one million sprinkles on one piece of bread.

✓ **Appreciating large numbers in money.** What sized container would be needed to carry a million dollars? Before solving this problem, the students should complete two tasks. The first involves making posters that are labeled with the amounts $1, $10, $100, $1,000, $10,000, $100,000 and $1,000,000. The students identify items in magazine and newspaper advertisements that approximately cost each of these amounts, and glue the pictures of items under the corresponding amounts. This activity raises students' awareness of the monetary value of expensive items. In the second task, the students calculate how much money is in a Monopoly game.

After completing these tasks, the students tackle the main problem of determining the container size needed to hold a million dollars. The students should use the Monopoly money to help them solve this problem. No containers are provided as the students are encouraged to model different container sizes with their hands. Through discussion, the students should realize that there is more than one answer to the problem. For instance, the size of the container is dependent on the denomination of the notes that are used to make one million dollars. Some students may observe that a larger-sized container would be required if notes of low value are used and vice versa.

✓ **Appreciating large numbers in distance.** How far away are the brightest stars? The purpose of this activity is to develop the students' understanding of large distances within the context of space travel. One approach is to have the students make 10 paper stars and label them with the names of the 10 brightest stars in the sky, their brightness, and their distance from Earth. The stars can be fastened onto upturned paper cups for ease of mobility. The students initially arrange the stars by order of brightness, beginning with the brightest star.

Next, consideration is given to the stars' distances from Earth. After the students discuss the notion of measuring stellar distances in light years, they rearrange the stars in order from the closest to Earth to the most distant. Extend the activity by asking the students to discuss whether there is a relationship between the brightness of a star and its distance from Earth.

To represent the stars' relative distances from Earth in light years, draw a time line and mark it in 100s from 0 to 1,000. Ask the students to position each star at the correct number of light years from Earth. Then they can discuss the fact that when we see a star today, the light from that star was actually emitted many years ago. Older students may be able to connect the year when light was emitted from particular stars to significant historic events on Earth. In this way, students make links between their mathematical understanding and their scientific knowledge.

Does the Lesson Deal With Estimation?

A close correlate to number sense is estimation. NCTM's *Curriculum Focal Points* (NCTM, 2006) state that students in Grade 3 should be able to "develop their understanding of numbers by building their facility with mental computation . . . by using computational estimation, and by performing paper-and-pencil computations." In Grade 4, students should "extend their understanding of place value and ways of representing numbers to 100,000 in various contexts. They use estimation in determining the relative sizes of amounts or distances."

Estimation is an extension of the brain's innate ability to subitize. Estimating how many animals to hunt or how many crops to plant to feed the village was a survival skill. Our ancestors were good at it. Are we? Mathematics educators often comment on the poor estimation skills of students. A frustrated teacher once told me that a middle school student felt very pleased with himself after

> *Estimation is an extension of the brain's innate ability to subitize. Estimating how many animals to hunt or how many crops to plant to feed the village was a survival skill. Our ancestors were good at it. Are we?*

calculating the size of a molecule to be just over one meter in length. The unreasonableness of this measurement never occurred to him. Yet, ironically, youngsters often successfully use estimation skills *outside* of school. For example, they can quickly make the computations needed to cross a street with traffic, decide if a sibling is sharing equally, or accurately throw, catch, or hit a ball in sports. Poor estimation skills, it seems, are more likely to appear *inside* school when dealing with arithmetic estimation, and they can result from at least three factors.

- First, students at an early age are programmed to get the exact answer in a problem, so they have few experiences with estimation. Furthermore, activities that ask students for both an estimated and exact answer undermine the value of estimation. Why should students estimate if they are going to find the exact answer, too?
- Second, when students use a calculator in their work, they assume the calculator's answer must be right, with no thought that they could have inadvertently entered an incorrect number or a misplaced decimal. Consequently, they rarely reflect on the reasonableness of their answers.
- Third, because students want to get the answer quickly, estimation is avoided because it often takes more time.

Activities involving estimation should begin as early as possible in the primary grades. However, they should not be isolated as a single unit of instruction, but rather should be taught in the context of other mathematics skills throughout all grade levels. If we want to emphasize the value of estimation, then students should be given assignments that require them only to estimate.

Methods of Estimation

The common methods of estimation include (1) rounding, which involves finding a number to the nearest ten, hundred, thousand, or the nearest one, tenth, hundredth, thousandth; (2) front-end estimation, which entails computing the higher place values or leftmost digits, then adjusting the rounded sum using the lower place values or digits to the right; and (3) clustering, which involves grouping numbers, and is useful whenever a group of numbers cluster around a common value. These methods of estimation are most helpful when students are doing computational tasks. They can check whether their answers come close to the estimated answer and to determine if their answer makes sense.

Students need to be aware that methods of estimation may not work in the real world. If you want to buy a shirt for $17.45, rounding down to the nearest dollar will not give you enough money to buy it. This is also true for estimations related to measurement. If you need exactly three and one-quarter yards of fabric to make a dress, you will not succeed if you round down to just three yards. Thus, rounding down of estimations of quantity in real-life situations will not give you enough. So what other types of estimation are available?

Types of Estimation

Taylor-Cox (2001) suggests four distinct types of estimation.

1. **True approximations** are used when an estimate is acceptable, especially when dealing with very large numbers. Is it really important to know that the average distance from the Earth to the sun is 92,955,630 miles, or will 93,000,000 miles suffice? True approximations are more applicable to problems in the intermediate and upper grades. Unfortunately, the numbers that youngsters work with in the primary grades are typically smaller and less complex than the numbers that lend themselves to true approximations. Making true approximations has little advantage with simpler numbers because we can easily calculate to ensure that we know the exact amount.
2. **Overestimating** is used when rounding up might be beneficial, such as overestimating the amount of food to buy for a child's birthday party. The major drawback for this option is that it may be wasteful if you get way too much. But if you underestimate, some kids may not get enough food.
3. **Underestimating** is used when rounding down is applicable. This can be helpful in certain situations. Better to underestimate the amount of profit a business will make so as to avoid overspending.
4. **Range-based estimations** broaden the applicability and understanding of estimation. Some situations call for underestimating and some for overestimating. Range-based estimation involves thinking about quantity in terms of the upper end and the lower end that encompass an estimate: "What are the minimum and maximum quantities I need for this?" In the primary grades, teachers can design mathematical tasks that are productive and worthwhile by using range-based estimation, thereby encouraging students to become better estimators.

Meaningful Estimation Activities

For estimation activities to be meaningful rather than futile, Taylor-Cox (2001) suggests that the activities include the following five components.

- ✓ **Purpose.** Whenever you ask students to estimate a number, give them a reason for doing so. These contexts offer a purpose and give students a reason to engage in real-life mathematical problem solving. Otherwise, students may ask, "Who cares?" Making the task relevant, interesting, and significant invites students to care and, consequently, invites them to engage in mathematics. Offering a purpose does not ensure that the "Who cares?" response will disappear. But by listening to students and reflecting on their perspectives and feelings, you can manage the continuing challenge of providing meaningful mathematics.

- ✓ **Referents (benchmarks).** To help students succeed, give them a referent or benchmark they can use when making estimations. For instance, if you ask students to estimate the number of marbles in a jar, it would be helpful to provide a smaller container with a known number of marbles of the same size. This container gives students a point of reference on which to base their estimates for the larger jar.

- ✓ **Pertinent information.** Clarify the actual mathematical problem to be solved so that the students can decide what type of estimation is most appropriate. For example, students do not need to estimate the number of marbles in a jar if they are going to open the jar and count the actual number of marbles. As explained earlier, doing so counteracts the purpose of, and time spent on, estimating. Rather, you should ask whether estimating or counting to find out the actual number is more appropriate. Which methods will be used to check for accuracy? What kind of information is pertinent to the given mathematical situation?

- ✓ **Diverse experiences.** Students need numerous and diverse experiences with estimation in the context of other content areas, such as in time and measurement. Primary-grade students often have difficulty estimating time. Teachers are no help when they attach inaccurate time constraints to their statements. When they say, "I will be there in just a minute" or "Wait one second," we really mean, "I will be there when I can" or "wait indefinitely." Perhaps asking students to actually time the teacher encourages them to check estimates of time while enhancing their experiences and improving their precision with estimating time.

  Young students work on measurement skills by comparing lengths, weights, and capacities. For estimating size they use comparative language, such as *larger, smaller, heavier,* and *lighter.* Figure 5.5 shows two examples of activities for different age groups that require estimating size. In these types of tasks, students engage in estimation that is related to size rather than quantity, they recognize that estimation is an important tool for dealing with real-life mathematical experiences.

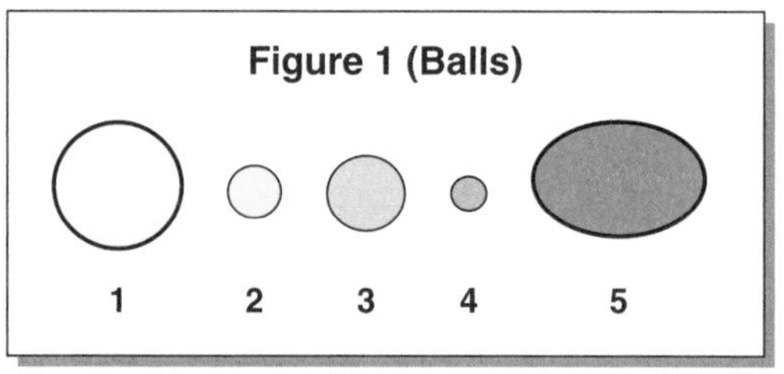

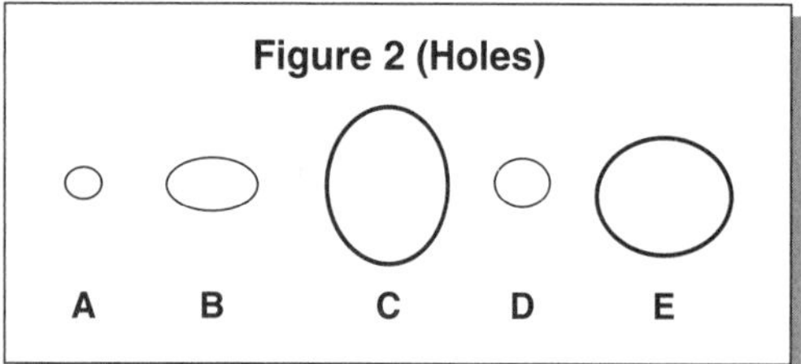

Primary grades: Which balls in Figure 1 can fit through the holes in Figure 2?

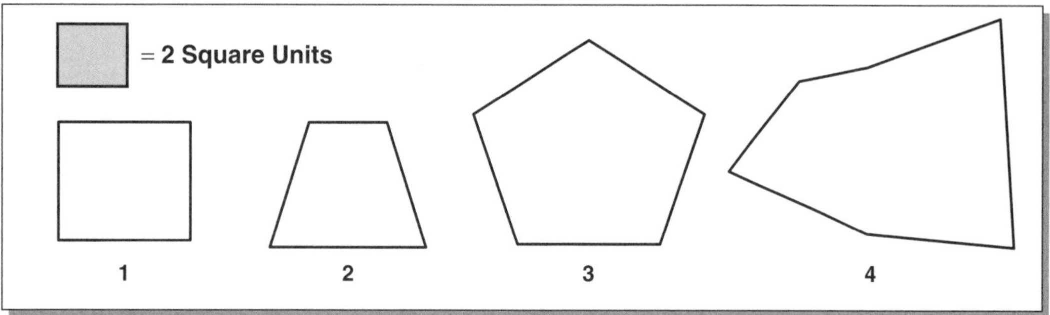

Intermediate grades: Estimate how many square units are in each of the four shapes.

Figure 5.5 These are sample activities that develop estimation skills in different grade levels.

✓ **Range-based techniques.** Estimation should involve using mathematical skill to predict information within a reasonable range. If, for example, the actual number of a quantity or measurement is in the 70s, an appropriate estimation may be in a range of 10 or less. But if the actual number is in the 700s, an appropriate range may include up to 60 or 70 numbers. Although suitable ranges vary with the problem situation, the aim is to estimate within an appropriate range. However, many students still want to estimate the precise amount. To combat this need for the right answer, it may help to use terminology such as the *actual answer*. A range of about 10 to 20 per hundred is reasonable. This type of ranged-based estimation is particularly helpful in situations that call for approximating a quantity that may need to be overestimated.

Estimation experiences improve the students' estimation skills, increase their confidence in their level of mathematical expertise, enhance their perception of the value of mathematics, and improve their mathematics achievement test scores (Booth & Siegler, 2006). Each estimation activity is an opportunity for teachers to connect mathematics with the everyday lives of students.

From Memorization to Understanding

We discussed earlier in this chapter the importance of teaching children the meaning of what they are doing when they manipulate numbers during arithmetic computations. Meaning not only increases the chances that information will be stored in long-term memory, but also gives the learner the opportunity to change procedures as the nature of the problem changes. Without meaning, students memorize procedures without understanding how and why they work. As a result, they end up confused about when to use which procedure. Teachers who use primarily a declarative approach emphasize not only arithmetic facts but how they are related to each other and connected to other concepts the students have already learned. They use elaborative rehearsal and provide for cognitive closure.

Are We Teaching Elementary-Grade Arithmetic for Understanding?

In some schools, we teach too much arithmetic through procedural approaches and very little with declarative methods. Could it be because that is how most teachers learned arithmetic themselves? Could this explain why arithmetic instruction in the primary grades has not changed very much over the years? We teach students a procedure for solving computation problems, which they then repeatedly practice (procedural memory). But the practice does not result in computational fluency because we rarely talk about how and why the procedure works. Consequently, when we give the students a problem to solve, they reflexively draw on their knowledge of the practiced procedure and apply that procedure quickly and efficiently, but with little understanding of the mathematical concepts involved.

> *To develop understanding and meaning, teachers should show students (at the earliest possible age) why they are performing certain arithmetic operations.*

Of course, students need to learn some basic procedural activities, such as memorizing a short version of the multiplication tables mentioned in Chapter 2, along with a few number facts. But the emphasis should be on showing students (at the earliest possible age) *why* they are performing certain arithmetic operations. The more arithmetic we can teach through declarative processes involving understanding and meaning, the more likely students will succeed and actually enjoy mathematics.

Example of a Declarative-Based Approach

A declarative-based approach focuses on capitalizing on the students's innate number sense, intuitive notions of counting by finger manipulation, and an understanding of a base-10 model for expressing quantities. It includes allowing students to create their own procedures for arithmetic computations so that they truly understand the algorithms involved. Researchers have long recognized that students in the primary grades are capable of constructing their own methods of computation (Carpenter et al., 1998; Fuson et al., 1997). In doing so, the primary-grades students pass through three predictable developmental levels.

- At the first level, students deal with all the quantities in a problem. To add a group of objects, they count out separate groups of objects, combine the groups, and then recount the total. To subtract, students count out and separate a group, and then recount what is left.
- At the next level, students consider all parts of the problem before solving it. They demonstrate this ability by counting on from, or back to, a quantity to determine an answer.
- At the most advanced level, students use abstract knowledge and consider quantities in flexible ways. They make use of what they already know to solve new problems. For example, students might use their prior knowledge to realize that $6 + 7$ is equal to $6 + 6 + 1$, or that $7 + 9$ is equal to $6 + 10$, by decomposing and recombining tens and ones.

Understanding the development of mathematical thinking in young students allows teachers to anticipate procedures that students are apt to invent and find ways to support students as they progress through the different levels. When teachers encourage students to invent alternative problem-solving strategies, the learning objectives are different from those that result from instruction using standard memorization procedures. The emphasis is on making sense and finding meaning in the methods that students create and successfully use (Scharton, 2004).

Mathematics educator, Susan Scharton, has been a strong advocate for giving primary-grade students opportunities to solve computational problems, to create their own procedures for solving them, and to explain their methods to others. She found that this approach improved the students' accuracy as well as their understanding of the methods they had created. When she asked students to explain their methods, their understanding of their own procedures deepened as a result of this elaborative rehearsal. Listening to the methods that others had used prompted some students to experiment with other students' methods of computing.

One example that Scharton (2004) has used to demonstrate how students can resort to different solution strategies involves the following problem: "Paul has 28 markers. He got 34 more. How many does he have?" One second-grade student wrote 34 under 28 and attempted classic addition of two-digit numbers in a column. Here is what he wrote down and then stopped:

$$\begin{array}{r} 1 \\ 28 \\ \underline{+\ 34} \\ 2 \end{array}$$

He tried to follow a standard procedure that typically begins by combining the numbers in the ones column. However, he did not understand how this step in the standard procedure works when the resulting sum is a two-digit number: He was unsure about where to place which digit. He treated each digit separately but did not associate each digit with a value. He was trying to use an efficient procedure that he did not understand and lacked confidence in his method because he could not recall the steps he thought he had learned. If he had devised his own solution strategy, he would have been forced to rely on his own understanding of the numbers and operations he was using, rather than on someone else's.

Another second-grade student, who came from a class that encouraged sharing problem-solving approaches, used a different method. She was able to accurately and efficiently solve the problem using the method she described in Figure 5.6. Her process demonstrated essential aspects of number sense and place-value relationships. She decomposed numbers into tens and ones and then recombined these parts. She understood that each digit in a two-digit number has a different and separate value. She recognized the commutative and associative properties of the problem, and she created her own sequence of steps to follow that were comfortable and meaningful to her. Not only could she use a method that made sense, she could clearly explain in writing why and how her method worked.

What I did was I put 20 from 28 together with 30 from 34 and got 50. I put 50 and 8 together and 58. Then I broke up 4 into 2 and 2. Then I put 58 plus one of the twos and got 60. I put 60 plus the other two and then I got 62.

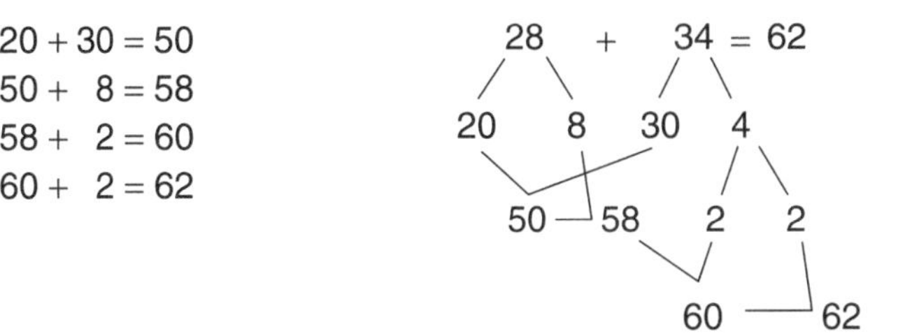

Figure 5.6 A second-grade student describes her method for solving the addition of a pair of two-digit numbers. (Adapted from Scharton, 2004)

An instructional model for first and second grades. Hoping to encourage young students to develop their own procedures for solving arithmetic problems, Scharton (2004) devised an instructional model in which students in first and second grades alternate between small-group sessions and whole-class discussions.

✓ The model focuses on the students' invention of meaningful computation methods and how they can effectively communicate these methods to one another through discussions and written work. Here's how it works.
  - *Small-group work.* Students first participate in a small, heterogeneous group of four to six students every week, usually during choice time. Give the group an arithmetic problem to solve. Meanwhile, the rest of the class works on activities that expose students to different types of problems and promote the development of various invented strategies for solution. In the small group, students independently solve the problem using methods they have invented or have learned from other students. They explain their methods to other group members (elaborative rehearsal) and discuss how their methods are similar to and different from one another, as well as the ways in which the methods are related. Students write down the ways in which they solved the problem.
  - *Whole-class discussion.* Following the small-group session, the whole-class discussion allows students to explain a range of methods to the larger group. Class discussions should focus on the efficiency of each method, the relationships between the methods, ways to effectively represent and communicate them, and how and why each method is successful. After the whole-class discussion, give students another similar problem to solve to determine the degree of transfer, that is, which strategies that were discussed the students will apply to solve the new problem. The students repeat this cycle weekly. Figure 5.7 illustrates this instructional model.

Too often, the goal of arithmetic instruction in most primary classrooms is the accurate and rapid use of a teacher-demonstrated algorithm. Scharton's model, however, helps young students build fluency by inventing their own computation procedures, explaining these procedures clearly to their peers, and analyzing their procedures for relevancy, efficiency, and effectiveness.

Multiplication With Understanding

An elementary school principal recently told me of conversations she had with parents about the third-grade mathematics curriculum. The parents felt there should be heavy emphasis on memorizing multiplication facts. To them, third-grade mathematics should include memorizing facts through drill

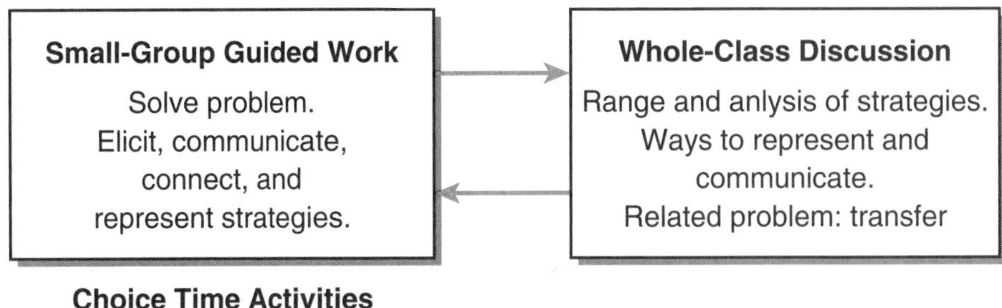

Figure 5.7 This instructional model by Scharton (2004) for first and second grades encourages students to develop strategies in small-group settings and to share them in whole-class discussions. (Used by permission of the author.)

and practice, worksheets, flash cards, and other memorization aids. But this school principal was promoting an approach that encouraged problem solving and understanding. She explained to the parents that this approach would help children remember the processes of multiplication for a much longer time. She recounted from her own experiences that students who had mastered their multiplication tables during third grade were barely able to remember them the following year. Apparently, memorizing multiplication facts during third grade had accomplished little because it did not build understanding of multiplication concepts. Despite having experienced a "back to basics" curriculum, they still did not know what multiplication is.

The *Principles and Standards for School Mathematics* (NCTM, 2000) states that "learning mathematics with understanding is essential" and that research shows "the alliance of factual knowledge, procedural proficiency, and conceptual understanding makes all three components usable in powerful ways." NCTM's *Curriculum Focal Points* (NCTM, 2006) emphasizes that "Students understand the meanings of multiplication and division of whole numbers through the use of representations."

Students typically develop the ability to add quite naturally, but multiplication is much more complex than addition and requires guidance to understand the actions that are important elements of the process. By memorizing facts before developing an understanding of multiplication, students get the mistaken impression about the need to understand what it means to multiply and the situations in which multiplying is the appropriate thing to do.

So what does it mean to understand multiplication? The mathematics education literature suggests that a basic understanding of multiplication requires four interconnected concepts:

(a) quantity, (b) problem situations requiring multiplication, (c) equal groups, and (d) units relevant to multiplication. Most of these understandings can develop from experiences using counting and grouping strategies to solve meaningful problems in the early grades (Smith & Smith, 2006).

- **Understanding quantity.** The meaning of quantity often gets overlooked in addition, but it provides an important foundation for understanding multiplication. A quantity is a characteristic of objects that can be counted or measured, and it consists of a *number* and a *unit*. Seven dollars is an example of a quantity because it includes both the number 7 and the unit, dollars. Number words (e.g., seven) are often used to describe the number portion of a quantity, but other representations, such as pictures (e.g., 7 bills representing 7 dollars), can be used. In addition to the number, a unit must be specified to know the complete quantity. A count is a particular type of number that is part of the quantity characteristic of collections of objects. It answers the question, "How many." Counting begins with counting by ones and progresses to skip counting using larger, equal-sized units. Students need sufficient experience in counting collections of objects to clearly understand these two aspects of quantities and the various ways of representing them. A measure (e.g., length) is a particular type of quantity that is a continuous characteristic of individual objects. Measuring includes selecting an appropriate unit of measure (e.g., an inch) and determining the number of these units in the continuous characteristic of the object. Thus, to fully understand quantity, students need to understand the differences between discrete and continuous quantities, recognizing they use both different units and different processes (counting versus measuring) to determine the number portion of the quantity.
- **Understanding problem situations requiring multiplication.** Students need experience interpreting word problems that require multiplication and distinguishing them from other situations requiring addition, subtraction, or division. Students also need to understand the relationships between multiplication and division and be able to find each of the three possible unknown quantities, providing any two of these three pieces of information are given (e.g., $3 \times 7 = ?$ or $3 \times ? = 21$).
- **Understanding equal groups.** Students need experience arranging objects into groups to understand the role of equal groups in multiplication and to understand the efficiency of multiplying equal groups instead of counting all of the objects in the problem. Number sense includes the ability to compose and decompose numbers. Reasoning in multiplication includes using factors and multiples as equal groups when composing and decomposing numbers instead of using adding. For example, eight objects can be arranged into groups

representing *multiplication* (one group of eight, two groups of four, four groups of two, or eight groups of one) rather than groups representing *addition* (one and seven, two and six, four and four, and eight and zero). Visual images are particularly helpful in understanding grouping (e.g., the difference between a disorganized collection of 60 items and the same 60 items organized into 5 groups of 12 items or an array of 6 rows and 10 columns).

- **Understanding units relevant to multiplication.** Students need experience with counting and arranging objects into groups to understand the differences between various kinds of units that are relevant to multiplication. Addition most often involves the joining of unequal quantities of the same unit (e.g., adding 35 cents and 24 cents). However, the two factors in multiplication most often refer to different units (e.g., multiplying 12 dogs by four legs for each dog). Students also need to understand how units are sometimes transformed in multiplication. For example, adding 7 oranges to 7 oranges makes 14 oranges, but multiplying the same units, such a 7 inches times 3 inches equals 21 *square inches.*

One way to increase the students' deeper understanding of the process of multiplication is to show different ways that multiplication can be carried out by hand. Figure 5.8 shows how to multiply a three-digit number by a two-digit number using the traditional method (a) as well as another way known as *lattice multiplication* (b). Multiplication requires three steps: multiply, carry, and add. In the traditional method, the multiplying and carrying steps are done together, so it is easy to get confused. In lattice multiplication, each step is clear. It was introduced to Europe by the famous mathematician, Fibonacci, in 1202 in his treatise, *Liber Abacii* (Book of the Abacus).

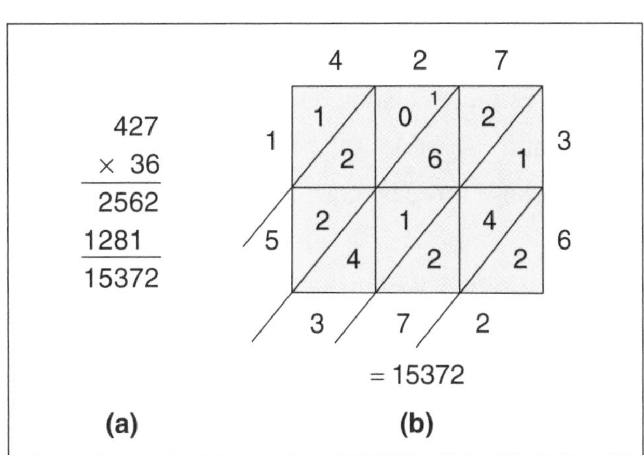

Figure 5.8 The numbers on the left in section (a) show the traditional method of multiplying two multidigit numbers. Section (b) illustrates the lattice method.

The process is simple. If we wish to multiply 427 by 36, we write 427 across the top of the lattice and 36 down the right-hand side of a 3 × 2 rectangle (because we have three- and two-digit numbers). We fill in the lattice by multiplying the digits at the head of the columns by the digits to the right of the row. If the partial product is two digits, the tens digit goes above the diagonal and the units digit is written below the diagonal. If the partial product is only one digit, a zero is placed above the diagonal and the unit digit below.

When all the combinations have been multiplied, we add the numbers along the diagonal, beginning in the upper right and placing the sum on the diagonal to the left outside the grid. If the sum is two digits, the tens digit is placed in the top row of the diagonal to the left and added to that diagonal's sum. Reading the digits outside the grid from upper left down across the bottom gives the final product of 15,372. This approach is not a cure-all, but it does provide novelty, and it may be just what some students need to better understand the process of multiplication.

Does the Lesson Develop Mathematical Reasoning?

The NCTM *Principles and Standards for School Mathematics* (NCTM, 2000) and the *Curriculum Focal Points* (NCTM, 2006) call for increased attention to developing mathematical reasoning as early as first grade, where students should be able to include ideas such as commutativity and associativity of tens and ones and can solve two-digit addition and subtraction problems with strategies that they understand and can explain. Mathematical reasoning also includes spatial and quantitative concepts as well as metacognition, which is thinking about what you are doing, why you are doing it, and making adjustments as needed.

Mathematical competence involves a blend of skills, knowledge, procedures, understanding, reasoning, and application. But too often, instruction focuses on skills, knowledge, and performance, that is, *what* students know and are able to do. Thus, students learn to use routine methods, leading to superficial understanding. We do not spend enough time on reasoning and deep understanding, that is, *why* and *how* mathematics works as it does. Knowledge and performance are not reliable indicators of either reasoning or understanding. For deep understanding, the what, the why, and the how must be well-connected. Then students can attach importance to different patterns and engage in mathematical reasoning.

> *Too often, mathematics instruction focuses on skills, knowledge, and performance but spends little time on reasoning and deep understanding.*

Can Preadolescents Do Mathematical Reasoning?

Have the brains of young children developed sufficiently to carry out reasoning skills? The answer: yes, but it depends on which reasoning skill. By the age of six, most students can demonstrate deductive reasoning using concrete objects. Abstract reasoning, on the other hand, is possible, but more difficult, and becomes easier in the early teen years and over the course of adolescence as the brain's frontal lobes mature. Teachers of preadolescents can find many activities in books and on the Web designed to enhance reasoning skills. Using activities that move students from concrete to abstract reasoning in effect also moves them from arithmetic thinking to algebraic thinking.

✓ Here is one example: Show students in the first and second grades a series of number sentences. Ask them to discuss the series and to make a general statement (conjecture) about that series (Carpenter & Levi, 2000).

Number Sentences	Conjecture by Students
7 – 9 = –2 10 – 14 = –4 15 – 20 = –5	When you subtract a number bigger than your starting number, you will always get a negative number for your answer. Then: 7 – 16 = ?
8 + 0 = 8 11 + 0 = 11 0 + 15 = 15	Zero plus a number equals that number. Then: 19 + 0 = ?
6 – 6 = 0 12 – 12 = 0 14 – 14 = 0	If you subtract the same number from the same number, you will get zero. Then: 21 – 21 = ?
4 – 0 = 4 13 – 0 = 13 21 – 0 = 21	If you subtract zero from a number, you will end up with the same number. Then: 18 – 0 = ?
3 + 3 = 6 6 + 6 = 12 11 + 11 = 22	If you add two identical whole numbers that are higher than zero, you will get an even number. Then: 14 + 14 = ?
5 + 3 = 8 11 + 7 = 18 15 + 9 = 24	If you add two odd whole numbers, you will get an even number. Then: 13 + 17 = ?

8 + 3 = 11	If you add an even and an odd whole number, you will always
14 + 7 = 21	get an odd whole number.
18 + 9 = 27	Then: 6 + 11 = ?

Interpreting the Equal Sign

Although most students in the primary grades can come up with these conjectures, they have difficulty interpreting the equal sign as expressing a relationship. Even into the upper elementary grades, most students interpret the equal sign as an operational symbol meaning to "find the total" or to "put the answer here." When asked to define the equal sign, students not only provide operational interpretations but also believe that interpretations such as "the total" and "the answer" are more accurate than interpretations such as "equal to" or "two amounts are the same" (McNeil & Alibali, 2005). One study provided evidence that age alone cannot account for students' operational—rather than relational—interpretation of the equal sign. When researchers asked first- through sixth-grade students what number should be placed on the line to make the number sentence 8 + 4 = __ + 5 true, they found that fewer than 10 percent in any grade gave the correct answer. Further, that performance did not improve with age (Carpenter, Franke, & Levi, 2003). The obvious question here is whether the preadolescents' difficulties in interpreting the equal sign are due to immature cognitive structures or to their earlier experiences with arithmetic.

Several studies were conducted to find the answer to this question. A case study of a second-grade classroom provided a systematic examination of the contexts in which students actually see the equal sign. The researchers analyzed two mathematics textbooks used by students in the classroom. They found that the equal sign was nearly always presented in the operations-equal-answer context (e.g., 4 + 5 = __). This finding is in line with the belief that students' understanding of the equal sign can be explained by their experiences (Seo & Ginsburg, 2003).

> *Most middle school students do not interpret the equal sign as a relational symbol, setting the stage for difficulties with algebraic operations. Their textbooks don't help.*

In an examination of four popular middle school mathematics textbooks, researchers found the textbooks frequently present the equal sign in an operations-equal-answer context, and rarely present the equal sign in an operations-on-both-sides context. This practice likely reinforces the students' interpretation of the equal sign as an operational symbol. Thus middle school mathematics textbooks may not be designed to help students acquire a relational understanding of the equal sign.

Although the proportion of equal signs presented in an operations-equal-answer context declined across the middle grades, even in eighth grade, many students continue to interpret the equal sign as an operational symbol (McNeil, Grandau, Knuth, Alibali, Stephens, Hattikudur et al., 2006).

Researchers found that students in middle school did not exhibit a relational understanding of the equal sign unless they had contextual support. Seventh-grade students were randomly assigned to view the equal sign in one of three contexts: alone (=), in an operations-equal-answer equation ($4 + 5 + 6 + 4 = \_\_$), and in an operations-on-both-sides equation ($4 + 5 + 6 = 4 + \_\_$). Only 11 percent of the students in the alone, and only 25 percent of the students in the operations-equal-answer contexts had a relational understanding of the equal sign. By contrast, 88 percent of the students in the operations-on-both-sides context exhibited a relational understanding of the equal sign. Apparently, students in seventh grade did not interpret the equal sign as a relational symbol of equivalence in general, but they were able to interpret the equal sign as a relational symbol in the context of an equation with operations on both sides of the equal sign (McNeil & Alibali, 2005). This finding is important because middle school (or upper elementary grades) is where students make the transition from arithmetic to algebra, and where a relational understanding of the equal sign is necessary for success.

Clearly, middle-school students benefit from seeing more equal signs in an operations-on-both-sides context. The notion of *equal* is complex and difficult for students to comprehend, yet it is a central mathematical idea within algebra. However, improving students' understanding of the equal sign and their preparation for algebra may require changes in teachers' instructional practices as well as changes in elementary and middle school mathematics curricula and textbooks. Teachers should present students with statements of equality in different ways to further develop their ideas of equivalence.

Using Practice Effectively With Young Students

We noted in Chapter 3 that practice allows the learner to use the newly learned skill in a new situation with sufficient accuracy so that it will be correctly remembered. Before students begin practice, the teacher should model the thinking process involved and guide the class through each step of the new learning's application.

Since practice makes permanent, the teacher should monitor the students' early practice to ensure that it is accurate and to provide timely feedback and correction if it is not. This guided practice helps eliminate initial errors and alerts students to the critical steps in applying new skills. Here are some suggestions by Hunter (2004) for guiding initial practice, especially as it applies to young students:

- ✓ **Limit the amount of material to practice.** Practice should be limited to the smallest amount of material or skill that has the most relevancy for the students. This allows for sense and meaning to be consolidated as the learner uses the new learning. Remember that most preadolescents can deal with only about five items in working memory at one time.
- ✓ **Limit the amount of time to practice.** Practice should take place in short, intense periods of time when the student's working memory is running on prime time. When the practice period is short, students are more likely to be intent on learning what they are practicing. Keep in mind the 5- to 10-minute time limits of working memory for preadolescents that are discussed in Chapter 3.
- ✓ **Determine the frequency of practice.** New learning should be practiced frequently at first so that it is quickly organized (massed practice). Vary the contexts in which the practice is carried out to maintain interest. Young students tire easily of repetitive work that lacks interest. To retain the information in long-term memory and to remember how to use it accurately, students should continue the practice over increasingly longer time intervals (distributed practice), which is the key to accurate retention and application of information and mastery of skills over time.
- ✓ **Assess the accuracy of practice.** As students perform guided practice, give prompt and specific feedback on whether the practice is correct or incorrect, and why. Ask the students to summarize your feedback comments in their own words. This process gives you valuable information about the degree of student understanding and whether it makes sense to move on or reteach portions that may be difficult for some students.

Testing as a Form of Practice

Most people think the purpose of a written test is to evaluate a student's achievement in the area being tested. That is a very limited view. Written tests can tell us so much more. For example, written tests can

- Allow students to practice what they have learned
- Give teachers information about what each student has learned
- Help teachers analyze how successful they were at teaching their lesson objectives

With younger students, teachers should consider using written tests mainly for practice and recording the score of only every third or fourth paper. Oral tests are a good substitute because they are less stressful, and some younger students are better at telling you what they know than writing it.

Graphic Organizers

We mentioned in Chapter 5 that today's students have grown up in a visual world. They are surrounded by television, computer screens, movies, portable DVD players, and cell phones with screen images. Using visual tools in the mathematics classroom, then, makes a lot of sense. Graphic organizers are one type of visual tool that not only get students' attention but are also valuable devices for improving understanding, meaning, and retention.

Many different types of graphic organizers are available in books and on the Internet (see Web sites in the **Resources** section of this book). The following are just two examples created by Dale Graham and Linda Meyer (2006) for use in middle school mathematics classes and used here with their permission.

What Are the Properties of the Real Number System?

PROPERTY	ADDITION	MULTIPLICATION
Closure		
Commutative		
Associative		
Identity		
Inverse		
Distributive		

Source: Graham & Meyer (2007). Adapted with permission of the authors.

What Are the Properties of Proportions?

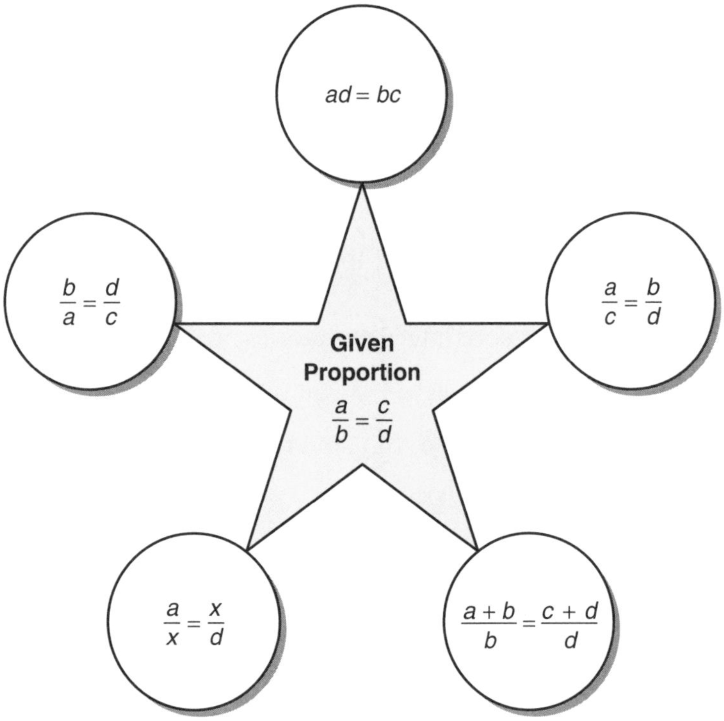

Given Proportion $\frac{a}{b} = \frac{c}{d}$

$ad = bc$

$\frac{a}{c} = \frac{b}{d}$

$\frac{a+b}{b} = \frac{c+d}{d}$

$\frac{a}{x} = \frac{x}{d}$

$\frac{b}{a} = \frac{d}{c}$

Source: Graham & Meyer (2007). Adapted with permission of the authors.

Don't Forget the Technology

Students today have grown up with technology. Using new technologies involves time, effort, and a rethinking of instructional approaches. Studies indicate that teachers are still not using technology as often as students expect, nor in ways that students perceive as helpful. In a recent study of 66 elementary, 143 middle school, and 163 high school classes, a majority of students responded that their teachers used technology only seldom or occasionally to explore mathematics concepts in depth, to gather and organize information, or as a tool for assessment and communication. Furthermore, a majority also rated the way the teachers used the technology as only somewhat helpful to their learning (Lawrenz, Gravely, & Ooms, 2006).

Why is technology not being used often in mathematics classes? One study of nearly 100 mathematics teachers found that a number of factors served to either inhibit or to encourage teachers to use technology in their mathematics classes (Forgasz, 2006). The top five inhibiting factors, in order of importance, were

1. Insufficient number of computers or computer laboratories
2. The need for more professional development with technology
3. Time needed to prepare lessons and set up computers
4. Lack of experience, confidence, skills
5. Old equipment, lack of technical support

The top five encouraging factors, in order of importance, were

1. Availability of computers or computer laboratories
2. Teachers' confidence, skills, experience, and enjoyment in using the technology
3. Software quality, variety, motivation, fun, and relevance
4. Students' enjoyment using the technology
5. Strong technical support

Which of these inhibiting and encouraging factors are operating in your school? What can be done to overcome the inhibiting factors and maintain or boost the encouraging factors?

Teachers are sometimes torn between the enthusiasm for using technology in mathematical investigations and the cautions about undermining students' computational skills. Research studies show that, particularly in middle-grade mathematics, technology can have positive effects on students' attitudes toward learning, on their confidence in their abilities to do mathematics, and on their motivation and time on task. Furthermore, technology use can help students make significant gains in mathematical achievement and conceptual understanding (Ninness et al., 2005).

> *Using technology for nonroutine mathematics applications leads students to greater conceptual understanding and higher achievement, whereas using technology for routine calculations does not.*

Research studies also suggest that using technology for *nonroutine* (that is, *novel*) applications, such as exploring number concepts and solving complex problems, leads students to greater conceptual understanding and higher achievement, whereas using technology for routine calculations does not. Students often perceive calculators as simply computational tools. But when they engage in mathematical exploration and problem solving with calculators, they broaden their perspective and see calculators as tools that can enhance their learning and understanding of mathematics (Guerrero, Walker, & Dugdale, 2004).

WHAT'S COMING?

As the brain's frontal lobes continue to mature during adolescence, students should be able to successfully engage in solving more complex and abstract problems. But many adolescents are not successful in high school mathematics courses. Why is that, and what can teachers do to improve mathematics achievement for this age group? The answers to these and other questions about adolescent performance in mathematics are found in the next chapter.

Chapter 5 — Teaching Mathematics to the Preadolescent Brain

Reflections

Jot down on this page key points, ideas, strategies, and resources you want to consider later. This sheet is your personal journal summary and will help to jog your memory.

Chapter 6

Teaching Mathematics to the Adolescent Brain

No employment can be managed without arithmetic, no mechanical invention without geometry.

—Benjamin Franklin

WHAT IS THE ADOLESCENT BRAIN?

Only in recent years have researchers begun to focus on understanding the capabilities and limitations of the adolescent brain. You will recall from Chapter 5 that the brain's frontal lobe matures much more slowly than the limbic area. So the processes that control voluntary behavior are not yet fully operational. Adolescents may look and sometimes even act like adults. But as recent studies indicate, differences in the development of the frontal lobe may be one of the most important distinctions between adolescents and adults. Although the strategies suggested in this chapter focus on adolescents, some of them can be easily adapted for use with preadolescents.

Overworking the Frontal Lobes

Much of the new information about brain growth and development has come from imaging studies using fMRIs. One extensive study involved scanning 8- to 30-year-old subjects performing

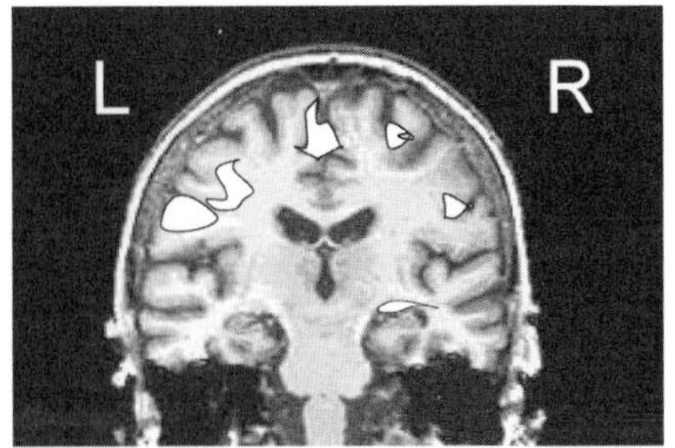

Children (ages 8 to 13)

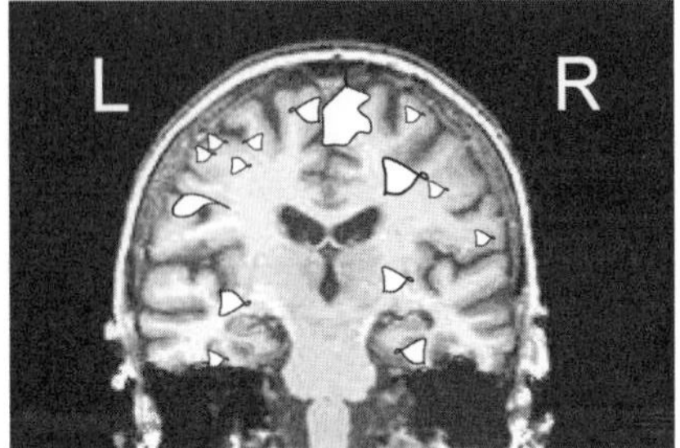

Adolescents (ages 14 to 17)

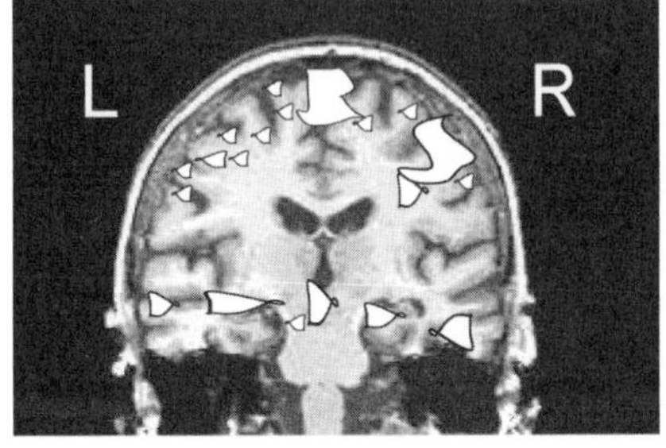

Adults (ages 18 to 30)

Figure 6.1 These representative fMRIs show that adolescent brains draw heavily on the frontal lobe areas to accomplish a visual-motor task, while adults distribute the workload over other brain regions. (Luna et al., 2001)

visual-motor tasks. The researchers found that adolescents used more of their prefrontal cortex than adults. Actually, the amount of prefrontal cortex used was similar to what adult brains use when performing much more complex tasks. The teens' excessive reliance on a brain region that is not mature can lead to problems. A mature prefrontal cortex makes it easier for an individual to use reason to override reflexive or emotional behavior. But for adolescent brains, deliberately overriding the automatic response is more difficult than it is for adult brains. Adults, on the other hand, recruit other parts of the brain to collaborate and better distribute the workload (Luna, Thulborn, Munoz, Merriam, Garver, Minshew et al., 2001).

Figure 6.1 shows how the workload to handle a visual-motor task is drawing heavily on frontal lobe resources in the adolescent brain. The adult brain recruits more resources from other parts of the brain to distribute the workload and collaborate to handle the task. Thus, if something unexpected occurs in an already stressful situation, an adolescent may exhaust his or her prefrontal cortex resources. That explains why adolescents often exhibit impulsive or thoughtless behavior.

Working Memory Still Developing

One of the functions of working memory is to control and guide voluntary behavior. Working memory is still developing in adolescents. Thus, fMRI images reveal that adolescents are not as efficient as adults in recruiting areas that support working memory. Investigations of spatial working memory showed that early adolescents performed well on spatial working-memory tests, but they needed to engage more neural circuits than older adolescents. Further, they also became much less efficient if they were stressed when asked to perform an additional task. This is likely due to cortisol, a hormone that is released in the blood when the body is under stress. Cortisol prepares the body to deal with the stress and reduces working memory's ability to focus on unrelated and less important learning tasks.

Older adolescents seem to recruit fewer neurons and use different strategies to perform the same job than younger adolescents. Researchers found the older teens solved the task through a verbal strategy rather than by rote spatial rehearsal. As adolescents mature, the brain uses more areas in general and distributes certain tasks to specialized regions. This process reduces the total neural effort necessary to achieve the same level of performance (Schweinsburg, Nagel, & Tapert, 2005).

We discussed in Chapter 5 the results of longitudinal brain imaging studies of individuals between the ages of 4 and 21. Table 6.1 summarizes the results of those studies along with additional scanning studies that have focused mainly on adolescents.

Table 6.1 Adolescent Brain Development and Some Implications

Research Finding	Possible Implications for Learning Mathematics
After puberty, gray matter volume continues to decrease to about the age of 20 to 22 as unneeded and unhealthy neurons are destroyed. Meanwhile, the white matter is thickening as more myelin surrounds neurons to increase protection and transmission of signals.	As neural networks begin to consolidate in the frontal lobes, learners can tackle more complex problem solving requiring inductive and deductive reasoning.
Some regions of the temporal lobes (located just above the ears) are the last to mature, even though some of the areas with which it is associated (like the visual and language-processing areas) mature earlier.	The temporal lobes are responsible mainly for auditory processing, but they also contribute to visual object identification and the association of vocabulary with objects. Older adolescents will be better able to name and discriminate plane and solid objects visually and auditorily than younger adolescents.
During problem solving, more frontal lobe areas are used than in adult brain.	Overworking of the frontal lobes leads to impulsive and more emotional (rather than rational) responses during problem solving.
Working memory (located mainly in frontal lobes) matures slowly.	Adolescents can have difficulty working with problems that have more variables and/or components than working memory's limited capacity can handle.

Sources: Gogtay et al., 2004; Luna et al., 2001; Schweinsburg et al., 2005.

Can Adultlike Challenges Accelerate Maturity?

I should point out that not all neuroscientists and psychologists accept the notion that the rate of maturation of the frontal lobes in adolescents is so closely linked to genetic influences. They point out that teens in other countries spend much more time with adults than with their peers and, consequently, do not exhibit the immature behavior of teens in North America (Sabbagh, 2006). If the environment can provide the adolescent brain with more adultlike experiences, then perhaps they can avoid the stress and antisocial behavior associated with this period of growth. Furthermore, they contend that allowing adolescents to make adult decisions (e.g., serving in the military) will accelerate frontal lobe maturation.

The extent to which genetic forces and environmental demands affect the developing brain will most likely be unique to each adolescent. Nonetheless, the implication of this approach is that schools should not view adolescents as being so biologically immature that they cannot take on challenging tasks, including those in mathematics.

The Search for Novelty

In Chapter 5 we discussed how the developing preadolescent brain responds to novelty. With the onset of puberty and during the adolescent years, the search for novelty becomes more intense. When curious adolescents try a new challenge, such as a video game, they play the game until they master it. Then the novelty wears off, they get bored with it, and move on to a new game. Cognitive neuroscientists attribute this phenomenon to the specialized functions of each cerebral hemisphere and how these functions affect new learning. Recent research seems to indicate that hemispheric specialization may center on the differences between novelty and routine. Closer examination of brain-damaged patients shows that those with severe right hemisphere problems experience difficulty in facing new learning situations, but can perform routine, practiced tasks, such as language, normally. Conversely, patients with severe left hemisphere damage can create new drawings and think abstractly, but have difficulty with routine operations (Goldberg, 2001).

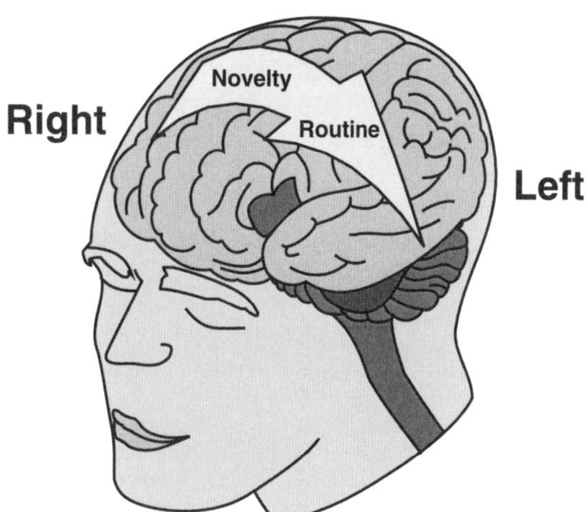

Figure 6.2 With repeated exposures, novel experiences become routine, and their cortical processing areas shift from the right hemisphere to the left hemisphere.

These findings give us a different way of looking at how the brain learns. They suggest that upon encountering a novel situation for which the individual has developed no coping strategy, the right hemisphere is primarily involved and attempts to deal with the situation. In mathematics, for instance, that could be the student's first encounter with solving quadratic equations. With repeated exposure to similar situations, coping strategies eventually emerge and learning occurs because it results in a change of behavior. In time, and after sufficient repetition, the responses become routine and shift to the left hemisphere (Figure 6.2). The amount of time and the number of situational exposures needed to accomplish this right-to-left hemisphere transition vary widely from one person to the next. But it may be that one component of mathematical aptitude is the ability of a student's brain to make right-to-left transitions involving mathematical operations in less time and with fewer exposures than average.

One component of mathematical aptitude may be the ability of a student's brain to make right-to-left hemisphere transitions involving mathematical operations in less time and with fewer exposures than average.

Studies using neuroimaging provide evidence to support this right-to-left transition. In one study, researchers used PET scans to measure the changes in brain flow patterns when subjects were asked to learn various types of information. Changes in blood flow levels indicate the degree of neural activation. When the information was novel, regions in the right temporal lobe were highly activated. After the information had been presented several times to the subjects, activity in the right temporal lobe decreased dramatically (Figure 6.3). In both instances, however, the level of activation in the left temporal lobe remained constant (Martin, Wiggs, & Weisberg, 1997).

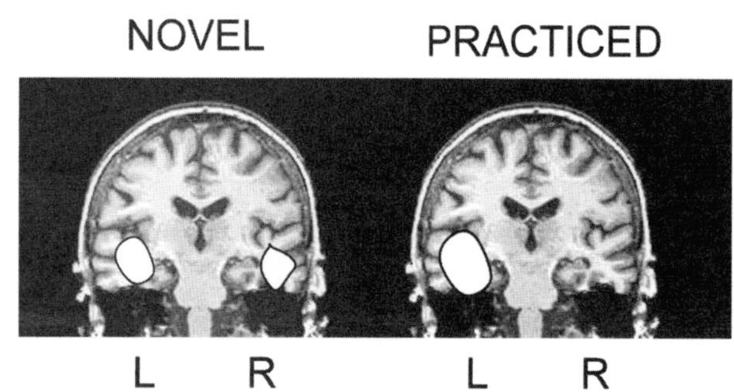

Figure 6.3 In this representation of PET scans, the white areas show the changes in regional blood flow for novel and practiced tasks. The images reveal areas of high activation in the left and right temporal lobes for novel tasks, but only in the left temporal lobe for practiced tasks.

Similar results were reported from other studies involving a variety of learning tasks, such as recognizing faces and symbols (Schwartz et al., 2003), learning a complex motor skill (Krakauer & Shadmehr, 2006), and learning and relearning different words or systems of rules (Berns, Cohen, & Mintun, 1997; Habib, McIntosh, Wheeler, & Tulving, 2003). The same shifts were detected no matter what type of information was presented to the subjects. In other words, the association of the right hemisphere with novelty and the left hemisphere with routine appears to be independent of the nature of the information being learned.

Novelty and Mathematics

Teachers ultimately decide whether mathematics is full or devoid of novelty. If adolescents have already mastered a mathematical operation yet we continue to give them more of the same assignments, they see no purpose in completing repetitive practice. They lose interest, they see mathematics as boring and hum-drum work, their motivation drops, and their grades slump. The key here is for the teacher to find different and meaningful applications of the mathematical operation or concept to maintain interest and attention, key components of motivation. And even more so, the teacher needs to recognize how much practice each student needs to show mastery, and no more.

Novelty and motivation are also undermined by a mathematics curriculum that focuses mainly on a strict formal approach, heavy in memorizing abstract axioms and theorems. This model, which emerged in the 1970s, was based on the brain-computer metaphor—the notion that cognitive processing in the human brain is similar to that in a computer. As neuroscience reveals more about the underlying mechanisms that power the brain's cognitive processes, it is clear that the differences between the brain's operations and those of a computer's are far greater than their similarities. An adolescent's brain, unlike that of a computer, is a structured entity that requires facts only insofar as they can be integrated into prior knowledge to elucidate new situations. It is adapted to represent continuous quantities and to mentally manipulate them in analogical form. Conversely, it is not innately prepared to handle vast arrays of axioms or symbolic algorithms. For most people, to do so requires heavy doses of motivation, interest, and novelty.

The Adolescent Brain and Algebra

The adolescent brain's heavy reliance on the frontal lobe for cognitive processing may have an upside. One curious finding from fMRI studies is that adolescents could have an advantage over adults when learning algebra. The studies indicate that after several days of practice, adolescents, like adults, rely on the prefrontal cortex regions for retrieving algebraic rules to solve equations. However, unlike adults, after practice, adolescents decrease their reliance on the brain's parietal region that is holding an image of the equation. To the researchers, this suggests that, compared to adults, the developing prefrontal regions of the adolescent brain are more plastic and thus change more with practice, resulting in an enhanced ability for learning algebra (Qin et al., 2004).

It seems that the adolescent brain may actually have an enhanced aptitude for learning algebra more easily than the adult brain.

LEARNING STYLES AND MATHEMATICS CURRICULUM

Qualitative Versus Quantitative Learning Styles

Cognitive researchers suggest that adolescent students approach the study of mathematics with different learning styles that run along a continuum from primarily quantitative to primarily qualitative (Augustniak, Murphy, & Phillips, 2005; Farkas, 2003; Sharma, 2006). Students with a quantitative style approach mathematics in a linear, routine-like fashion. They prefer working with numbers over concrete models and may run into difficulty with solutions requiring multistep procedures. On the other hand, students with a qualitative style prefer concepts over routine steps and models over numbers. The implication of this research is that students are more likely to be successful in learning mathematics if teachers use instructional strategies that are compatible with their students' cognitive styles, but that exposure to both kinds of strategies can strengthen a student's weakness.

✓ Tables 6.2 and 6.3 illustrate teaching strategies that are appropriate for the mathematical behaviors exhibited by quantitative and qualitative learners, respectively. The strategies are meant to help teachers address specific mathematical behaviors that they identify in individual students. Such strategies target specific needs and, with practice, can strengthen a student's weakness. It is unrealistic, however, to expect teachers to identify and select individual strategies for problems encountered by all of their students during a single learning episode.

Table 6.2 Teaching Strategies for Learners With Quantitative Style

Mathematical Behaviors	**Teaching Strategies to Consider**
Approaches situations using recipes	Emphasize the meaning of each concept or procedure in verbal terms.
Approaches mathematics in a mechanical, routine fashion	Highlight the concept and overall goal of the learning.
Emphasizes component parts rather than larger mathematical constructs	Encourage explicit description of the overall conceptual framework. Look for ways to link parts to the whole.
Prefers numerical approach rather than concrete models	Use a step-by-step approach to connect the model to the numerical procedure.
Prefers the linear approach to arithmetic concept	Start with the larger framework and use different approaches to reach the same concept.
Has difficulty in situations requiring multistep tasks	Separate multiple tasks into smaller units and explain the connections between the units.

Table 6.3 Teaching Strategies for Learners With Qualitative Style

Mathematical Behaviors	Teaching Strategies to Consider
Prefers concepts to algorithms (procedures for problem solving)	Connect models first to the concept, and then to procedures before introducing algorithms.
Perceives overall shape of geometric structures at expense of missing the individual components	Emphasize how individual components contribute to the overall design of the geometric figure.
Difficulties with precise calculations and in explaining procedure for finding the correct solution	Encourage explicit description of each step used.
Can offer a variety of approaches or answers to a single problem.	Use simulations and real word problems to show application of concept to different situations.
Prefers to set up problems but cannot always follow through to a solution	Provide opportunities for the student to work in multistyle cooperative learning groups. To ensure full participation, give one grade for problem approach and setup, and one grade for exact solution.
Benefits from manipulatives and enjoys topics related to geometry	Provide a variety of manipulatives and models (e.g., Cuisenaire rods, tokens, or blocks) to support numerical operations. Look for geometric links to new concepts.

By understanding the different approaches to the learning of mathematics, teachers are more likely to select instructional strategies that will result in successful learning for all students.

Developing Mathematical Reasoning

As teenage brains mature over the course of adolescence, teachers should present challenging mathematical problems involving increasingly complex reasoning. Inductive and deductive reasoning are among the most common types of reasoning used in mathematics. Inductive reasoning, sometimes called the bottom-up approach, moves from parts to a whole or from the specific to the general. In inductive reasoning, we begin with specific observations and measures, look for patterns and regularities, formulate some tentative hypotheses that we can explore, and develop general conclusions or theories. "The sun rose today, and yesterday, and the day before, etc. I conclude the sun will rise tomorrow."

In deductive reasoning, sometimes called the top-down approach, one draws a conclusion from principles (or premises) that are already known or hypothesized. "Triangle A has three 60-degree angles. Triangles with three 60-degree angles are called equilateral triangles. Therefore, triangle A must be an equilateral triangle." Inductive reasoning is often used to make a guess at a property, and deductive reasoning is then used to prove that the property must hold for all cases, or for some set of cases.

Table 6.4 suggests a sequence for using inductive and deductive approaches when introducing a new mathematical concept. The order first accommodates qualitative learners and then moves to techniques for quantitative learners.

Table 6.4 Inductive to Deductive Approach for Introducing a New Concept in Mathematics

Steps for the Inductive Approach for Qualitative Learners	✓ Explain the linguistic aspects of the concept ✓ Introduce the general principle or law that supports the concept ✓ Provide students opportunities to use concrete materials to investigate and discover proof of the connection between the principle and the concept ✓ Give many specific examples of the concept's validity using concrete materials ✓ Allow students to discuss with each other what they discovered about how the concept works ✓ Demonstrate how these individual experiences can be integrated into a general principle or rule that applies equally to each example
Steps for the Deductive Approach for Quantitative Learners	✓ Reemphasize the general principle or law that the concept relates to ✓ Demonstrate how several specific examples obey the general principle or law ✓ Allow students to state the principle and suggest specific examples that follow it ✓ Ask students to explain the linguistic elements of the concept

Instructional Choices in Mathematics

We have already discussed in earlier chapters the irony that although people are born with a number sense, many feel they are not able to learn or remember basic mathematical operations. This feeling of incompetence is particularly evident in high school classrooms and poses a significant obstacle for both students and teachers to overcome. Motivation, of course, has a lot to do with this attitude, and there are plenty of research studies showing that low motivation leads to low achievement in mathematics, as in other subjects.

Educators for years have explored strategies and models to help motivate students to higher achievement levels. Kathie Nunley (2004, 2006) has developed a student-centered teaching method based on research in cognitive neuroscience. Her model is called *Layered Curriculum®* and consists of three layers of differentiated instruction that enhance student motivation and encourage complex thinking.

Nunley notes that mathematics teachers who strive for brain-compatible classrooms share three basic goals. First, they want to increase student motivation by engaging students emotionally in their learning. Second, they want to enable students to master mathematics skills to a level of proficiency that allows practical use of the skill, thus creating meaning. And third, they look for ways to encourage higher-level thinking and to connect new learning to prior knowledge in a complex manner. Engaging students is first and foremost, because without engagement and motivation, teachers cannot begin to address the other two goals. Improving motivation and engagement in students requires only that teachers add one simple thing to their classroom—choice.

Lack of motivation, Nunley suggests, remains one of the major reasons students do not succeed in mathematics, or any other subject (Legault, Pelletier, & Green-Demers, 2006; Pintrich, 2003). In mathematics class, students may feel that they lack the ability to be successful, or they may feel they cannot sustain the effort long enough for success, or they may simply be bored and unable to concentrate on the task. Some students experience lack of motivation due to learned helplessness—the feeling that no amount of effort will ever lead to success, so there is no point in trying. Other unmotivated students simply have placed no personal value on the learning task (Bigelow & Zhou, 2001). Whatever the cause, they all have one common thread: Students without self-determined motivation are generally not successful in school.

> *Layered Curriculum® consists of three layers of differentiated instruction that enhance student motivation and encourage complex teaching.*

In order to be motivated, Nunley continues, students must see a relationship between their behavior and the outcome. This requires that they perceive they have some sense of control in their environment. With a sense of control comes a sense of responsibility. Unfortunately, traditional teacher-centered, autocratic classrooms do little to encourage responsibility in students (Ryan & Deci, 1999). If the teacher makes all the decisions regarding rules and instruction, the student is immune from all responsibility.

Thus we see the shift in education to student-centered classrooms. In student-centered classrooms, students are allowed some choice and decision making through differentiated instruction. Studies reveal that student-centered classrooms have higher-achieving students, higher standardized test scores, fewer classroom-management problems, more on-task behavior, and fewer dropouts (Pekrun, Maier, & Elliot, 2006). So, mathematics teachers want to create classrooms of motivated learners because motivated learners actively process information, have better conceptual understanding of material, and show greater problem-solving skills. Such an approach is also consistent with what we know about how today's students want to actively participate in their learning (Sousa, 2006).

Three Steps to Layering the Curriculum

Layering the curriculum is a simple way to differentiate instruction, encourage higher-level thinking, prepare students for adult-world decision making and hold them accountable for learning. Any lesson plan can be converted into a layered unit with three easy steps (Nunley, 2004, 2006).

✓ **Step One: Add some choice.** Choice transforms a classroom instantly. Choice suddenly turns unmotivated students into motivated ones, ensures student attention, and gives students the perception of control. Choice is the centerpiece to student-centered, differentiated classrooms. Traditionally, mathematics teachers have seen their subject as one that is so regimented and sequential that it has little room for student choice. But within even the tightest structured curriculum, some student choice is possible.

- Take your teaching objectives and offer two or three assignment choices as to how students can learn those objectives. Not all objectives need to be taught through choices, but offer as many as you can. These can include teacher lecture, small-group peer instruction, hands-on tactile projects, or independent study.
- For example, if your objective is that students can determine the area of a triangle, you may offer a quick chalkboard lesson on that topic. Then allow the students to do some practice problems themselves, work in small groups, play a computer game that practices that concept, or complete a task using manipulatives.
- One suggestion worth considering is to make your lectures optional and award points for them. Tell the students that they can either listen to your lecture (direct instruction) or work on another assignment from the unit instead. What you will discover is that all students will probably listen to the lecture. But the fact that it is now their decision,

rather than the teacher's mandate, changes the whole perception of the task and increases attention.

✓ **Step Two: Hold students accountable for learning.** One of the unfortunate developments in our traditional grading system is the wide variation in how grading points are awarded in our classrooms. Some teachers award points simply for practicing a skill, some for just doing assignments, and of course some points are eventually awarded for demonstrating mastery in the test. Because grading schemes are nearly as numerous and varied as the number of teachers, a heavy weight is frequently put on the points awarded for doing assignments. This means that students can earn enough points to pass a course without actually learning much at all. In fact, so many points have been awarded for doing class work and homework that many students never understand that the purpose of doing an assignment is to actually *learn* something from it. They say, "I did it; doesn't that count?"

- A key to layering the curriculum is to award grade points for the actual learning of the objective rather than the assignment that was chosen for the learning. For example, if our objective is that students learn how to determine the area of a triangle, then points are awarded for the assignment based on whether or not the student can do that. Whether they chose to do the book work, a manipulative exercise, or a computer game is immaterial. What is important is that they learned the objective. This can be done through oral defense, small-group discussions, or unannounced quizzes. Have sample problems on index cards that you or their classmates can pull at random. Two or three sample problems can easily check for the skill. Award points for acquiring the skill rather than for the journey chosen to get there.

✓ **Step Three: Encourage higher-level thinking.** One of the main components of brain-compatible learning is helping students make complex connections with new information. Finding relationships, hooking new learning to previous knowledge, and cross-connecting between memory networks. These are the keys to real learning. Layering the curriculum encourages more complex learning by dividing the instructional unit into three layers: (1) basic rote information, (2) application and manipulation of that information, and (3) critical analysis of a real-world issue. Rather than just calling them layer 1, layer 2 and layer 3, the complexity of the learning is tied into the actual grade a student will earn, so the layers are called C layer, B layer and A layer.

- The C layer consists of all the objectives that have to do with the lower levels of Bloom's taxonomy. This layer consists of rote learning and concrete facts. All students begin in this layer. Even the highest-ability students can add to their current bank of knowledge, so the entire class starts here.

- After students complete this C layer, they move to the B layer, which asks them to connect the new information gained in the C layer to prior knowledge. This layer includes assignments that require problem solving, application, demonstration of mastery, or unique creations. The purpose of this layer is to attach new knowledge to prior knowledge to make a more complex picture or network in the student's brain. Interdisciplinary assignments work beautifully in this layer. A student who satisfactorily completes the C and B layer would then earn the grade of a B on this unit.
- Finally, the A layer asks students to mix the facts and basic information they have learned with more sophisticated brain concepts such as values, morality, and personal reflection, in order to form an opinion on an adult-world issue or current event. This layer asks for critical thinking and prepares students for their role as voters and decision makers in the real world. Many educators may refer to this area as the essential question. A student who successfully completes this layer will earn the grade of an A on this unit.

All students are expected to complete the three layers. Many students may not be able to show sufficient mastery of a skill or handle an A layer issue with the sophistication needed to gain enough points for a letter grade of A or B. Nonetheless, they all must still tackle the three layers. We are preparing these students for an adult world that will ask them to gather and manipulate information and to make community decisions based on that information. Thus all students need to practice these types of thinking. At the outset, teachers help students walk through all the layers so they experience success and understand the process. As the year progresses, units may be left more open in their structure so that students are free to move among the layers as they are ready.

Examples of Layered Curriculum Units

✓ **Eighth-Grade Layered Curriculum Unit**
Content: Understanding Graphs and Data Analysis
Objectives:

- Collect, organize, analyze, and display data (including scatter plots) to solve problems.
- Approximate a line of best fit for a given scatter plot; explain the meaning of the line as it relates to the problem and make predictions.
- Identify misuses of statistical and numerical data.

C Layer:

1. Listen to the teacher "chalk talk" lesson each day (5 points/day)
2. Book Practice problems: Choose one from each section (10 points each)
   a. page 235, numbers 1 to 20, any 7 problems

b. page 238, numbers 1 to 21, any 7 problems
c. page 240, numbers 1 to 17, any 6 problems

3. Choose one of the lab analysis projects. With one or two classmates, calculate mean, median, mode, and range and draw a linear regression line. Answer the prediction questions. (10 points each)

B Layer: Choose one (20 points)

1. What will be the price of gasoline in the year 2010? Research a 10-year history of gas prices, plot the data, and use it for your prediction.
2. What will be the price of school lunch in the year 2010? Research a 10-year history as in Question 1 above.
3. What's the value of a scatter plot? Surf the Internet. Find 30 Internet sites that use scatter plots to make predictions or explain situations. Compile an annotated bibliography of your findings.

A Layer: Choose one (20 points)

1. Do you feel that politicians misuse statistical data? If yes, find three to five pieces of evidence to support your argument. If your answer is "no," choose another question.
2. The media often misuse graphs and data. Find three to five examples and make an argument for being an educated consumer of media.
3. How many people will die on our highways next year? Find the research to support your answer. Are our laws helping to reduce highway deaths? What else could be done?

✓ **Sample of a Layered Curriculum Unit in Calculus**
Content: Introducing Derivatives
C Layer:

Day One: Topic: Define Derivatives and Rules for Finding Derivatives:

1. Lecture (5 points)
2. Practice: Choose one (5-point quiz)
   a. Problem set 3.1, numbers 1 to 9
   b. Work derivatives unit on our *Journey Through Calculus* software.

Day Two: Topic: Derivatives of Trigonometric Functions

1. Lecture (5 points)
2. Practice: Choose one (5-point quiz)
   a. Problem set 3.2, numbers 1 to 10
   b. Find a Web site that teaches this topic. Create a mini-lesson and teach it to two classmates.

Day Three: Topic: The Chain Rule

1. Lecture (5 points)
2. Practice: Choose one (5-point quiz)
   a. Problem Set 3. 3, numbers 1 to 12
   b. Make a poster that teaches the chain rule. Give a mini-lesson to two classmates.

B Layer: Choose one (10 points)

1. Write a one-page library report on tides and explain how derivatives are used to predict high tide and low tide.
2. Write a one-page library report on the actual use of derivatives in business transactions and corporate risk management.
3. Solve these 3 problems:

   (a) A rectangular piece of paper measures 20 cm by 28 cm. Equal-sized squares are to be cut out from each corner of the paper, and the remaining flaps are to be folded up to make an open-topped box. Find the dimensions of the square that should be cut out to maximize the volume of the box.

   (b) A metal cylindrical soda can is to be constructed to have a known volume, V. What is the ratio of the diameter of the can to the height of the can if the amount of metal used in the construction of the can is to be a minimum? Assume that the metal used is of uniform thickness.

   (c) A Norman window, one that is formed by placing a semicircle on top of a rectangle, still remains a popular architectural feature. If the perimeter of the window is 300 cm, find the radius of the semicircle that will maximize the window's area and let in the most light.

A Layer: Choose one. Find and summarize three pieces of research on your topic. Write a two-paragraph opinion using the research as a basis. (15 points)

1. Asteroid A2004 MN4 is heading toward Earth and projected to impact our planet in 2029. Impact dates continue to be revised. How do they calculate this event? Should we be worried?
2. When Hurricane Katrina hit New Orleans in 2005, how did the tide position at the time the hurricane made landfall impact the devastation of New Orleans? Would a change in tidal position have made the impact worse or better? How much importance should be placed on tidal position during coastal storms for making evacuation decisions?

You will also have a 50-point quiz over this unit.

For more information on Nunley's Layered Curriculum, see the **Resources** section.

Graphic Organizers

We mentioned in Chapter 5 that today's adolescents have grown up in a visual world. They are surrounded by television, computer screens, movies, portable DVD players, and cell phones with screen images. Using visual tools in all mathematics classrooms, then, makes a lot of sense. Graphic organizers are one type of visual tool that not only get students' attention but are also valuable devices for improving understanding, meaning, and retention.

Many different types of graphic organizers are available in books and on the Internet (See Web sites in the **Resources** section of this book). The following are just a few examples created by Dale Graham and Linda Meyer (2006) for use in high school mathematics classes and used here with their permission.

How to Determine if a Function Is Continuous

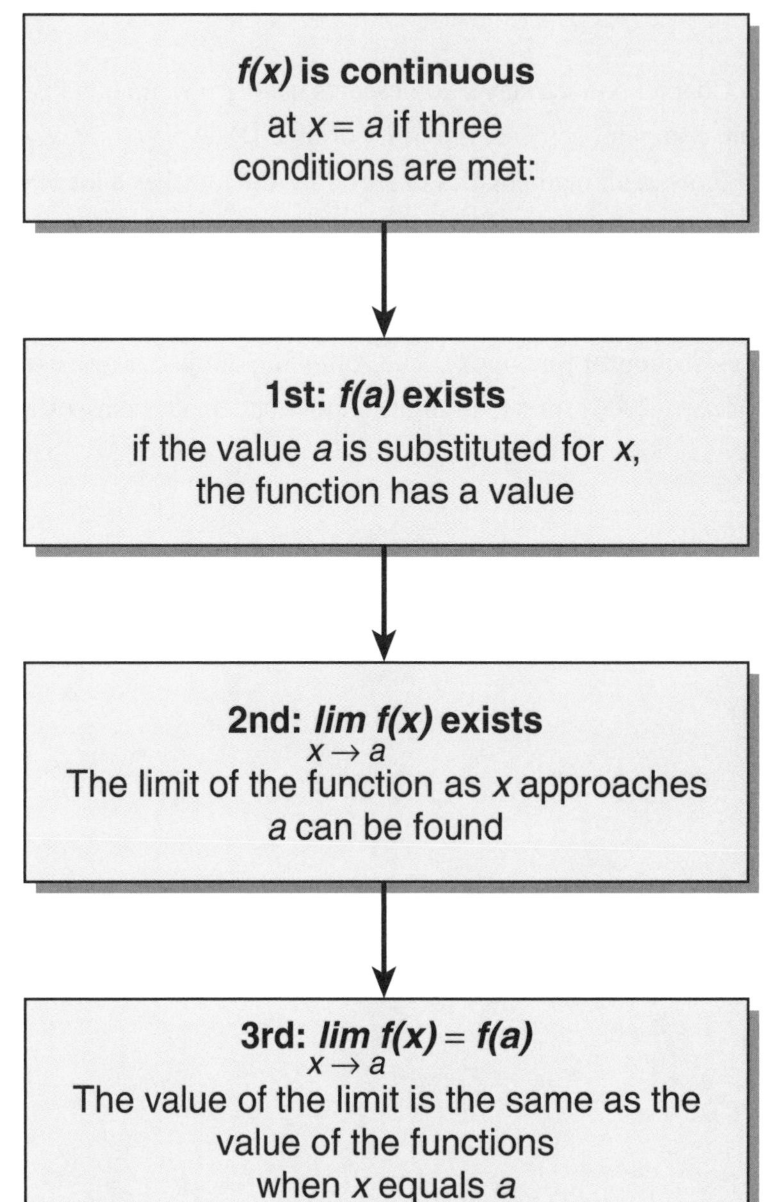

Source: Graham & Meyer (2007). Adapted with permission of the authors.

How to Graph Quadratic Functions

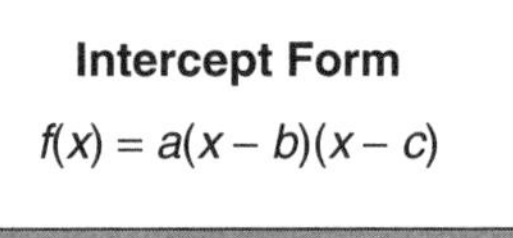

Intercept Form

$f(x) = a(x - b)(x - c)$

	Example	**Your Turn**
	$f(x) = 0.5(x + 5)(x - 4)$	$f(x) = -\frac{1}{2}(x - 3)(x + 1)$
Find and plot the x-intercepts and the vertex $x = \dfrac{b + c}{2}$		
Find and sketch the axis of symmetry		
Make a table of values using two values of *x* higher than the vertex. Plot these points.		

Using symmetry, find two other points on the curve and plot them

Connect the points with a smooth curve

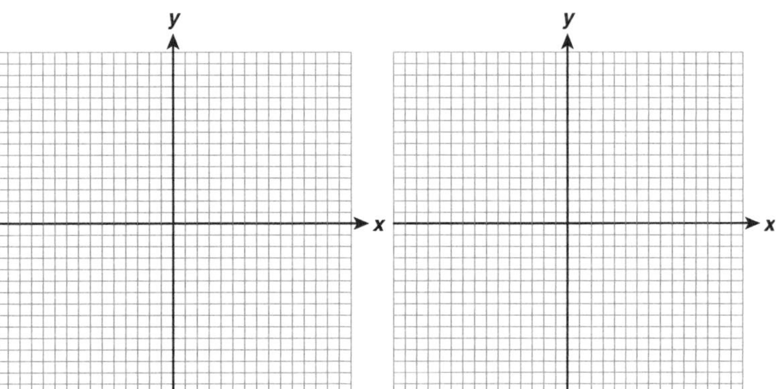

Source: Graham & Meyer (2007). Adapted with permission of the authors.

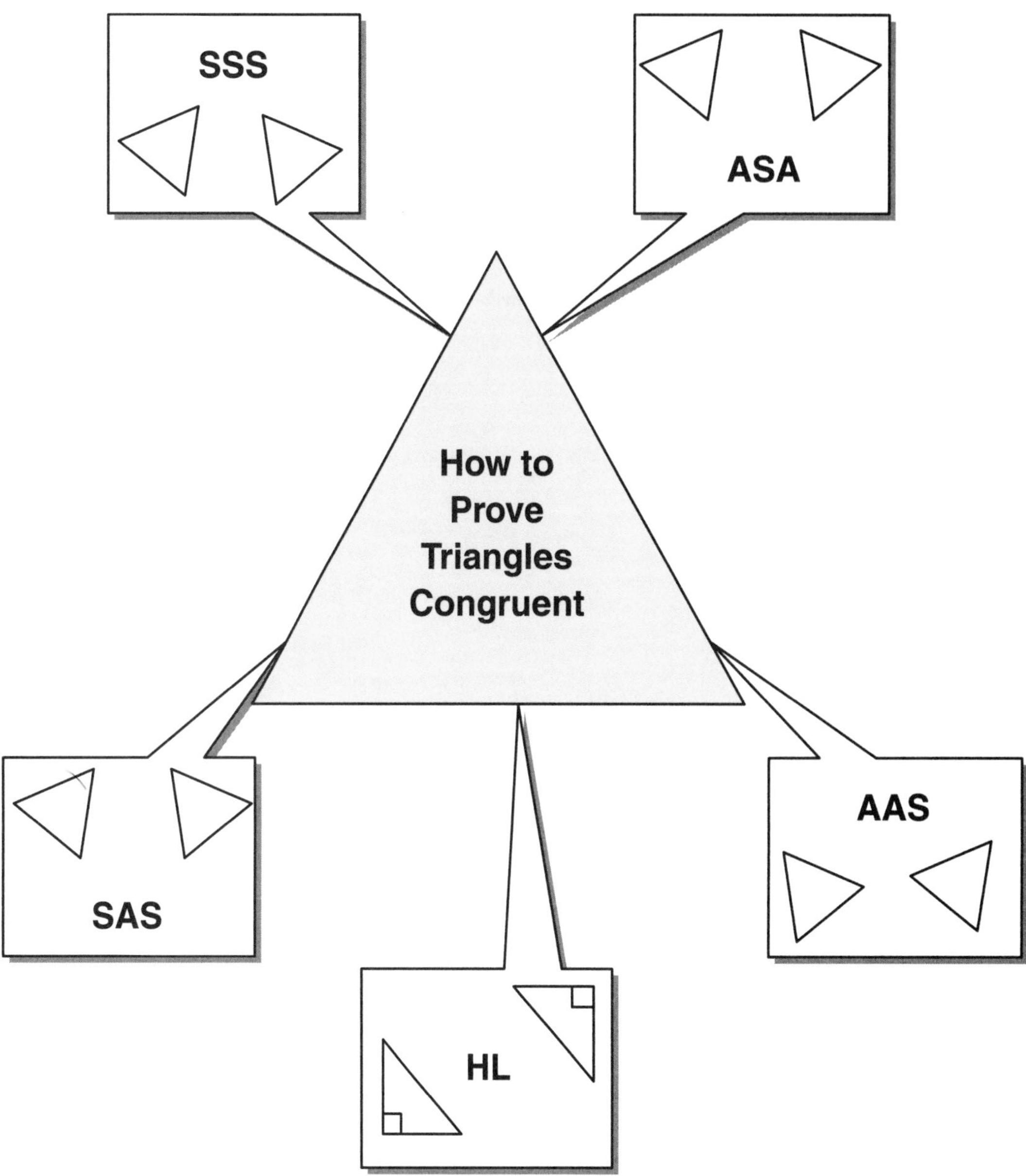

Source: Graham & Meyer (2007). Adapted with permission of the authors.

How to Write the Equation of a Line

Given	Example	Your Turn
Slope and *y*-intercept Use the slope intercept form of the equation: $y = mx + b$ Substitute for m and b	Slope = $\frac{3}{4}$, y-intercept = –2	Slope = –1/2, y-intercept = 5
Slope and a Point Use the point-slope form of the equation: $y - y_1 = m(x - x_1)$ Substitute for m, x_1 and y_1. Solve for y. Solve for y.	Slope = –3, Point = (–2, 4)	Slope = 4, Point = (–6, –4)
Two Points Use the slope formula and the coordinates of the two points to find the slope. $m = \frac{rise}{run} = \frac{y_2 - y_1}{x_2 - x_1}$ Use this slope and one of the given points to write the equation of the line following the **Slope and a Point** method above.	Points are (–6, 3) and (2, –7)	Points are (–9, –2) and (1, –8)

Source: Graham & Meyer (2007). Adapted with permission of the authors.

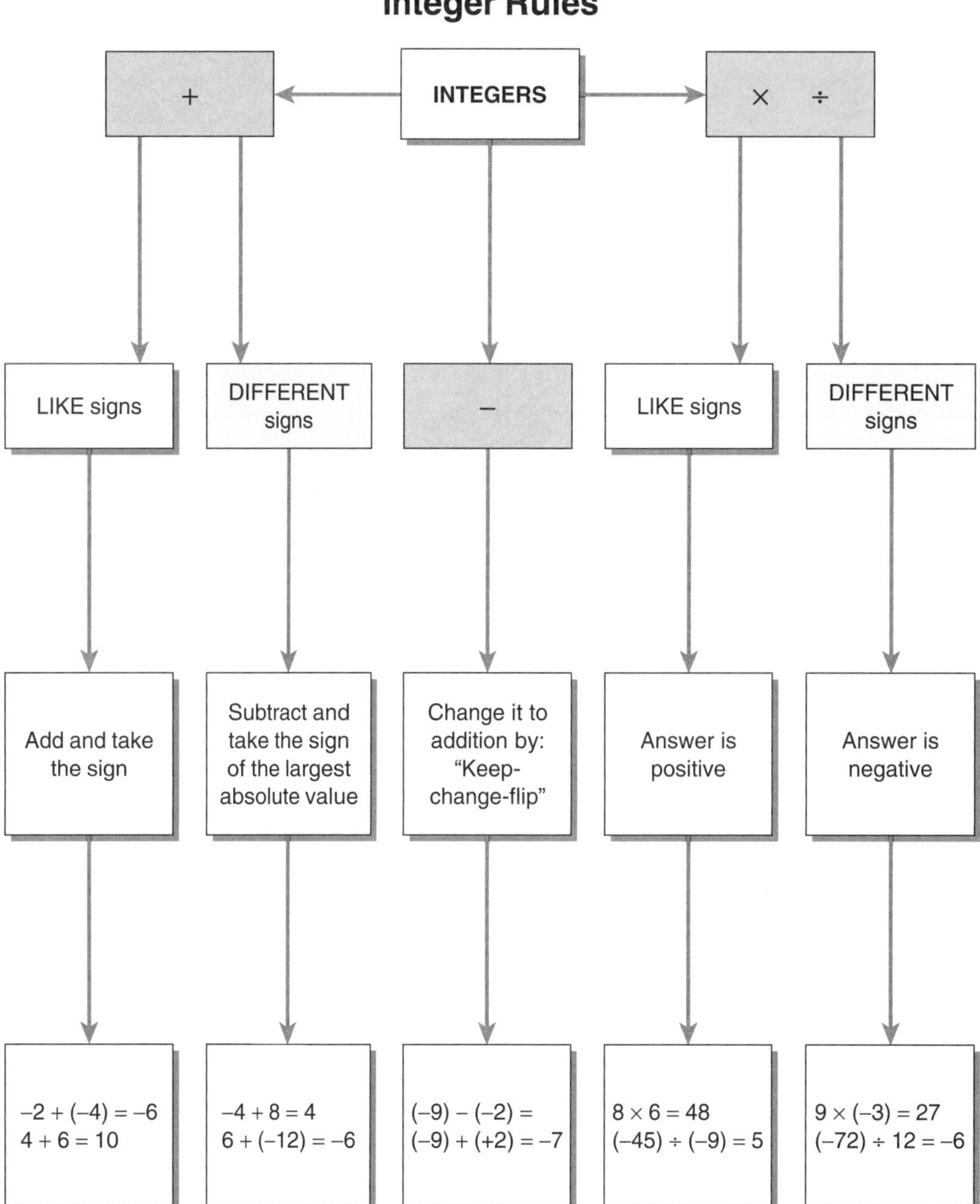

Source: Graham & Meyer (2007). Adapted with permission of the authors.

Interpreting Word Problems

Even students who are proficient at solving mathematical expressions can have difficulty interpreting the meaning of word problems. Barton and Heidema (2002) suggest that authors of mathematics texts do not always follow the principles of writing that students have learned in their language arts classes. For example, students learn that an author's main idea usually appears in the passage's opening sentences. In mathematics problems, however, the main idea often appears in the last sentence. Here's a typical example:

> Billy is sorting out blue, green, and yellow marbles into single color groups. He has 58 marbles altogether. There are twice as many blue marbles as green marbles, and three more yellow marbles than blue marbles. How many marbles of each color does Billy have?

Students must wade through numerous details before they get to the point of the problem: "How many marbles of each color does Billy have?" Teachers can help students interpret word problems by using strategies designed to focus on what the problem is asking and to select a solution.

The SQRQCQ Process

✓ One way to help students get to important information in a word problem is through a six-step process called SQRQCQ (Barton & Heidema, 2002). This strategy is designed to help students think through what the problem is asking and to determine the method for solving it. The six steps are

- Survey: Read the problem quickly to get a general understanding of it.
- Question: Ask what information the problem requires.
- Read: Reread the problem to identify relevant information, facts, and the details that are needed to solve it.
- Question: Ask what must be done to solve the problem. "What operations must be performed and in what order?"
- Compute: Do the computations or construct a solution.
- Question: Ask whether the solution process seems correct and the answer reasonable.

Note that in this strategy the student is specifically told to reread the problem. Students often rely on their working memory to retain all the relevant information after one quick reading. Rereading the problem (a form of rehearsal) increases the likelihood that important details will be found, processed, and retained in working memory.

Making Mathematics Meaningful to Teenagers

As mentioned in Chapter 3, it is important for students to find meaning in what they are learning because meaning is one of the criteria the brain uses to identify information for long-term storage. One way to help learners find meaning is to connect what they are learning to their daily life. Yet too often students in secondary school mathematics classes have difficulty seeing the practical and concrete applications of mathematics to everyday living. Here are just a few suggestions as to how mathematical concepts can be meaningfully related to common experiences.

Probability

✓ **Determining odds.** Millions of people visit casinos, buy lottery tickets, play the stock market, join in the office football pool, and meet with friends for a game of poker. They invest their money in chance, believing they can beat the odds. The mathematical principle of probability can tell us how often we are likely to win, helping us decide whether to risk the odds and our money.

How do we determine probability? Let's say there are 12 apples in a fruit basket. Five are red and seven are green. If you close your eyes, reach into the basket, and grab one apple, what is the probability that it would be a red apple? Five of the 12 apples are red, so your chances of picking a red apple are 5 out of 12, or as a fraction, 5/12, which is about 42 percent. Or, if you are choosing between two colleges, one in Texas and one in Connecticut. You decide to flip a coin. The chances are one out of two, or 1/2, of getting heads or tails. The odds are 50 percent for each.

What could the odds be for winning the state lottery if you buy only one ticket?

✓ **Does gambling pay off? Odds in roulette.** Is roulette a good bet at a casino? Actually, the casino will win more often than the player. Here's why. The roulette wheel is divided into 38 numbered slots. Two of these slots are green, 18 are red, and 18 are black. To begin the round, the wheel is spun, and a ball is dropped onto its outside edge. When the wheel stops, the ball drops into 1 of the 38 slots. Players bet on which slot they believe the ball will land in. If you bet your money that the ball will land in any of the 18 red slots, your chances of winning are 18 out of 38, or about 47 percent. If you bet your money on a certain number, such as the red slot numbered with a 10, your chances of winning fall to 1 in 38, or 2.6 percent.

The mathematics of probability guarantee that the roulette wheel will make money even if the casino doesn't win every time. Remember there are 18 each of the red and black slots. There are also 2 green slots. Whenever the ball lands in one of those green slots, the house wins everything that was bet on that round. So again, let's say you bet that the ball will land in a red or black slot. This is the safest possible bet in roulette, since the odds are 18 out of 38 (47 percent) that you will win. But there are 20 out of 38 chances (53 percent) that you will lose.

Calculating Interest on Buying a Car

- ✓ **How much are you actually paying when you finance a car purchase?** Understanding interest can help you manage your money and help you determine how much it will cost you to borrow money to pay for your car purchase. Interest is expressed as a rate, such as three percent or 18 percent. The dollar amount of the interest you pay on a loan is figured by multiplying the money you borrow (called the principal) by the rate of interest.

  Suppose you want to buy a used car for $10,000. The car salesman says that the dealership will finance your car at a rate of 8.4 percent, and estimates your monthly payments at about $200 over a period of five years. How much money are you actually paying back to the dealer over the term of the loan? Is this a good deal, or should you shop around? What if a bank offered to loan you the $10,000 at a rate of 9.0 percent for four years? Which offer is better?

Exponential Changes/Progressions

- ✓ **Population growth.** The number of people living on Earth has grown dramatically in the last few centuries. There are now 10 times more people on our planet than there were 300 years ago. How can population grow so fast? Think of a family tree. At the top are two parents, and beneath them the children they had. Listed beneath those children are the children they had, and so on down through many generations. As long as the family continues to reproduce, the tree increases in size, getting larger with each passing generation. This same idea applies to the world's population.

  New members of the population eventually produce other new members so that the population increases exponentially as time passes. Population increases cannot continue forever. Living creatures are constrained by the availability of food, water, land, and other vital resources. Once those resources are depleted, a population growth will plateau, or even decline, as a result of disease or malnutrition.

  How fast will population grow? Arriving at a reasonable estimate of how the world's population will grow in the next 50 years requires a look at the rates at which people are being born and dying in any given period. If birth and death rates stayed the same across the years in all parts of the world, population growth could be determined with a fairly simple formula. But birth and death rates are not constant across countries and through time because disease or disaster can cause death rates to increase for a certain period. A booming economy might mean higher birth rates for a given period.

The rate of Earth's population growth is slowing down. Throughout the 1960s, the world's population was growing at a rate of about two percent per year. By 1990, that rate was down to one and a half percent, and is estimated to drop to one percent by the year 2015. Family planning initiatives, an aging population, and the effects of diseases such as AIDS are some of the factors behind this rate decrease. Even at these very low rates of population growth, the numbers are staggering. Can you estimate how many people will be living on Earth in 2015? By 2050? Can the planet support this population? When will we reach the limit of our resources? How could this affect the lifestyle of your children or grandchildren?

✓ **Is this job offer a good deal?** Looking to make a million dollars? Let us examine a plan for earning a million dollars based on a contract between an employee and an employer. First let us agree upon a contract.

Contract for Employment

Employee ____________ (enter your name)

Employer ____________ (a company agreeing with these terms)

Points of Agreement

1. The employee will work a five-day work week.
2. The employee will be paid for the week's wages each Friday.
3. The employee will be hired for a minimum of 30 work days.
4. The salary schedule is as follows:
   - The base pay for Day 1 is one penny.
   - Each subsequent day, the salary is double that of the previous day.

Signed ____________________________ (Employee)

Signed ____________________________ (Employer)

Date: ________________________

Is this a good deal? Take a guess how much money this employee will have earned in the 30 working days: My guess: $__________________. Calculate the amount one would earn working six weeks (40 hours a week) at minimum wage? Minimum wage salary (before taxes and other deductions) $___________. Now let's calculate the earnings for this contract and see whether the employer or the employee has made the better deal. In week one, the wages would be: Monday, 1 cent; Tuesday, 2 cents; Wednesday, 4 cents; Thursday, 8 cents; and Friday, 16 cents, for a total weekly earnings of 31 cents. Doesn't seem like much does it? Now continue calculating the daily wages for the next five weeks.

There is a formula that allows one to calculate a particular day's wages without having to calculate every step. This is an example of a geometric progression, a sequence of numbers in which the ratio of any number to the number before it is a constant amount, called the common ratio. For example, the sequence of numbers 1, 2, 4, 8, 16, ... has a common ratio of 2. A geometric progression may be described by calling the first term in the progression *X* (in this example *X* is one cent), the common ratio as *R* (in this example, $R = 2$), and in a finite progression, the number of terms as *n*. Then the *n*th term of a geometric progression is given by the expression: $X_n = X_1 R^{n-1}$

Questions about this job:

1. How does the total amount of money earned compare with your original guess?
2. Suppose you wanted to buy a car. On which day could you purchase your car and pay in cash?
3. Can you develop a formula for the daily salary? (Answer: Daily Salary = $2^{n-1} X$ where n = the number of days you've been working, and X = your base pay on Day 1.

This counting principal can be applied also to social causes. Efforts to address social issues are often started by just a scant few individuals who are committed to a cause. Suppose you tell one person a day about your issue. A one-on-one plea will be much more effective in convincing the listener. On the second day, there will be two of you who can approach two more people. On day three, there are four of you to approach four more people. On day five, the eight of you convince eight more people, and so on. By day 12, there are over 2,000 people who know about your cause, and by day 30, over one billion people are talking about the issue that is so close to your heart! Yet you personally talked to only 30 people. By the way, now you know why unfounded rumors spread so quickly.

Ratio/Proportion

✓ **The challenges of cooking: Altering recipes.** Recipes involve mixing together ingredients that have relationships to each other. In mathematics, this relationship between two quantities is called a ratio. If a recipe calls for one egg and two cups of flour, the relationship of eggs to cups of flour is 1 to 2. In mathematical language, that relationship can be written in two ways: 1/2 or 1:2.

All recipes are written to serve a certain number of people or yield a certain amount of food. For example, suppose you have a cookie recipe that makes 2 dozen cookies. What if you want 1 dozen or 4 dozen cookies? Understanding how to increase or decrease the yield without spoiling the ratio of ingredients is a valuable skill for any cook.

Let's look at the cookie recipe:

1 cup flour	1/2 tsp. baking soda
1/2 tsp. salt	1/2 cup butter
1/3 cup brown sugar	1/3 cup sugar
1 egg	1/2 tsp. vanilla
1 cup chocolate chips	

This recipe yields 3 dozen cookies. If you want 9 dozen cookies, you will have to increase the amount of each ingredient in the recipe, while ensuring that the relationship between the ingredients stays the same. To do this, you will need to understand proportion. A proportion exists when you have two equal ratios, such as 2:4 and 4:8. Two unequal ratios, such as 3:16 and 1:3, do not result in a proportion. The ratios must be equal.

In the cookie recipe, you will need to set up a proportion to make sure you get the correct ratios to make 9 dozen. Start by figuring out how much flour you will need to make 9 dozen cookies by setting up this proportion:

$$\frac{1(\text{cup})}{X(\text{cups})} = \frac{3(\text{dozen})}{9(\text{dozen})}$$

To find X (number of cups of flour needed in the new recipe), multiply the numbers like this: X times $3 = 1$ times 9 or $3X = 9$. Now find the value of X by dividing both sides of the equation by 3. The result is $X = 3$. To extend the recipe to make 9 dozen cookies, you will need 3 cups of flour. Follow the same process to determine how much of each ingredient is needed for 9 dozen cookies.

These are just a few examples of activities that can help make seemingly abstract mathematical operations more interesting and practical to students. For suggestions on where to find more examples, see some of the Web sites in the **Resources** section of this book.

WHAT'S COMING?

Although many students have occasional difficulties learning mathematics, they often find ways to overcome them. But some students have persistent difficulties with even simple arithmetic operations. The next chapter discusses how teachers can recognize those students who have persistent problems and what can be done to help them learn mathematics concepts.

Chapter 6 — Teaching Mathematics to the Adolescent Brain

Reflections

Jot down on this page key points, ideas, strategies, and resources you want to consider later. This sheet is your personal journal summary and will help to jog your memory.

Chapter 7

Recognizing and Addressing Mathematics Difficulties

Do not be troubled by your difficulties with Mathematics. I can assure you mine are much greater.

—Albert Einstein

Some children are very adept at mathematical calculations while others struggle despite much effort and motivation. In the past three decades, the percentage of school-age children who experience difficulties in learning mathematics has been growing steadily. Why is that? Is the brain's ability to perform arithmetic calculations declining? If so, why? Does the brain get less arithmetic practice because technology has shifted computation from brain cells to inexpensive electronic calculators? What makes a child do poorly in mathematics? The answer to this question is complicated by at least two considerations:

1. We need to distinguish whether the poor achievement is due to inadequate instruction or some other environmental factor, or whether it is due to an actual cognitive disability.

2. Exactly *how* is mathematics being taught? Instructional approaches can determine whether a cognitive deficit is really a disability at all. For example, one instructional approach emphasizes conceptual understanding while de-emphasizing the learning of procedures and mathematical facts (NCTM, 2000). Another approach places heavy emphasis on procedures and facts as in the California Department of Education standards (1999). A student with a deficit in retrieving arithmetic facts might not be considered as having a learning disability in the first approach because of the de-emphasis on memory-based information. However, that deficit would be a serious disability in the second approach.

The growing number of students who are having trouble learning mathematics has spurred research interest in how the brain does calculations and the possible causes of mathematical difficulties. In this chapter, I use the term *mathematics difficulties* to include those students performing in the low average range, regardless of whether their difficulties are due to environmental factors or cognitive deficits. It is important to remember that because mathematics achievement tests include many types of items, it is possible that students may demonstrate average performance in some areas of mathematics and show deficits in other areas.

DETECTING MATHEMATICS DIFFICULTIES

As with any learning difficulty, the earlier it is detected, the better. Studies have shown that using intense tutoring with first graders who display problems with calculations significantly improved their end-of-year achievement in mathematics (Fuchs et al., 2005). The key, of course, is early detection so that interventions can begin as soon as practicable.

Determining the Nature of the Problem

The first task facing educators who deal with students with mathematics difficulties is to determine the nature of the problem. Obviously, environmental causes require different interventions than developmental causes. Low performance on a mathematics test *may* indicate that a problem exists, but tests do not provide information on the exact source of the poor performance. Standardized tests, such as the *Brigance Comprehensive Inventory of Basic Skills—Revised*, are available and provide more precise information on whether the problems stem from deficits in counting, number facts, or procedures.

Educators should examine the degree to which students with mathematics difficulties possess the prerequisite skills for learning mathematical operations. What skills are weak, and what can we do about that? They also should look at the mathematics curriculum to determine how much mathematics is being taught and the types of instructional strategies that teachers are using. Are we trying to cover too much? Are we using enough visual and manipulative aids? Are we developing student strengths and not just focusing on their weaknesses?

Prerequisite Skills

Examining the nature of mathematics curriculum and instruction may reveal clues about how the school system approaches teaching these topics. A good frame of reference is the recognition that students need to have mastered a certain number of skills before they can understand and apply the principles of more complex mathematical operations. Mathematics educators have suggested that the following seven skills are prerequisites to successfully learning mathematics (Sharma, 2006). They are the ability to

1. Follow sequential directions
2. Recognize patterns
3. Estimate by forming a reasonable guess about quantity, size, magnitude, and amount
4. Visualize pictures in one's mind and manipulate them
5. Have a good sense of spatial orientation and space organization, including telling left from right, compass directions, horizontal and vertical directions
6. Do deductive reasoning, that is, reason from a general principle to a particular instance, or from a stated premise to a logical conclusion
7. Do inductive reasoning, that is, come to a natural understanding that is not the result of conscious attention or reasoning, easily detecting the patterns in different situations and the interrelationships between procedures and concepts

Students who are unable to follow sequential directions, for example, will have great difficulty understanding the concept of long division, which requires retention of several different processes performed in a particular sequence. First one estimates, then multiplies, then compares, then subtracts, then brings down a number; and the cycle repeats. Those with directional difficulties will be unsure which number goes inside the division sign or on top of the fraction. Moving through the division problem also presents other directional difficulties: One reads to the right, then records a number up, then multiplies the numbers diagonally, then records the product down below while watching for place value, then brings a number down, and so on.

Diagnostic Tools

Primary-Grades Assessments

Teachers in the primary grades, of course, often rely on their own observations of students' performance to determine when a particular child is having problems with arithmetic computations. Although teacher observations are valuable, other measures should be considered as well. Research studies have shown that several measures are reliable in detecting and predicting how well young students are mastering number manipulation and basic arithmetic operations. Table 7.1 summarizes the screening measures that can be used with kindergarten and first-grade students to determine whether mathematics difficulties exist (Gersten, Jordan, & Flojo, 2005; Griffin, 2002).

Table 7.1 Description of Selected Screening Measures in Early Mathematics

Measure	Description
Digit Span	Student repeats a string of number either forwards or backwards
Magnitude Comparison	Student chooses the largest of four visually or verbally presented numbers
Missing Number	Student names a missing number from a sequence of numbers between 0 and 20
Number Knowledge Test	Basic measure of number sense (See Chapter 5)
Numbers From Dictation	Student writes numbers from oral dictation
Number Identification	Student identifies numbers between 0 and 20 from printed numbers
Quantity Discrimination	Student identifies the larger of two printed numbers

Sources: Gersten, Jordan, & Flojo, 2005; Griffin, 2002.

Postprimary Grades Assessments

Past the primary grades, research studies over the last 15 years suggest that five critical factors affect the learning of mathematics. Each factor can serve as a diagnostic tool for assessing the nature of any learning difficulties students may experience with mathematical processing (Augustyniak, Murphy, & Phillips, 2005; Sharma, 2006). Here are the factors you will need to consider:

✓ Level of cognitive awareness. Students come to a learning situation with varying levels of cognitive awareness about that learning. The levels can range from no cognitive awareness to high levels. Your first task is to determine the students' level of cognitive awareness and the strategies that each student brings to the mathematics task. This is not easy, but it can be accomplished by doing the following:

- Interview the students individually and observe how each one approaches a mathematical problem that needs to be solved
- Ask "What is the student thinking?" and "What formal and informal strategies is the student using?"
- Determine what prerequisite skills are in place and which are poor or missing
- Determine if a mathematics answer is correct or incorrect and ask students to explain how they arrived at the answer

Knowing the levels of the students' cognitive awareness and prerequisite skills will give you valuable information for selecting and introducing new concepts and skills.

✓ **Mathematics learning profile.** As discussed in Chapter 6, researchers agree that each person processes mathematics differently and that these differences run along a continuum from primarily quantitative to primarily qualitative. You will recall that quantitative learners prefer entities with definite values, use procedural approaches to problem solving, and focus on deductive reasoning. Qualitative learners, on the other hand, prefer holistic and intuitive approaches, look for relationships between concepts and procedures, are social learners, and focus on visual-spatial aspects of mathematical information.

Because both types of learning styles are present in mathematics classes, teachers need to incorporate multiple instructional strategies. Teaching to one style alone leaves out students with the other style, many of whom may do poorly in mathematics as a result. In fact, some may even exhibit the symptoms of mathematics difficulties.

✓ **Language of mathematics.** Mathematical difficulties often arise when students fail to understand the language of mathematics, which has its own symbolic representations, syntax, and terminology. Solving word problems requires the ability to translate the language of English into the language of mathematics. The translation is likely to be successful if the student recognizes English language equivalents for each mathematical statement. For example, if the teacher asks the class to solve the problem "76 take away 8," the students will correctly write the expression in the exact order stated, "76 - 8." But if the teacher says, "Subtract 8 from 76," a student following the language order could mistakenly write,"8 - 76." Learning to identify and correctly translate mathematical syntax becomes critical to student success in problem solving.

Language can be an obstacle in other ways. Students may learn a limited vocabulary for performing basic arithmetic operations, such as "add" and "multiply," only to run into difficulties when they encounter expressions asking for the "sum" or "product" of numbers. You can avoid this problem by introducing synonyms for every function: "Let us *multiply* 6 and 5. We are finding the *product* of 6 and 5. The product of 6 *times* 5 is 30."

✓ **Prerequisite skills.** As noted earlier, the seven prerequisite skills necessary to learn mathematics successfully are nonmathematical in nature. However, they must be mastered before even the most basic understandings of number concepts and arithmetic operations can be learned. You should assess the extent to which these seven skills are present in each student.

Consider using this simple profile diagram (see example on the next page) to assist in their assessment. After assessing the student's level on each skill, analyze the results and decide on a plan of action that will address any areas needing improvement.

Students with four or more scores in the 1 to 2 range will have significant problems learning the basic concepts of mathematics. They will need instruction and practice in mastering these skills before they can be expected to master mathematical content.

Prerequisite Skills Profile for Mathematics

Student's Name: ____________________ Date: ___________

Directions: On a scale of 1 (lowest) to 5 (highest), circle the number that indicates the degree to which the student displays mastery of each skill. Connect the circles to see the profile.

Skill					
Follows sequential directions	5	4	3	2	1
Recognizes patterns	5	4	3	2	1
Can estimate quantities	5	4	3	2	1
Can visualize and manipulate mental pictures	5	4	3	2	1
Sense of spatial orientation and organization	5	4	3	2	1
Ability to do deductive reasoning	5	4	3	2	1
Ability to do inductive reasoning	5	4	3	2	1

Action Plan: As a result of this profile, we will work together to ________________

____

by doing ____

✓ **Levels of learning mastery.** How do you decide when a student has mastered a mathematical concept? Certainly, written tests of problem solving are one of the major devices for evaluating learning. However, they are useful tools only to the extent that they actually measure mastery rather than rote memory of formulas and procedures. Cognitive research suggests that a person must move through the following six levels of mastery to truly learn and retain mathematical concepts:

- Level One: Connects new knowledge to existing knowledge and experiences (Example: Recognizes that three multiplied by four is the same as three plus three plus three plus three and the same as four plus four plus four)
- Level Two: Searches for concrete material to construct a model or show a manifestation of the concept (Example: Uses manipulatives such as blocks or coins to lay out four groups of three objects or three groups of four objects)
- Level Three: Illustrates the concept by drawing a diagram to connect the concrete example to a symbolic picture or representation (Example: Draws four groups of three objects or three groups of four objects, such as animals or stars)

- Level Four: Translates the concept into mathematical notation using number symbols, operational signs, formulas, and equations (Example: Writes $3 \times 4 = 3 + 3 + 3 + 3 = 12$ or $3 \times 4 = 4 + 4 + 4 = 12$)
- Level Five: Applies the concept correctly to real-world situations, projects, and story problems (Example: Solves prewritten or student-created story problems)
- Level Six: Can teach the concept successfully to others, or can communicate it on a test (Example: Explains the concept orally to a peer or to the class)

Too often, paper-and-pencil tests assess only Level Six. Thus, when the student's results are poor, the teacher may not know where learning difficulties lie. By designing separate assessments for each level, teachers will be in a much better position to determine what kind of remedial work will help each student.

ENVIRONMENTAL FACTORS

Students without cognitive deficits may still display difficulties with arithmetic and mathematical operations. Environmental factors, such as emotional responses to mathematics and instructional quality, can play a vital role in determining how well young students and adolescents will achieve in their mathematics classes.

Student Attitudes About Mathematics

In modern American society, reading and writing have become the main measures of a good student. Mathematics ability has been regarded more as a specialized function rather than as a general indicator of intelligence. Consequently, the stigma of not being able to do mathematics was reduced and became socially acceptable. Just hearing their parent say "I wasn't very good at math" allowed children to embrace the social attitudes that regard mathematics failure as acceptable and routine.

Despite higher standards and high-stakes testing, student attitudes about mathematics have not improved much.

In recent years, schools have placed a heavy emphasis on raising standards in all curriculum areas. At the same time, the No Child Left Behind Act requirements include high-stakes assessments in reading and mathematics. Despite these initiatives, student attitudes about mathematics have not improved much. Surveys show that most students (including those who like mathematics) find making nonmathematical mistakes much more embarrassing than making mathematical mistakes (Latterell, 2005). Furthermore, regardless of the efforts toward gender equity, female high school students still rate themselves as less confident in mathematics than their male peers (Morge, 2005).

These findings are unsettling, especially because other research studies have shown that attitudes are formed by social forces and predict academic performance. Not surprisingly, students with positive attitudes about what they are learning achieve more than students with poor attitudes (Singh, Granville, & Dika, 2002). Apparently, higher standards and increased testing are not sufficient as yet to improve how students feel about learning mathematics. They do not yet view competency in mathematics as a basic life skill. Until this view changes, students will have little incentive to master it, and teachers will continue to have their work cut out for them.

Fear of Mathematics (Math Anxiety)

Anxiety about learning and doing mathematics (commonly referred to as "math anxiety") has been around a long time. It can be described as a feeling of tension that interferes with the manipulations of numbers and the solving of mathematical problems in academic and ordinary life situations. It occurs in many individuals regardless of age, race, or gender, and can prevail in the home, classroom, or society. Some studies suggest that over 60 percent of adults have a fear of mathematics (Burns, 1998).

Students at all grade levels often develop a fear (or phobia) of mathematics because of negative experiences in their past or current mathematics class or have a simple lack of self-confidence with numbers. Math anxiety conjures up fear of some type. Perhaps it is the fear that one won't be able to do the calculations, or the fear that it's too difficult, or the fear of failure that often stems from having a lack of confidence. In people with math anxiety, the fear of failure often causes their minds to draw a blank, leading to more frustration and more blanks. Added pressure of having time limits on mathematics tests also raises the levels of anxiety for many students.

Typically, students with this phobia have a limited understanding of mathematical concepts. They may rely mainly on memorizing procedures, rules, and routines without much conceptual understanding, so panic soon sets in. Mathematics phobia can be as challenging as any learning disability, but it is important to remember that these students have neurological systems for computation that are normal. They need help primarily in replacing the memory of failure with the possibility of success. As we shall see later, students with mathematical disorders, on the other hand, have a neurological deficit that results in persistent difficulty in processing numbers.

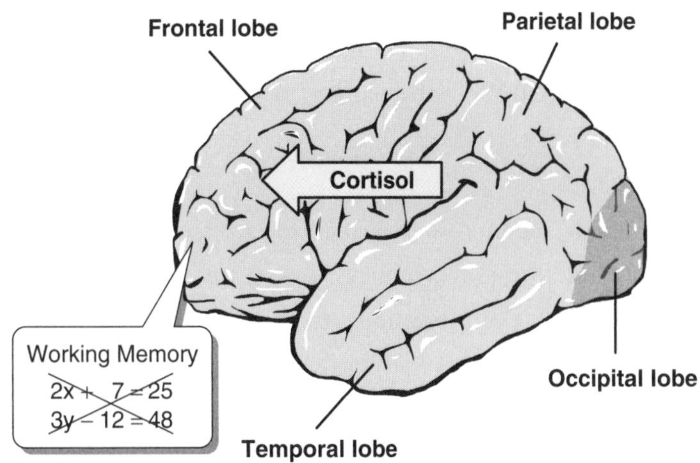

Figure 7.1 Math anxiety causes the release of cortisol in the blood. Cortisol refocuses the frontal lobe to deal with the anxiety. Meanwhile, any unrelated learning in working memory is disrupted and lost.

Regardless of the source, the most prevalent consequences of this anxiety are poor achievement and poor grades in mathematics. One reason for the poor performance is biological. Anxiety of any type causes the body to release the hormone cortisol into the bloodstream. Cortisol's main function is to refocus the brain on the source of the anxiety and to determine what action to take to relieve the stress (Figure 7.1). Heart rate increases and other physical indicators of worry appear. Meanwhile, the frontal lobe is no longer interested in learning or processing mathematical operations because it has to deal with what appears to be a threat to the individual's safety. As a result, the student cannot focus on the learning task at hand and has to cope with the frustration of inattention. Furthermore, the anxious feelings disrupt working memory's ability to manipulate and retain numbers and numerical expressions (Ashcraft & Kirk, 2001).

Alleviating Math Anxiety in the Classroom

Shields (2005) suggests that five areas contribute in one way or another to math anxiety: teachers' attitudes, curriculum, instructional strategies, the classroom culture, and assessment. Let's take a look at what research studies say about each of these five areas as well as what can be done to lessen anxiety and improve student achievement in mathematics (Figure 7.2).

✓ **Teacher attitudes.** Research studies confirm that teacher attitudes greatly influence math anxiety and represent the most dominating factor in molding student attitudes about mathematics (Harper & Daane, 1998; Ruffell, Mason, & Allen, 1998). Here are some things you can do to maintain a positive attitude in yourself as well as in your students:

- Present an agreeable disposition that shows mathematics to be a great human invention.
- Show the value of mathematics by how it contributes to other disciplines as well as society.
- Promote student confidence and curiosity by assigning appropriate, interesting, and relevant tasks.

Figure 7.2 Math anxiety is a common problem with both students and adults. In schools, math anxiety can be lowered by making modifications in the five areas shown in the figure.

- Focus on the goals and process of learning rather than searching for just the correct answer.
- Create opportunities for success. Studies suggest that teachers need to build in a 70-percent success rate in order for students to remain engaged with work that is challenging enough to demand effort but easy enough to expect success (Sowder & Schappelle, 2002).
- Resist the temptation to believe that males have a greater innate ability than females to do mathematics, or that females have to put forth more effort than males to succeed.
- Display confidence in your teaching. Teachers, especially at the elementary grade levels, who are math anxious themselves or who lack confidence with the subject often inadvertently transmit this fear to students.

✓ **Curriculum.** Studies of mathematics curriculum in Grades 2 through 8 reveal much repetition of subject matter. An analysis of the TIMSS 1999 video study showed that 53 percent of instruction in mathematics at these grade levels consisted of review problems and only 23 percent of the time was spent on dealing with new concepts and problems (TIMSS, 2003). In the primary grades, students usually rate mathematics as one of the subjects they like most. Through positive learning experiences, the students believe that they have the competence to do mathematics and that hard work will bring success. But by fourth grade, math anxiety often surfaces because the curriculum shifts from using manipulatives and concrete applications to more abstract thinking.

By middle school, the abstract nature of the curriculum content causes students to believe that success in mathematics is due to innate ability and that effort matters little. The material gets even more abstract in high school, and students realize that memorization is not sufficient to succeed. You help students make this transition to abstract thinking when you

- Devote more time in the elementary and middle school grades to new material, discovery, and application
- Provide activities that constantly train students to apply their knowledge to new ideas and to use mathematics as a tool for discovery
- Prune the mathematics curriculum to eliminate the less important items so that it focuses on a deeper understanding of major topics and enhances skills
- Avoid repeating the same topics annually unless they are critical to learning, applying, and discovering new opportunities in mathematics

✓ **Instructional strategies.** One critical factor in how well students learn mathematics is the quality of the teaching. Studies show that student achievement in mathematics is strongly linked to the teacher's expertise in mathematics. Students of a teacher expert in mathematics perform better on achievement tests than students of a teacher with limited training in mathematics (NSF, 2004). Teaching techniques that center on "explain-practice-memorize" are among the main sources of math anxiety because the focus is on memorization rather than on understanding the concepts and reasoning involved. Students taught with this approach do not have the skills to successfully deal with material that goes beyond memorization. Students are more successful in mathematics classes where you do the following:

- Possess a mathematics skill level that goes beyond basic understanding
- Show an awareness of and understand student confusion and frustration
- Pose questions in an effort to help students continuously learn
- Limit the frequency of memorizing, doing rote practice, searching for one right answer, and making calculations that can be performed by computers and calculators
- Develop meaning by showing practical applications that are related to students' lives
- Incorporate projects that allow students to explore solutions to problems individually and in groups
- Encourage students to investigate and formulate questions involving mathematical relationships

- Provide opportunities for students to represent everyday situations verbally, numerically, graphically, and symbolically

✓ **Classroom culture.** Classroom culture can be defined as the norms and behaviors that regularly guide classroom interactions. Structured, rigid classes where there is little opportunity for debate can become a source of math anxiety. If the culture includes that inevitable search for the one right answer, then students feel there is no recognition or reward for the cognitive processes involved. The culture may also place a strong emphasis on answering quickly and on timed tests. Placing a strong emphasis on speed does not encourage students to reflect on their thinking processes or to analyze their results. Math anxiety is likely to be lower in classrooms where you do the following:

- Create a culture where students can ask questions, discover learning, and explore ideas
- Provide an environment where students can feel secure in taking risks and not feel embarrassed for giving wrong answers
- Discourage valuing speed over time for reflection
- Encourage students to make sense of what they are learning rather than just memorize steps or procedures. Remember that making sense is one of the criteria (along with meaning) that the brain uses to determine whether information is worth tagging for long-term storage.

Flewelling and Higginson (2001) suggest that students can overcome math anxiety and find learning mathematics to be a rewarding and successful experience when teachers establish a classroom culture oriented toward making sense rather than a more traditional culture oriented toward memorizing, being correct, recalling quickly, and listening. More specifically, their comparison of some of the characteristics of the sense-making classroom to the traditional classroom is shown in Table 7.2.

Table 7.2 Comparison of Sense-Making and Traditional Classroom Cultures	
Traditional Classroom	**Sense-Making Classroom**
Mathematics is a collection of procedures	Mathematics is a way of thinking
Working with the inexplicable	Working with things that make sense
Significance of material lost on learner	Material significant to learner
Student is passive	Student is active
Validated by teacher	Validated by student
Truth is as presented	Truth is as constructed
Teacher-owned	Student-owned
Described/explained in teacher language	Described/explained in student language
Often forgotten, not retrievable	Remembered, retrievable
Pops into existence	Grows into being
Ignores student readiness	Considers student readiness
Nonexperiential	Experiential
Presented at beginning of lesson	Developed at end of lesson
Reliance on memory aids	Minimal reliance on memory aids
Isolated and superficial	Connected and thorough
Follow procedures	Develop procedures
Anxious about mathematics	Sense of personal efficacy and confidence
Deadens the mind and spirit	Enlivens the mind and spirit

Source: Flewelling & Higginson (2001).

Flewelling and Higginson (2001) further suggest that changing the typical classroom culture to a sense-making culture in mathematics can be achieved by having students and their teacher focus on, engage in, and experience rich learning tasks. They need to see what learning looks and feels like and the kind of interaction that is involved when they are so engaged. They define rich learning tasks as those that give learners the opportunity to (1) use their knowledge in an integrated, creative, and purposeful fashion to conduct investigations, inquiries and experiments, and to solve problems, (2) acquire knowledge with understanding, and (3) develop the attitudes and the habits of a lifelong sense-maker. Table 7.3 offers a comparison of traditional and rich tasks that can be conducted in the mathematics classroom.

Table 7.3 Comparison of Traditional and Rich Tasks

Traditional Tasks	Rich Tasks
Prepare for success in school	Prepare for success outside of school
Address learning outcomes in mathematics	Address learning outcomes in mathematics and other subject areas
Focus on the use of relatively few skills	Provide an opportunity to use broad range of skills in an integrated and creative fashion
Are more artificial and out of context	Are authentic and in context
Encourage recollection and practice	Encourage thinking, reflection, and imagination
Allow for demonstration of a narrow range of performance	Allow for demonstration of a wide range of performance
Usually require enrichment to be added after the task	Provide enrichment within the task
Permit the use of fewer teaching and learning strategies	Encourage the use of a wide variety of teaching and learning strategies
Keep students and teachers distanced from the task	Encourage greater engagement of students and teachers in the task

Source: Flewelling & Higginson (2001).

✓ **Assessment.** Tests can be the primary source of students' anxiety in any subject. But the anxiety may be greater in those subjects, such as mathematics, that are the basis for the high-stakes tests that have emerged since the adoption of curriculum standards and minimum competencies. Tests often diminish the students' confidence because they have no flexibility in the testing process, and as a result, the tests do not stir their curiosity or inventiveness. Furthermore, tests are often used to determine which students will enter classes of advanced mathematics. One can question whether poor assessment techniques should be used to determine how students advance in the mathematics curriculum, especially since these decisions can affect their post–high school choices. You can alleviate the math anxiety caused by testing when you do the following:

- Limit class tests and do not time them. Timed tests increase the pressure on students, which disrupts processing in both working and long-term memories (Beilock, Kulp, Holt, & Carr, 2004).

- Reduce the weight given to tests in determining grades, ranking students, or measuring isolated skills.
- Assess students on how they think about mathematics.
- Include multiple methods of assessment such as oral, written, or demonstration formats.
- Provide feedback that focuses on a lack of effort rather than a lack of ability so that students remain confident in their ability to improve (Altermatt & Kim, 2004).
- Use the six NCTM Assessment Standards for School Mathematics (1995) as a guide for their testing practices. In brief, these standards state that assessment should (1) include real-life activities, (2) enhance mathematics learning, (3) promote equity, (4) be an open process, (5) promote valid inferences about mathematics learning, and (6) be a coherent process.

Research studies clearly indicate that student performance in mathematics improves when anxiety is alleviated (Ashcraft, 2002). Teachers alleviate that anxiety when they demonstrate excitement and confidence in the subject, develop a relevant mathematics curriculum, use effective instructional strategies, create classrooms centered on discovery and inquiry, and assess students in a meaningful and fair manner (Shields, 2005).

NEUROLOGICAL AND OTHER FACTORS

Apart from environmental factors that can cause poor performance in mathematics, researchers look also at potential neurological causes. Just a few years ago neuroscientists studied reading disabilities and were finally able to separate the factors that *cause* reading problems from those that are the *consequences* of these factors. Most researchers now agree that the major causal deficits in reading difficulties result from impairments in the brain regions responsible for phonological processing (Sousa, 2005).

The problem facing researchers in the field of mathematics disabilities is similar: distinguishing those factors that are causal from those that are consequences. Because students with moderate mathematical difficulties are often of average or higher intelligence and possess good reading skills, the brain regions involved in mathematics difficulties are likely localized or modular. In other words, the neurological causes of mathematics difficulties can be limited and not affect other cognitive areas. As we have noted in previous chapters, there is already a substantial body of brain imaging and case studies research supporting the existence of number modules.

Dyscalculia

About 5 to 8 percent of school-age students have serious difficulty processing mathematics (Fuchs & Fuchs, 2002; Geary, 2004). This is about the same number as students who have serious reading problems. However, because of the strong emphasis that our society places on the need to learn reading, many more research studies have focused on problems in this area than on mathematics.

The condition that causes persistent problems with processing numerical calculations is referred to as *dyscalculia* (pronounced, dis-kal-KOOL-ee-ah). Dyscalculia is a difficulty in conceptualizing numbers, number relationships, outcomes of numerical operations, and estimation, that is, what to expect as an outcome of an operation. If the condition is present from birth, it is called *developmental dyscalculia.* Genetic studies reveal that developmental dyscalculia is inheritable (Shaley et al., 2001). If the condition results from an injury to the brain after birth, it is called *acquired dyscalculia.* Whether developmental or acquired, for most individuals, this disorder is the result of specific disabilities in basic numerical processing and not the consequence of deficits in other cognitive abilities (Landerl, Bevan, & Butterworth, 2004). People with dyscalculia have difficulty:

- Mastering arithmetic facts by the traditional methods of teaching, particularly the methods involving counting
- Learning abstract concepts of time and direction, telling and keeping track of time, and the sequence of past and future events
- Acquiring spatial orientation and space organization, including left/right orientation, trouble reading maps, and grappling with mechanical processes
- Following directions in sports that demand sequencing or rules, and keeping track of scores and players during games such as cards and board games
- Following sequential directions and sequencing (including reading numbers out of sequence, substitutions, reversals, omissions and doing operations backward), organizing detailed information, remembering specific facts and formulas for completing their mathematical calculations

The neurological basis of developmental dyscalculia is an impairment in the child's innate ability to subitize. Because they cannot see the "twoness" or "threeness" of a group of objects, they learn to count in a way different from other students, relying heavily on sequencing and memorizing. They typically have no difficulty remembering the sequence of number words, and they can place those

> *The neurological basis of developmental dyscalculia is an impairment in the child's innate ability to subitize.*

words into a one-to-one correspondence with objects in an array. But even when they say that four objects are present, they do not have an innate sense of the "fourness." They simply have confidence that their counting process has led them to the correct answer.

We explained in Chapter 2 that after children learn to count, their brains will quickly associate a digit with a quantity, that is, the digit "5" automatically produces a mental image of five items. But in individuals with developmental dyscalculia, seeing the digit does not generate this mental representation of quantity, making it very difficult to perform mental arithmetic operations involving symbols (Rubinstein & Henik, 2005). On the other hand, these individuals can still differentiate the number of objects contained in concrete (nonsymbolic) collections of objects. Apparently, it is the symbol (digit) that causes the problem (Rouselle & Noël, 2007).

Dyscalculia can be (1) quantitative, which is a difficulty in counting and calculating, (2) qualitative, which is a difficulty in the conceptualizing of mathematics processes and spatial sense, or (3) mixed, which is the inability to integrate quantity and space.

Some simple tests are available that could indicate the presence of dyscalculia. A common one is a reaction time test in which subjects are asked which is the larger of two numbers. You will recall from Chapter 1 that as the distance between two numbers increases, most people find it easier to say which is larger. It is easier to recognize that 8 is larger than 3 than to recognize that 4 is larger than 3. But the responses from people with dyscalculia are exactly the opposite. Because they cannot subitize, people with dyscalculia must rely on counting and sequencing. Counting takes longer to get from 3 to 8 than from 3 to 4.

Possible Causes

The difficulty that individuals with developmental dyscalculia have in subitizing may be due to deficits in the number-processing regions of the brain. Recent fMRI studies have found that the parts of the brain responsible for making the approximations necessary to subitize are much less activated in children with developmental dyscalculia than in typical children. However, brain activation during exact calculations was similar for both groups (Castelli, Glaser, & Butterworth, 2006; Kucian et al., 2006). Figure 7.3 shows only a small activated area in the brain of children with dyscalculia during approximate calculations compared to typical children, but a similar amount of activation during exact calculations.

Because the parietal lobe is heavily involved with number operations, damage to this area can result in mathematics difficulties. Studies of individuals with Gerstmann's syndrome—the result of damage to the parietal lobe—showed that they had serious problems with mathematical calculations as well as right-left disorientation, but no problems with oral language skills (Lemer, Dehaene, Spelke, & Cohen, 2003; Suresh & Sebastian, 2000).

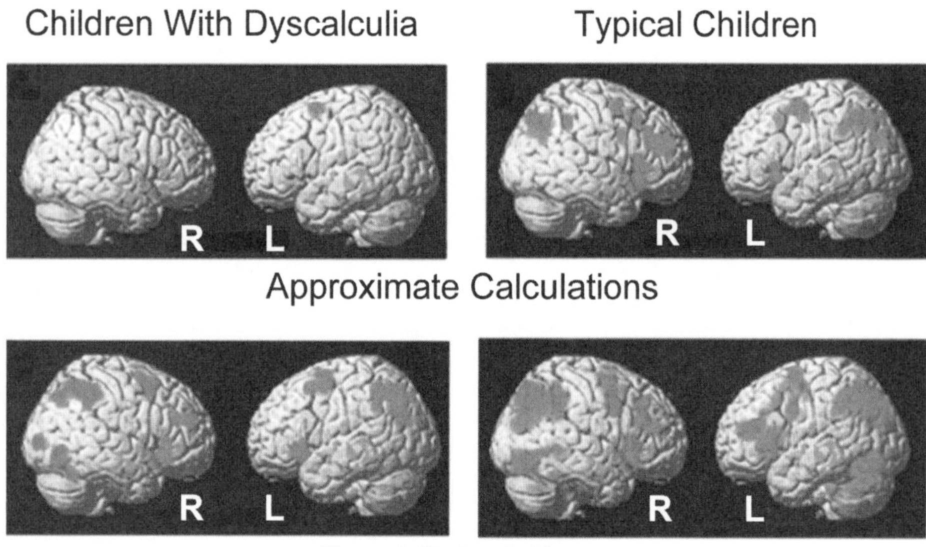

Figure 7.3 These representative fMRIs show that during approximate calculations, the right (R) and left (L) hemispheres of children with dyscalculia are much less activated than typical children. During exact calculations, however, the activation is very similar in both groups. (Kurcian et al., 2006)

Individuals with visual processing weaknesses almost always display difficulties with mathematics. This is probably because success in mathematics requires one to visualize numbers and mathematical situations, especially in algebra and geometry. Students with sequencing difficulties also may have dyscalculia because they cannot remember the order of mathematical operations or the specific formulas needed to complete a set of computations.

Genetic factors also seem to play a significant role. Studies of identical twins reveal close mathematics scores. Children from families with a history of mathematical giftedness or learning disorders show common aptitudes with other family members. Girls born with Turner's syndrome (a condition caused by the partial or complete absence of one of the two X chromosomes normally found in females) usually display dyscalculia, among other learning problems (Murphy, Mazzocco, Gerner, & Henry, 2006).

Types of Mathematical Disorders

The complexity of mathematics makes the study of mathematical disorders particularly challenging for researchers. Learning deficits can include difficulties in mastering basic number concepts, counting skills, and processing arithmetic operations as well as procedural, retrieval, and visual-spatial deficits (Geary, 2004). As with any learning disability, each of these deficits can range from mild to severe.

Number concept difficulties. As discussed in Chapter 1, an understanding of small numbers and quantity appears to be present at birth. The understanding of larger numbers and place value, however, develops during the preschool and early elementary years. A poor understanding of the concepts involved in a mathematical procedure will delay the adoption of more sophisticated procedures and limit the child's ability to detect procedural errors. Studies show that most children with mathematical disorders nevertheless have their basic number competencies intact. However, they often are unable to use their number concept skills to solve arithmetic problems (Geary, 2004).

Counting skill deficits. Studies of children with mathematical disorders show that they have deficits in counting knowledge and counting accuracy. Some may also have problems keeping numerical information in working memory while counting, resulting in counting errors.

Difficulties with arithmetic skills. Children with mathematical disorders have difficulties solving simple and complex arithmetic problems, and they rely heavily on finger counting. Their difficulties stem mainly from deficits in both numerical procedures (solving 6 + 5 or 4 × 4) and working memory. They tend to use developmentally immature procedures, such as counting all rather than counting on.

At the same time, they do not show the shift from procedure-based problem solving to memory-based problem solving that is found in typically achieving children, most likely because of difficulties in storing arithmetic facts or retrieving them from long-term memory. Moreover, deficits in visual-spatial skills can lead to problems with arithmetic because of misalignment of numerals in multicolumn addition. Although *procedural, memory,* and *visual-spatial* deficits can occur separately, they are often interconnected.

Procedural disorders. Students displaying this disorder:

- Use arithmetic procedures (algorithms) that are developmentally immature
- Have problems sequencing multistep procedures, such as 52 × 13 or 317 + 298
- Have difficulty understanding the concepts associated with procedures
- Make frequent mistakes when using procedures

The exact cause of this disorder is unknown, but research studies have yielded some intriguing findings. Children with developmental or acquired dyscalculia can still count arrays of objects, say the correct sequence of number words while counting, and understand basic counting concepts, such as cardinality. However, they have difficulties in solving complex arithmetic problems. Researchers suspect one possible cause may be a dysfunction in the brain's left hemisphere, which specializes in procedural tasks.

Memory disorders. Students displaying this disorder:

- Have difficulty retrieving arithmetic facts

- Have a high error rate when they do retrieve arithmetic facts
- Retrieve incorrect facts that are associated with the correct facts
- Rely on finger counting because it reduces the demands on working memory

This disorder likely involves the manipulation of information in the language system. Here again, a dysfunction of the left hemisphere is suspected, mainly because these individuals frequently have reading disorders as well (D'Amico & Guarnera, 2005). This association further suggests that memory deficits may be inheritable.

Memory disorders can be caused by two separate problems. One involves disruptions in the ability to retrieve basic facts from long-term memory, resulting in many more errors than typically achieving children. Research findings indicate that this form of memory disorder is closely linked to the language-processing system and may indicate developmental or acquired deficits in the left hemisphere.

The second possibility involves disruption in the retrieval process caused by difficulties in inhibiting the retrieval of irrelevant associations. Thus the student seems impulsive. For example, when asked what is 7 + 3, a student might quickly blurt out 8 or 4 because those numbers come next in counting (Passolunghi & Siegel, 2004). Solving arithmetic problems becomes much easier when irrelevant information is prevented from entering working memory. When irrelevant information is retrieved, it lowers working memory's capacity and competes with correct information for the individual's attention. This type of retrieval deficit may be caused by deficits in the brain's executive areas of the prefrontal cortex responsible for inhibiting working-memory operations.

Visual-spatial deficits. Students with this disorder:

- Have difficulties in the spatial arrangement of their work, such as aligning the columns in multicolumn addition
- Often misread numerical signs, rotate and transpose numbers, or both
- Misinterpret spatial placement of numerals, resulting in place value errors
- Have difficulty with problems involving space in areas, as required in algebra and geometry

Studies indicate that this disorder is closely associated with deficits in the right parietal area, which specializes in visual-spatial tasks. Individuals with injuries to this area often show a deficit in spatial orientation tasks and in the ability to generate and use a mental number line (Zorzi, Priftis, & Umiltá, 2002). Some studies suggest that the left parietal lobe also may be implicated.

Many students eventually overcome procedural disorders as they mature and learn to rely on sequence diagrams and other tools to remember the steps of mathematical procedures. Those with visual-spatial disorders also improve when they discover the benefits of graph paper and learn to

> *Children often outgrow procedural and visual-spatial difficulties, but memory problems may continue throughout life.*

solve certain algebra and geometry problems with logic rather than through spatial analysis alone. However, memory deficits do not seem to improve with maturity. Studies indicate that individuals with this problem will continue to have difficulties retrieving basic arithmetic facts throughout life. This finding may suggest that the memory problem exists not just for mathematical operations, but may signal a more general deficit in retrieving information from memory.

Associating Dyscalculia With Other Disorders

Reading disorders. Some students with dyscalculia can also have developmental reading difficulties, or dyslexia, but these disorders are not genetically linked (Fletcher, 2005). Students with both disorders are less successful in solving mathematics problems than those who have only dyscalculia, mainly because they have difficulty translating word problems into mathematical expressions.

Attention-deficit hyperactivity disorder (ADHD). Because many children with ADHD have difficulty with mathematics, some researchers wondered if these two conditions had related genetic components, increasing the possibility that they would be inherited together. But studies show that these two disorders are transmitted independently and are connected to distinctly different genetic regions (Monuteaux, Faraone, Herzig, Navsaria, & Biederman, 2005). These findings underscore the need for separate identification and treatment strategies for children with both conditions.

Nonverbal learning disability (NLD). This disability is thought to be caused by deficits in the brain's right hemisphere. Individuals with NLD have difficulty processing nonverbal information, but are very good at processing verbal information. They tend to be excessively verbal and expressive and show weaknesses in visual and spatial tasks. Although there is little evidence that NLD is directly associated with dyscalculia, NLD affects one's ability to manage and understand nonverbal learning assignments. Thus students with NLD will have problems with handwriting, perceiving spatial relationships, drawing and copying geometric forms and designs, and grasping mathematics concepts and skills. We will discuss later in this chapter some of the strategies that can help these individuals.

ADDRESSING MATHEMATICS DIFFICULTIES

Research Findings

Numerous research studies have looked at the effectiveness of instructional strategies on improving achievement by students with mathematics difficulties. As expected, some strategies work better than others, and a particular strategy's effectiveness can depend on the nature of the learning difficulties found in the individuals being studied. Three recent projects looked at more than fifty studies to determine which instructional strategies worked best for students with difficulties in mathematics (Baker, Gersten, & Lee, 2002; Gersten et al., 2006; Kroesbergen & van Luitt, 2003). Their meta-analyses focused on six aspects of instruction and their effectiveness with low-achieving students in mathematics and special education students. Effectiveness of the strategies was determined by effect sizes (0.2 small effect, 0.4 moderate effect, and 0.6 or above large effect). Table 7.4 lists the six strategies along with the effect size for teaching low-achieving students with learning difficulties in mathematics and special education students.

Table 7.4 Effect Sizes for Instructional Strategies for Low-Achieving and Special Education Students

Instructional Strategy	Effect Size for Low-Achieving Students	Effect Size for Special Education Students
Systematic and explicit instruction	0.58 (moderate to large)	1.19 (large)
Student think-alouds	NA	0.98 (large)
Visual and graphic depictions of problems	NA	0.50 (moderate)
Structured peer-assisted learning activities with heterogeneous ability groupings	0.62 (large)	0.42 (moderate)
Formative assessment data provided to teachers	0.51 (moderate)	0.32 (small to moderate)
Formative assessment data provided directly to students	0.57 (moderate to large)	0.33 (small to moderate)

Sources: Baker et al., 2002; Gersten et al., 2006; Kroesbergen & van Luitt, 2003.

In these studies, systematic and explicit instruction provided consistently strong effects for both groups. The effect size of 1.19 for the special education students would indicate that more than

80 percent of the participants improved their test scores after the strategy was used. This strategy involved teachers demonstrating a specific plan for solving a problem and the students using that plan to find their way to a solution. These plans provided highly explicit models of steps and procedures or of the questions that students should ask when solving problems.

Student think-alouds showed a strong effect size for special education students. This strategy encourages students to express their thinking by talking, writing, or drawing the steps they used to solve a problem. This process may be effective in part because it reduces the impulsive approach that many of these students use to solve problems.

Strategies that involved the visual and graphic depictions of problems resulted in a moderate effect size (0.50) for special education students. Of particular interest was the finding that the specificity of the visual representation determined the effectiveness of the intervention. Effect sizes were much larger when teachers (1) presented graphic depictions with multiple examples, (2) helped students select which visuals to use and why, and (3) had students practice with their own graphic organizers.

Although using peer-assisted learning and formative data improved the performance of both groups, the effect sizes were larger with low-achieving students than with the special education groups.

The Concrete-Pictorial-Abstract Approach

Students who have difficulties with mathematics can benefit significantly from lessons that include multiple models that approach a concept at different cognitive levels. Mathematics educators have recognized a substantial body of research showing that the optimal presentation sequence for new mathematical content is *concrete-pictorial-abstract,* or the CPA approach. This approach has also been referred to as concrete-representational-abstract (CRA) or concrete, semiconcrete, abstract (CSA). Regardless of the name, the instructional approach is similar and originally based on the work of Jerome Bruner in the 1960s (Bruner, 1960). Concrete components include manipulatives (for example, Cuisenaire rods, foam-rubber pie sections, and markers), measuring tools, or other objects the students can handle during the lesson. Pictorial representations include drawings, diagrams, charts, or graphs that are drawn by the students or are provided for the students to read and interpret. Abstract refers to symbolic representations, such as numbers or letters, that the student writes or interprets to demonstrate understanding of a task.

When using the CPA approach, the sequencing of activities is critical. Activities with concrete materials should come first to impress on students that mathematical operations can be used to solve real-world problems. Pictured relationships show visual representations of the concrete manipulatives and help students visualize mathematical operations during problem solving. It is important here that the teacher explain how the pictorial examples relate to the concrete examples. Finally, formal work with symbols is used to demonstrate how symbols provide a shorter and efficient way to represent numerical operations. Ultimately, students need to reach that final abstract level by using symbols proficiently with many of the mathematical skills they master. However, the meanings of those symbols must be firmly rooted in experiences with real objects. Otherwise, their performance of the symbolic operations will simply be rote repetitions of meaningless memorized procedures.

This CPA approach benefits all students but has been shown to be particularly effective with students who have mathematics difficulties, mainly because it moves gradually from actual objects through pictures and then to symbols (Jordan, Miller, & Mercer, 1998). These students often get frustrated when teachers present mathematics problems only in the abstract. Mathematics teachers need to organize content into concepts and provide instruction that allows students to process the new learning in meaningful and efficient ways.

Research studies support the effectiveness of this approach. Witzel and his colleagues conducted a study of sixth- and seventh-grade students identified as having difficulties in learning algebra. Students who learned how to solve algebra transformation equations through CPA scored higher on postinstruction and follow-up tests than the control peers receiving traditional instruction. Furthermore, students who used the CPA sequence of instruction performed fewer procedural errors when solving for algebraic variables (Witzel, Mercer, & Miller, 2003).

Teachers of mathematics in elementary schools have recognized the importance of using concrete and pictorial activities when introducing new concepts. Yet despite newer research in cognitive neuroscience lending support for the CPA method, it is not in widespread use in middle and high school mathematics classrooms. Perhaps teachers at the secondary level feel that concrete objects may be perceived by students as too elementary, or it may be that the content demands of the curriculum push teachers directly to the abstract level to save time.

Concrete and pictorial representations should be used at all grade levels. By using cognitive strategies such as CPA, teachers provide students a technique for tackling mathematics problems rather than just searching for an answer. Here is a simple example of presenting an algebraic word problem at the three cognitive levels.

✓ **Example: Algebraic Word Problem**

High school students Bob and John both work part-time on weekends at the local fast-food restaurant, and are paid at the end of the day on Sunday. When they receive their pay, Bob gets \$10 more than John. Together they have \$130. How much money does each person have?

- **Concrete**: Count out \$130 in play money. Give Student A (Bob) \$10. Then divide the rest of the money (\$120) between Student A (Bob) and Student B (John). Find out how much money each student has. Bob has \$70 and John has \$60.
- **Pictorial:** Represent the \$130 as \$10 drawings on an overhead or on a board:

  \$10 \$10 \$10 \$10 \$10 \$10 \$10 \$10 \$10 \$10 \$10 \$10 \$10

  Identify the \$10 for Bob (shown in bold italic):

  (\$10) \$10 \$10 \$10 \$10 \$10 \$10 \$10 \$10 \$10 \$10 \$10 \$10

  Count how much money is left. (\$120)

  Divide the remaining money equally between Bob and John:

  Bob: ***(\$10)*** + \$10 \$10 \$10 \$10 \$10 \$10

  John: \$10 \$10 \$10 \$10 \$10 \$10

  Count how much money Bob has: \$70

  Count how much money John has: \$60

✓ **Abstract:**

Bob = x John = $(x - \$10)$

$x + (x - \$10) = \$130$

$2x - \$10 = \$130$

$2x = \$130 + \$10$

$2x = \$140$

$x = \$70$ (Bob)

$x - 10 = \$60$ (John)

Figure 7.4 is an example of a simple planning worksheet that reminds teachers to select instructional strategies that address all three cognitive levels.

Using Process Mnemonics

Many teachers are aware of the value of mnemonic devices to help students remember important facts. But a less widely known mnemonic technique, called a *process mnemonic,* is designed to help remember rules, principles, and procedures. They are called process mnemonics because they serve to recall the orderly cognitive processes required in problem solving. A common process mnemonic in spelling is the "use i before e, except after c," rule. In mathematics, "Please excuse my dear Aunt Sally" helps recall the order of operations for solving algebraic equations (parentheses, exponents, multiplication, division, addition, and subtraction). Process mnemonics are useful when teaching the computational skills of addition, subtraction, multiplication, and division, and for remembering rules and procedures in spelling, trigonometry, mathematics and science.

Planning Sheet for CPA Representational Levels	
Mathematics Concept:	
Level	Instructional Strategy
Concrete	
Pictorial	
Abstract	

Figure 7.4 A planning grid for selecting instructional strategies at three representational levels.

> *Process mnemonics are powerful memory devices that help students with mathematics difficulties learn basic arithmetic operations.*

Originating in Japan as "Yodai," which means "the essence of structure," process mnemonics has been used in that country to teach mathematical rules, computational skills, and chemical formulas. Process mnemonics incorporate vivid images, such as representing mathematical rules (e.g., "to divide fractions, multiply by a reciprocal") with more memorable phrases (e.g., "flip the fool into the pool"). Sentences, phrases, songs, and rhymes are used to teach the steps in solving the problems. The components of computation are explained in elaborate stories, and the concepts are explained through things familiar to students, such as warriors, joggers, swimmers, and bugs.

Several research studies have shown process mnemonics to be particularly effective with students who have difficulties in mathematics. In one study, Emmanuel Manalo and his colleagues investigated the effects of process mnemonic instruction on the computational skills performance of 13- to 14-year-old students with mathematics learning disabilities. Students were randomly assigned to one of four instruction groups: process mnemonics, demonstration-imitation, study skills, or no instruction. After instruction, students in both the process mnemonics and demonstration-imitation groups made significant improvements in addition, subtraction, multiplication, and division.

However, the improvements were greater for the process mnemonics students. More important, the improvements they made were maintained better than the students in the demonstration-imitation group during the follow-up periods (Manalo, Bunnell, & Stillman, 2000). The specific strategies that Manalo et al. used can be found in the article or on the Internet. See the **Resources** section.

Process mnemonics are so effective with students who have mathematics difficulties because they are powerful memory devices that actively engage the brain in processes fundamental to learning and memory. They incorporate meaning through metaphors that are relevant to today's students, they are attention-getting and motivating, and they use visualization techniques that help students link concrete associations with abstract symbols.

Numeracy Intervention Process

Many students with dyscalculia have difficulties with basic numerical knowledge and conceptual knowledge. Interventions designed to address these deficits can be effective in improving student achievement in basic arithmetic. Kaufman, Handle, and Thöny (2003) reported the results of a pilot study that used an intervention program involving third-grade students with dyscalculia. The interventions were conducted three times weekly for a period of about six months. Figure 7.5 lists the components of the intervention program, which were conducted in semi-hierarchical order from the bottom up. Results from subtests administered before and after the interventions showed that the students with dyscalculia exhibited positive and partly significant improvement in basic numerical knowledge, in conceptual knowledge, and in arithmetic fact and procedural knowledge.

Students With Nonverbal Learning Disability

Students with nonverbal learning disability (NLD) have good verbal processing skills but will have problems comprehending the visual and spatial components of mathematics skills and concepts, especially when dealing with geometric shapes and designs. Although it may be difficult for students with NLD to understand mathematics concepts and solve problems, they may have no trouble applying a mathematical formula that has been explicitly taught. They generally learn verbal information quickly. But when they look at a diagram for the first time, they look at a detailed piece. When they look a second time they see a different piece and then another piece when they look for the third time. Because there is no visual overview, the diagram may not make sense. Additionally, due to their poor spatial-organization ability, they may have difficulty aligning problems on a page to solve them correctly.

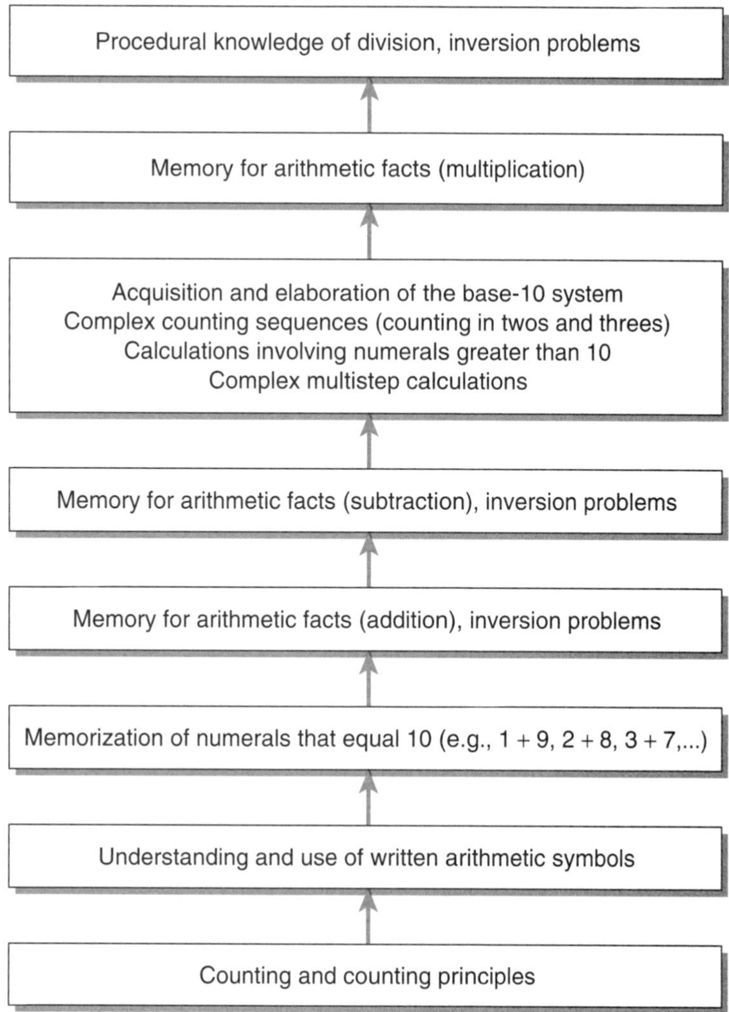

Figure 7.5 The modules in the intervention program are shown here. They were conducted in semi-hierarchical order from the bottom up. (Kaufmann, Handl, & Thöny, 2003)

Teachers of arithmetic and mathematics who work with students with NLD should consider the following strategies (Foss, 2001; Serlier-van den Bergh, 2006):

✓ Rely heavily on the student's verbal and analytic strengths. These students begin to work when speech is used, so use speech as the starting point. For example, have students read the mathematics problem aloud before attempting to solve it.

✓ Gain a commitment from the student to collaborate to improve visual and spatial weaknesses. Drawing diagrams and graphic organizers that are related to mathematics concepts and problems may help considerably.

- ✓ Use words to describe visual and spatial information. Ask the student to do the same while pointing to the corresponding places on the diagram or concrete model.
- ✓ Provide sequential verbal instructions for nonverbal tasks.
- ✓ Young students with NLD may feel awkward handling manipulatives because their tactile sense is not developed. However, manipulatives can help students develop mental images of geometric shapes and visualize spatial relationships as well as improve their visual memory skills. Ask them to touch objects first with their dominant hand, then with the non-dominant hand, and finally with both hands at once.
- ✓ Encourage the student to slowly integrate sensory information: Read it, say it, hear it, see it, write it, do it.

Students With Both Mathematics and Reading Difficulties

Students who have both reading and mathematics difficulties are obviously at a double disadvantage. However, even though the reading and mathematical processing areas of the brain are separate from each other, these two cerebral regions interact whenever the learner must translate word problems into symbolic representations. Here are some strategies that are effective with these students.

- ✓ **Cue words in word problems.** Help these students decode language into mathematical operations by alerting them to common phrases or cue words found in word problems that identify which operation to use. For example:

Common Phrases/Cue Words	Example	Operation
Add how many, altogether, in all, put together	When the apples were put together, how many were there?	Addition
Took away, take, left, give away	How many apples did they give away?	Subtraction
Problems that start with one and then ask for a total	Each rock weighed six pounds. How much did five rocks weigh?	Multiplication
Problems that start with many and then ask about one	Four boxes of the same cereal cost 12 dollars. How much did each box cost?	Division

✓ **Word problem maps.** Give students with reading problems a story map to highlight certain important aspects of the story such as introduction, plot line, characters, time line, and story climax. Gagnon and Maccini (2001) have developed a similar learning aid, called a word problem map, to help students with mathematics difficulties organize their thoughts as they tackle word problems. The map can be completed by an individual student or by students working in groups of two or three. Figure 7.6 is one variation of the word problem map (Gagnon & Maccini, 2001).

✓ **The RIDD strategy.** The RIDD strategy was developed by Jackson (2002) in 1997 for students with learning disabilities. In practice, it has shown to be particularly helpful to students who have difficulties in both reading and mathematics. RIDD stands for Read, Imagine, Decide, and Do. The following is a description of these four steps.

- *Step 1: Read the problem.* Read the passage from beginning to end. This helps students focus on the entire task rather than just one line at a time. Good readers often skip words within a text, or they substitute another word and continue reading. In this step, students decide ahead of time what they will call a word that they do not recognize. In mathematics word problems, substitutions can be made for long numbers rather than saying the entire number on the first reading. Teachers should model this substitution when they read the problem aloud to the class.
- *Step 2: Imagine the problem.* In this step, the students create a mental picture of what they have read. Using imagery when learning new material activates more brain regions and transforms the learning into meaningful visual, auditory, or kinesthetic images of information. This makes it easier for the new information to be stored in the students' own knowledge base. Imagery helps students focus on the concept being presented, and provides a way of monitoring their performance.

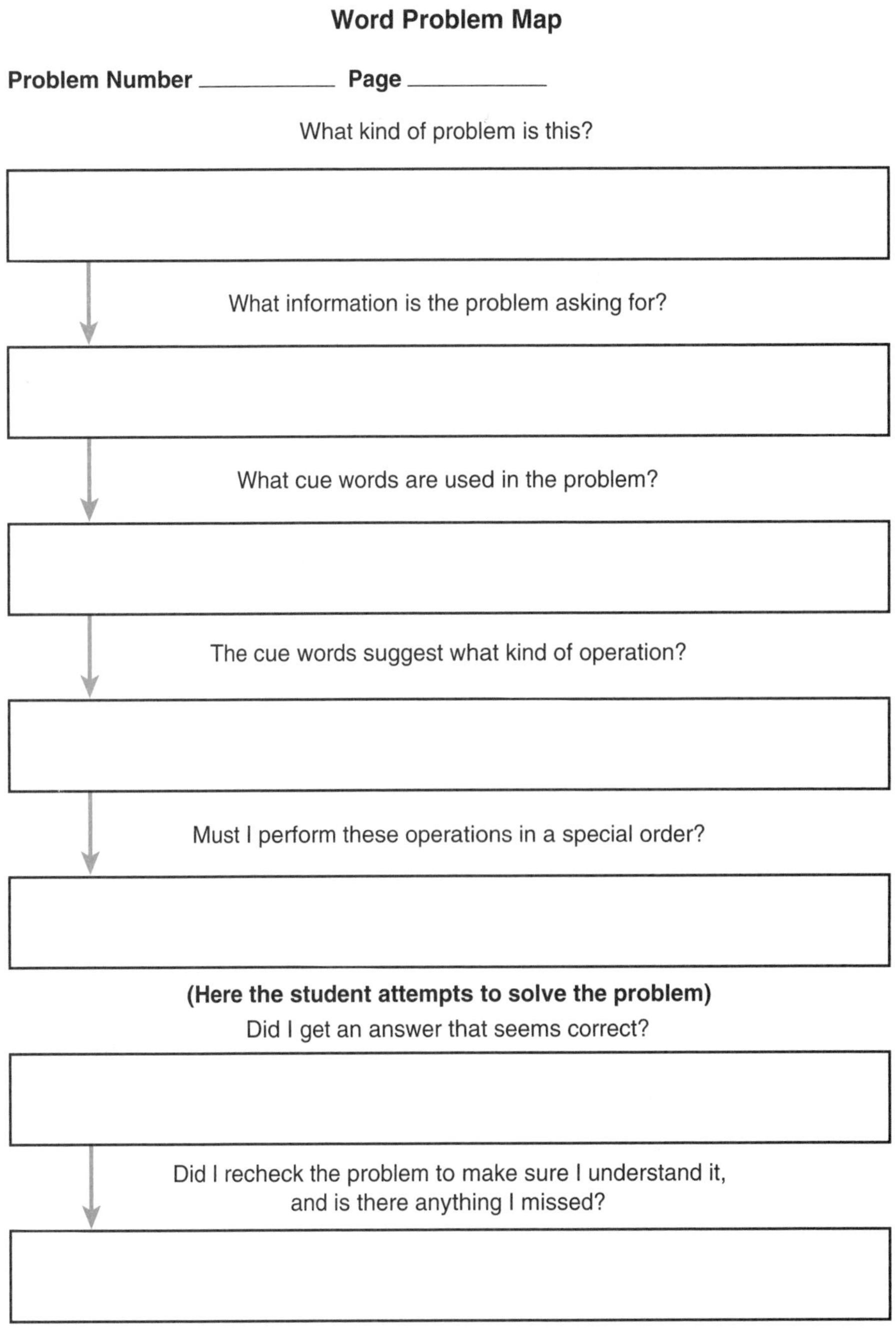

Word Problem Map

Problem Number ____________ **Page** ____________

What kind of problem is this?

What information is the problem asking for?

What cue words are used in the problem?

The cue words suggest what kind of operation?

Must I perform these operations in a special order?

(Here the student attempts to solve the problem)

Did I get an answer that seems correct?

Did I recheck the problem to make sure I understand it, and is there anything I missed?

Figure 7.6 This is one example of a word problem map that can help students with mathematics difficulties organize their approach to solving the problem.

- *Step 3: Decide what to do.* In order to generate a mental picture of the situation, this step encourages students to read the entire mathematics problem without stopping. They then decide what to do and in what order to solve the problem. For example, in a word problem requiring addition and then subtraction, students would read the problem, create a mental picture, and then decide whether to add or subtract first. For young students, teachers can guide them through this step with appropriate questioning so the students can decide what procedures to use. Note how this step combines reading, visualization, and problem solving.

- *Step 4: Do the work.* During this step the students actually complete the task. Often, students start reading a mathematics problem, stop part way through it, and begin writing numerical expressions. This process can produce errors because the students do not have all the information. By making this a separate step, students realize that there are things to do between reading the problem and writing it down. Jackson (2002) observed that when students used RIDD to solve mathematics problems, they liked this strategy because they perceived the last step as the only time they did work. Apparently, the students did not realize that what they did in the first three steps was all part of the process for solving problems.

> The RIDD Strategy
> R Read the problem
> I Imagine the problem
> D Decide what to do
> D Do the work

✓ **Computer assistance.** Computer programs are now available for elementary level students that address both reading and mathematics weaknesses. For example, *Knowledge Adventure* has several software titles that focus on teaching basic mathematics and reading skills while adhering to national and state standards. Each program provides instruction at a student's own pace and includes automatic progress tracking for each student so teachers can provide additional instruction to those who need it.

Other Considerations

The Power of Immediate Feedback

Students with difficulties in mathematics are apt to get frustrated at their lack of success, especially if they are unaware of the specific deficit responsible for their poor achievement. Several research studies have demonstrated how the timing of teacher feedback affects the performance of students with learning disabilities in preschool and in elementary and secondary schools. The results are consistent: Immediate feedback improves performance, but delayed feedback has little impact on performance (Dihoff et al., 2004; Epstein et al., 2003).

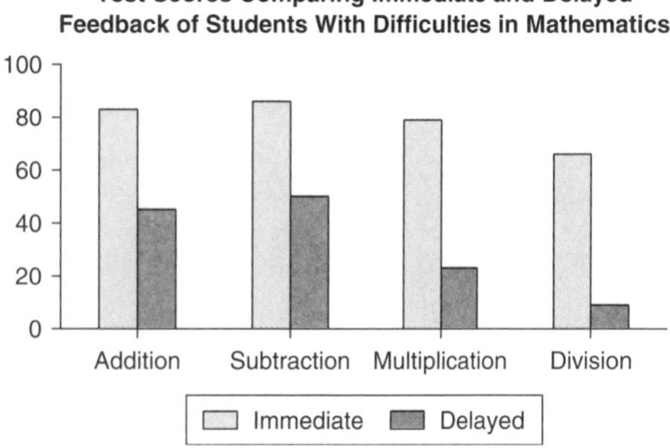

Figure 7.7 The graph compares the average scores of students with mathematics difficulties on tests of arithmetic operations receiving immediate or delayed feedback on their performance. (Adapted from Brosvic et al., 2006)

One recent study of 40 third-grade students identified as having learning difficulties in mathematics demonstrated the power of immediate feedback versus delayed feedback (Brosvic, Dihoff, Epstein, & Cook, 2006). After instruction in separate lessons on arithmetic operations, one half of the group was given immediate feedback after each lesson while the other half was not given feedback until the end of 20 lessons. Feedback was either corrective or affirming and provided by the teacher or through a paper-and-pencil feedback assessment form.

Both groups were tested after 20 lessons on what they had learned about arithmetic operations. Figure 7.7 compares the average results of the students in the immediate and delayed feedback groups on tests of addition, subtraction, multiplication, and division. Clearly, students with mathematics difficulties can achieve more in classrooms where teachers find ways to provide immediate affirming or corrective feedback.

Linguistically Diverse Students

Research on mathematical problem solving by elementary-grade linguistically diverse students has been limited. A few studies found that bilingual students with learning disabilities had difficulties with extraneous information in word problems in both their native language and English but were successful in solving word problems without extraneous information in both languages. By using diagrams and pictures, teachers helped students remember the number line and interpret what the word problem was asking. Also, if students can understand the process of solving an arithmetic problem, their native language may make translating a word problem difficult but not interfere with solving the arithmetic expressions (Bernardo, 2005; Rodriguez, Parmar, & Signer, 2001).

Findings from the studies suggest that teachers of mathematics who have bilingual students in their classes keep the following in mind:

- ✓ **Draw pictures and symbols.** These students need considerable help in representing word problems through symbols and pictures. This includes providing the necessary pictures or having the students draw their own diagrams, which help translate the word problem into a visual representation.

✓ **Help students to select the correct operation.** These students often are able to solve the arithmetic algorithm. Their difficulty arises in deciding which arithmetic operation to use, based on interpreting the language in the word problem.

✓ **Reinforce basic concepts.** Do not assume that these students have a sound understanding of number relationships. Instruction should include activities that continuously reinforce basic concepts, such as manipulating the number line, estimating, evaluating answers, and representing number relationships.

✓ **Use all the information.** Encourage these students to use all the information sources provided, including diagrams, to solve the problem.

We have noted in previous chapters that the brain regions responsible for language processing are separate and distinct from those that process numerical operations. Of course, these centers communicate with each other when necessary, but each can perform its individual tasks without much input from the other. The impact of native language on solving word problems in mathematics depends on the nature of the specific component processes involved. More research is needed to thoroughly understand how bilingual students engage in mathematics. For now, it seems clear that there are cognitive processes that have a mathematically abstract language of their own and that may be unaffected by the languages of the bilingual individual.

WHAT'S COMING?

What is mathematics? What inherent constructs of mathematics should be a consistent part of mathematics instruction? What do the findings from research in cognitive neuroscience tell us about how lessons should be planned and delivered so that the new learning is likely to be remembered? These are some of the questions we will tackle in the next, and final, chapter.

Chapter 7 — Recognizing and Addressing Mathematics Difficulties

Reflections

Jot down on this page key points, ideas, strategies, and resources you want to consider later. This sheet is your personal journal summary and will help to jog your memory.

Chapter 8

Putting It All Together

Planning Lessons in PreK–12 Mathematics

It is hard to convince a high-school student that he will encounter a lot of problems more difficult than those of Algebra and Geometry.

—Edgar W. Howe

At first glance, the title of this chapter could give the reader the impression that planning lessons in mathematics might be different from planning lessons in other subject areas. To some extent it is. Studying mathematics requires not only the mastery of content but also the acquisition and enhancement of certain process skills needed for that study to be successful. Consequently, teachers planning lessons in mathematics at *any* grade level should consider whether those lessons will provide learners with both the content and requisite process skills. To find out more about what those skills are, we need to delve a little deeper into understanding exactly what we mean by mathematics.

WHAT IS MATHEMATICS?

To most people, mathematics is about calculating numbers. Some may even expand the definition to include the study of quantity (arithmetic), space (plane and solid geometry), and change (calculus). But even this definition does not encompass the many areas where mathematics and mathematicians are found. A broader definition of mathematics comes from W. W. Sawyer. In the 1950s, he described mathematics as the "classification and study of all possible patterns." He explained that *pattern* was meant "to cover almost any kind of regularity that can be recognized by the mind" (Sawyer, 1982).

Other mathematicians who share Sawyer's view have shortened the definition even further: Mathematics is the science of patterns. Devlin (2000) not only agrees with this definition but has used it as the title of one of his books. He explains that patterns include order, structure, and logical relationships and go beyond the visual patterns found in tiles and wallpaper to patterns that occur everywhere in nature. For example, patterns can be found in the orbits of the planets, the symmetry of flowers, how people vote, the spots on a leopard's skin, the outcomes of games of chance, the relationship between the words that make up a sentence, and the sequence of sounds we recognize as music. Some patterns are numerical and can be described with numbers, such as voting patterns of a nation or the odds of winning the lottery. But other patterns, such as the leopard's spots, are visual designs that are not connected to numbers at all.

Mathematics can be defined simply as the science of patterns.

Devlin (2000) further points out that mathematics can help make the invisible visible. Two thousand years ago, the Greek mathematician Eratosthenes was able to calculate the diameter of Earth with considerable accuracy and without ever stepping off the planet. The equations developed by the eighteenth-century mathematician Daniel Bernoulli explain how a jet plane flying overhead stays aloft. Thanks to Isaac Newton, we can calculate the effects of the unseen force of gravity. More recently, linguist Noam Chomsky has used mathematics to explain the invisible and abstract patterns of words that we recognize as a grammatical sentence.

If mathematics is the science of patterns and if visible and invisible patterns exist all around us, then mathematics is not just about numbers but about the world we live in. If that is the case, then why are so many students turned off by mathematics before they leave high school? What happens in those classrooms that gives students the impression that mathematics is a sterile subject filled with meaningless abstract symbols? Clearly, educators have to work harder at planning a mathematics curriculum that is exciting and relevant and at designing lessons that carry this excitement into every day's instruction.

I will leave the discussion of what content to include in a PreK to 12 mathematics curriculum to experts in that area. My purpose here is to suggest how the research in cognitive neuroscience that we have discussed in the previous chapters can be used to plan lessons in mathematics that are more likely to result in learning and retention.

QUESTIONS TO ASK WHEN PLANNING LESSONS

After deciding a lesson's content objective, one of the next steps is to design the learning episode. When teachers keep in mind what is now known about how the brain learns, they are more likely to develop lessons wherein students learn and remember the content objective while they enhance their process skills. Here are some questions to keep in mind while planning for effective instruction.

Is the Lesson Memory-Compatible?

Do you remember the capacity and time limitations we discussed in Chapter 3? These limitations become very important when deciding *how much* and *how long* to present new learning to students.

- ✓ **Capacity limitations** of working memory must be considered when planning lessons. The elementary-grade teacher who tells the class, "We have seven mathematical facts to learn today," is already in trouble. So is the high school teacher who plans to cover eight different ideas in one lesson. By keeping the number of items in a lesson objective within the capacity limits of working memory, students are likely to remember more of what you presented. Less is more!

> *Keep the number of items in a lesson objective within the capacity limits of working memory, and students are likely to remember more of what you presented. Less is more!*

- ✓ **Time limitations** mean that lessons in the elementary grades should be taught in 12- to 15-minute segments and those in secondary classes in 15- to 20-minute segments. So, for example, one segment could be direct instruction, and the next could be practice or computer work or research. These time restrictions are particularly critical in high schools that have block scheduling. In this format, periods are from 80 to 90 minutes in length. Teachers

> *Teaching within the time limits of working memory will enable students to stay focused and remember more of what you presented. Shorter is better!*

have already learned from experience that doing direct instruction (mainly through teacher talk) for this entire period of time is not generally effective. Breaking the 90-minute block into four segments of 20 minutes or so is much more productive because each new segment starts the time-limit clock all over again. Sometimes, incorporating a brief off-task activity between segments also serves to refresh to working memory clock. Shorter is better!

Does the Lesson Include Cognitive Closure?

Cognitive closure describes the covert process whereby the learner's working memory summarizes for itself its perception of what has been learned. It is during closure that a student often completes the rehearsal process and attaches sense and meaning to the new learning, thereby increasing the chances that it will be retained in long-term memory.

✓ **Initiating Closure.** Give directions that focus the students on the new learning, such as "I'm going to give you two minutes to think of what we learned today about how to multiply two double-digit numbers (or How did we calculate the area of a polygon?). Be prepared to talk about it with a partner." In this statement, you told the students how much quiet time they have for the mental summarizing to occur, and you identified the overt activity (discussion) that will be used for student accountability. During the discussion, listen carefully, assess the quality and accuracy of what occurred during closure, and make any necessary adjustments in teaching.

✓ **Closure Is Different From Review.** In review, you do most of the work, repeating key mathematics concepts made during the lesson and rechecking for student understanding. In closure, the student does most of the work by mentally rehearsing and summarizing those concepts and deciding whether they make sense and have meaning. It also gives the students an opportunity to think of questions that can clarify any misunderstandings.

✓ **When to Use Closure.** Closure can occur at various times in a lesson.

- It can start a lesson: "Think of the steps we learned yesterday about adding fractions and be prepared to discuss them."

- It can occur during the lesson (called *procedural closure)* when you move from one sublearning to the next: "Review those two geometry rules in your mind before we learn the third rule."

> *Cognitive closure is a small investment in time that can pay off dramatically in increased retention of learning.*

- It should almost always take place at the end of the lesson (called *terminal closure)* to tie all the sublearnings together. Remember, this may be the last opportunity the learner has to make sense and attach meaning to the new learning.

Cognitive closure is a small investment in time that can pay off dramatically in increased retention of learning.

Will the Primacy-Recency Effect Be Taken Into Account?

In Chapter 3 we discussed the impact of the primacy-recency effect on retention. This impact should be taken into account when planning and teaching a lesson. The learning episode begins when the learner focuses on the teacher with intent to learn (this is indicated by "0" in Figure 8.1). New information or a new skill should be taught first, during prime-time-1, because it is most likely to be remembered. Keep in mind that the students will remember almost any information coming forth at this time. It is important, then, that only *correct* information be presented. This is not the time to be searching for what students *might* know about something. I remember watching a teacher of mathematics start a class with, "Today, we are going to learn the differences between the *mean,* the *median,* and the *mode.* Does anyone have any idea what the differences are?" After several wrong guesses, the teacher finally explained thedifferences. Regrettably, those same wrong guesses appeared as answers in the follow-up test. And why not? They were mentioned during the most powerful retention position, prime-time-1.

> *When you have the students focus, teach the new information. Don't let prime-time get contaminated with incorrect information.*

Presenting new material right at the beginning of the class without student input might seem to contradict other views of teaching that encourage students to construct their own model of what they are learning. This "constructivist" approach is valid but not very useful if the students have little or no knowledge of the concept that the teacher is introducing. We cannot construct a concept with ignorance. Keep in mind, too, that

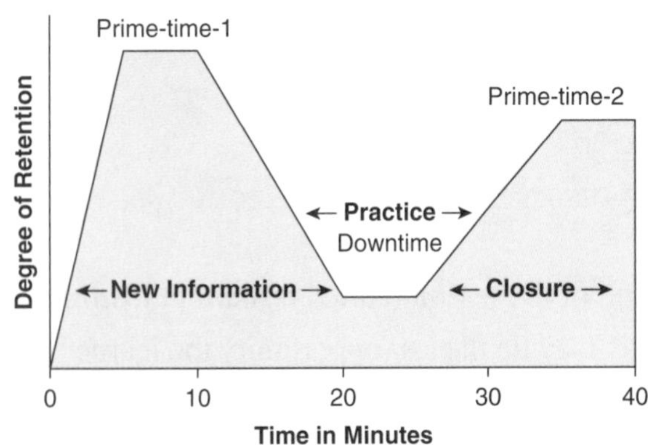

Figure 8.1 New information should be presented in prime-time-1 and closure in prime-time-2. Practice is appropriate during downtime.

nature did not prepare our brains for the variety of symbols, ratios, and abstract correlations that are found in advanced algebra and calculus. Consequently, there are no intuitive constructs that the student can use to develop a model.

The new material being taught should be followed by practice or review during the downtime. At this point, the information is no longer new, and the practice helps the learner organize it for further processing. Cognitive closure should take place during prime-time-2, since this is the second most powerful learning position and an important opportunity for the learner to determine sense and meaning. Adding these activities to the graph in Figure 3.5 shows how we can take advantage of research on retention to design a more effective lesson.

Should a Lesson Start With Mathematics Homework?

A standard practice with many teachers of mathematics is to start a lesson by reviewing the students' homework from the previous day. This can be an effective strategy, but there are some cautions to be observed. Because this review is being carried out during prime-time-1, the teacher should emphasize the *correct* way to solve the homework problems. Spending too much time focusing on student errors might cause students to inadvertently remember the errors during this powerful memory segment. Do not use up valuable prime-time if the homework review is merely casual (about the mechanics of *doing* it) rather than substantive (about its *content*). Get on with today's learning objective and collect the homework during downtime.

Here is a summary of how to take advantage of the primacy-recency effect in the classroom.

- ✓ **Teach the new material first** (after getting the students' focus) during prime-time-1. This is the time of greatest retention. Alternatively, this would also be a good time to reteach any concept that students may be having difficulty understanding.

- ✓ **Avoid asking students** at the beginning of the lesson if they know anything about a *new* topic being introduced. If it is a new topic, the assumption is that most students do not know it. However, there are always some students eager to make a guess—no matter how unrelated. Because this is the time of greatest retention, almost anything that is said, including incorrect information, is likely to be remembered. Give the information and examples yourself to ensure that they are correct.

✓ **Avoid using precious prime-time** periods for classroom management tasks, such as collecting absence notes or taking attendance. Do these before you get focus, or during the downtime when students are engaged in practice.

✓ **Use the downtime** portion to have students practice the new learning or to discuss it by relating it to past learnings. "How does what we learned today about calculating the area of a polygon tie into what we already learned about calculating the area of a triangle?" Remember that retention of learning does occur during the downtime, but it just takes more effort and concentration.

✓ **Do cognitive closure during prime-time-2.** This is the learner's last opportunity to attach sense and meaning to the new learning, to make decisions about it, and to determine where and how it will be transferred to long-term memory. It is important, then, that the student's brain do the work at this time as in prime-time-1. If you wish to do a review, then do it *before* closure to increase the chances that the closure experience is accurate. But doing review *instead* of closure is of little value to retention.

✓ **When packaging lesson objectives** (or sublearnings) into teaching episodes of about 20 minutes, link the sublearnings with procedural closure. This approach helps students recognize why these sublearnings should be integrated into the same memory network.

What About Practice?

We noted in Chapter 3 that practice makes permanent, not perfect. Practice is more likely to be effective when you do the following:

✓ **Start by selecting the smallest amount of material** that will have maximum *meaning* for the learner. Stay within the capacity limits of working memory for the students' age group. Excessive homework erodes motivation, builds frustration, and often leads to poor attitudes about studying mathematics.

- ✓ **Model the application of the concept step-by-step.** Use concrete manipulative whenever possible. This helps students develop visual and spatial representations of the concept or skill being taught. Studies show that the brain uses observation as a means for determining the spatial learning needed to master a skill (Petrosini et al, 2003).

- ✓ **Insist that the practice occur in your presence** (guided practice) over a short period of time while the student is focused on the learning.

- ✓ **Watch the practice** and provide the students with prompt and specific feedback on what variable needs to be altered to correct and enhance the performance. When the guided practice is correct, then assign limited independent practice.

What Writing Will Be Involved?

Chapter 3 noted how important writing is in communicating mathematical concepts. Adding this kinesthetic activity engages more neurons and causes students to organize their thoughts about the concept.

Strategies for Using Writing in Mathematics

Here are some strategies for incorporating writing in the mathematics classroom that I think can be effective, along with some recommended by Burns (2004) and Ediger (2006):

- ✓ **Clarify the purpose.** Students, especially in the secondary schools, may not be thrilled about writing in mathematics class, nor may they see its purpose. Make clear that writing activities are for students to use as a tool to help gain understanding of the mathematical concepts involved in their lessons. Treating writing as a learning and memory tool and not as an assignment to be graded helps students feel more comfortable with using writing in the mathematics classroom.

- ✓ **Review vocabulary.** Before beginning the writing activity, review and explain any new vocabulary terms encountered in the lesson. Do they know the meaning of *proper* and *improper* fractions, or of *complementary* and *supplementary* angles. Posting a chart in the front of the room containing all the new words is also helpful.

✓ **Discuss before writing.** By talking about their ideas in class before writing, students are able to formulate and clarify their thinking, select appropriate vocabulary, and decide on the main points that will be included in their writing sample. They can write about any mathematical idea they heard during the discussion, as long as they can explain it.

✓ **Work individually or in groups.** Although writing is often done working alone, some students may prefer to work in groups so they can discuss what they are writing with others. Working in groups also allows students to share their written ideas and to hear different points of view. Allow for both types of opportunities.

✓ **Add interest.** Maintaining student interest is an important component of motivation. Writing activities can be made interesting by including historical information, such as how the Roman and Arabic number systems developed, the invention of the zero placeholder, or negative numbers. People have been using geometry for thousands of years. How did it develop, and what was its impact on the development of ancient societies?

✓ **Prompt when necessary.** Sometimes younger students need prompts to get them started. Write some prompts on the board, such as: *I think the answer is_____ because_______*, or *Today I learned __________. It is important to know this because_____________*.

✓ **Avoid rewriting the textbook.** Students are expected to use their own thoughts, phrasing, and vocabulary to write their sample and not simply copy what is in their textbook. The point here is to get the brain to do elaborative rehearsal of the new concepts learned so that the likelihood of retaining the learning is significantly increased.

✓ **Provide individual assistance.** Some students, especially in the elementary grades or English language learners, will no doubt have difficulty getting their thoughts down. Talk with these students individually to ensure that they understand what they have learned and what they are expected to do in the writing activity. Get them to talk to you by asking, "What have you learned about this idea? What do you think about other people's ideas?" For younger students, just the physical act of writing can be such an effort that they have difficulty keeping their thoughts in working memory. Suggest they repeat silently to themselves what they intend to write before and while they are writing it down.

✓ **Use students' ideas.** Student writings can often provide useful ideas for clarifying or extending a mathematics concept. Sharing student notions in this manner places value on their work and provides motivation for future writing activities.

Writing as an Assessment Tool

✓ Writing can be an effective assessment tool for both students and teachers. Because writing provides a permanent record of students' thoughts, it documents the students' progress in learning. Students reflect on their own learning when they return to their writing. Once the writing is complete, students have a permanent record of their learning that can help them revise information or expand their application of knowledge in the future. The writing can help you by

- Diagnosing error patterns
- Giving you insights about where instruction should begin or what topics need to be retaught
- Providing evidence of where and why a student has failed to make connections
- Showing the beliefs and attitudes that students hold about mathematics

✓ Consider keeping student writing samples in individual folders. They provide a chronological collection of each student's thoughts and progress and can be very helpful in parent conferences as well.

Are Multiple Intelligences Being Addressed?

Dozens of books are available that suggest specific activities in all subject areas for applying Gardner's theory in the classroom. My purpose here is to offer some general activities that mathematics teachers can use to apply and strengthen the eight intelligences through instruction.

In Table 8.1, simply replace the term "M.C." with the mathematical concept you are teaching. The variety of activities helps you to differentiate instruction. Some activities serve as enrichment for students who have already mastered the concept while others serve to provide additional information to help students whose understanding of the concept may be shaky. Of course, it might not be appropriate to require all students to practice all of the activities because they may not be suitable for students with a weakness in any particular area, or for those who, for example, might not be comfortable doing performance-style activities in some situations. Students should have some choice in selecting which of these activities to do.

Table 8.1 Activities for Multiple Intelligences

Intelligence	Activity for the Mathematical Concept (M.C.)
Linguistic "The word player"	• Use storytelling to explain the M.C. • Write a poem, myth, legend, or news article about the M.C. • Give a presentation on the M.C. • Lead a class discussion on the M.C. • Create a talk show radio program about the M.C.
Logical/Mathematical "The questioner"	• Translate the M.C. into a mathematical formula • Design an proof for the M.C. • Make a strategy game that includes the M.C. • Collect and interpret data related to the M.C. • Write a computer program for the M.C.
Spatial "The visualizer"	• Chart, map, or graph the M.C. • Design a poster, bulletin board, or mural about the M.C. • Create a piece of art that demonstrates the M.C. • Make a film or advertisement of the M.C.
Musical "The music lover"	• Write a song that explains the M.C. • Give a presentation with appropriate musical accompaniment on the M.C. • Explain how the music of a song relates to the M.C. • Create a musical game that relates to the M.C.
Bodily/Kinesthetic "The mover"	• Rehearse and perform a play that explains the M.C. • Choreograph a dance that shows the M.C. • Build a model that explains the M.C. • Plan and attend a field trip that will show or explain the M.C.
Interpersonal "The socializer"	• Conduct a class meeting that discusses the M.C. • Organize or participate in a group that will deal with the M.C. • Suggest ways to accommodate learning differences and the M.C. • Participate in a service project that uses the M.C.
Intrapersonal "The individual"	• Create a personal analogy for the M.C. • Set a goal to accomplish the M.C. • Describe how you feel about the M.C. • Use some form of emotional processing to understand the M.C.
Naturalist "The nature lover"	• Describe any patterns you detect in the M.C. • Explain how the M.C. can be found in the environment • Show how the M.C. could be applied in nature • Demonstrate how this M.C. can be linked to other M.C.s we have learned

Multiple Intelligences and the NCTM Process Standards

Activities can be designed to address both student strengths in multiple intelligences and the NCTM *Principles and Standards for School Mathematics* (2000). Table 8.2 shows some overlapping activities suggested by Adams (2000) for Gardner's original seven intelligences (omitting naturalist).

Table 8.2 **Overlapping Multiple Intelligences and NCTM Process Standards**

Intelligence	Problem Solving	Reasoning and Proof	Communication	Connection	Representation
Linguistic	Write stories as context for word problems. Write about problem solving.	Express arguments in ways that make sense to others. Refute/support a mathematics idea.	Respond to prompts for writing with or about mathematics. Define terms.	Write about relationships between mathematical concepts.	Translate word problems to algebraic expressions and vice versa.
Logical/ Mathematical	Gather, record, and use numerical data to solve problems Calculate to solve problems.	Generalize mathematical conclusions. Provide non-examples.	Develop and use categories to classify written and oral mathematical information.	Categorize and classify numbers. Explore the use of numbers in other disciplines.	Use technology to represent and sort data. Represent numbers in various ways.
Spatial	Use drawings and diagrams as problem-solving strategies. Explain a drawn solution.	Use paper folding and cutting to prove concepts.	Describe characteristics of two-dimensional shapes and three-dimensional objects.	Explore the uses of mathematics in architecture. Describe classroom and school.	Use diagrams, charts, pictures, and tables to solve problems.
Bodily/ Kinesthetic	Use dramatization as a strategy for problem solving.	Use parts of the body to reason about conceps (e.g., proportion).	Use body language or charades to convey a mathematical message.	Investigate connections between body and various restrictions in the world.	Model division by distribution of objects to people.

Table 8.2 **Overlapping Multiple Intelligences and NCTM Process Standards**

Musical	Translate problem-solving strategies to a musical tune to help recall strategies.	Compare patterns to songs that have patterned rounds that "never end."	Listen to counting songs in other cultures and languages.	Create a mathematical musical in connection with the music program.	Use objects to model music rhythms. Explore the sound of concrete objects.
Interpersonal	Solve problems through cooperative learning. Lead a problem-solving excursion.	Collaborate with others to develop arguments and proofs.	Share communicative roles in cooperative groups.	Lead peers in discussions about mathematical connections.	Debate the applicability of various representations.
Intrapersonal	Set goals for growth in problem solving. Monitor problem-solving process.	Use personal and previous knowledge to build a basis for a conjecture.	Describe feelings and attitudes about mathematics. Think aloud.	Consider ways in which mathematics is used in own life.	Organize thinking according to various representations. Use different representations.

Source: Adams (2000). Reprinted with permission of the author.

Mathematical experiences of the types suggested in Table 8.2 can help in designing mathematical curriculum, instruction, and assessment. Activities that are challenging and meaningful not only develop students' cognitive strengths but also raise motivation and, thus, enhance the enjoyment of learning mathematics.

Does the Lesson Provide for Differentiation?

Today's teachers work in classrooms filled with a broad diversity of students. Besides their different learning capabilities, students come from different cultures, speak many languages, and possess varying learning styles. Direct instruction based mainly on a one-size-fits-all approach does not work effectively with such a diverse group. What *can* work is an approach whereby teachers differentiate their instruction by using a variety of techniques and strategies that address the varying needs of all students. In differentiated instruction, teachers enhance learning by matching their students' characteristics to instruction and assessment. Teachers can differentiate content, process, and/or product for students (Tomlinson, 1999).

- **Differentiation of content** refers to a change in the material being learned by an individual student. For example, if the classroom objective is for all students to determine whether two triangles are congruent, some students may learn this by working with diagrams of triangles while others may learn it through solving word problems.
- **Differentiation of process** describes the method by which a student accesses material. One student may explore a learning center, another may conduct an interview, while a third student collects information from the Internet.
- **Differentiation of product** refers to the way students demonstrate what they have learned. For instance, to demonstrate understanding of a geometric concept, one student may solve word problems, while another builds a model.

When teachers commit themselves to using differentiated instruction, they switch their goal from teaching a collective class to teaching individual students. This is a major paradigm shift, and to do so successfully, teachers respond to an individual student's readiness, interest, and learning profile. A teacher may differentiate based on any one of these factors or any combination of factors (Tomlinson, 1999).

- **Readiness** describes the skill level and background knowledge of the student in mathematics. Some of this information can be gathered at the beginning of the year by reviewing student records, standardized test scores, and previous mathematics grades. Diagnostic assessments can also be used to determine student readiness. These assessments can be formal or informal. Teachers can give pretests or question students about their background knowledge of a particular topic.
- **Interest** refers to topics related to mathematics that the student may want to explore or that will motivate the student. This can be done by using interest inventories throughout the year. Teachers may discover, for example, that some students are interested in sports statistics or architecture. Including students in the lesson planning process is another way to explore interests. Teachers ask students what specific interests they have in a topic, and then try to incorporate these interests into their lessons.
- **Learning profile** includes learning style (i.e., is the student's preference for visual, auditory, tactile, or kinesthetic input?), grouping preferences (i.e., individual, small group, or large group), and environmental preferences (i.e., lots of space or a quiet area to work). Learning styles can be measured using learning style inventories. Teachers can also get information about student learning styles by asking students how they learn best and by observing student activities.

Some Guidelines for Differentiating Instruction

Dozens of books and Internet sites suggest specific ways to differentiate instruction in mathematics at every grade level (see the **Resources** section). Here are some general guidelines:

- ✓ If you are new to differentiation, start small. Try it first with one short unit and then use your regular method for the next unit. Reflect upon what was successful and what needs improvement. Students also need to adjust to this method of learning, so do not get discouraged if at first it does not go as well as planned. Like any new strategy, learning to differentiate instruction is a process. To succeed, implement it gradually, and constantly revise what does not work.

- ✓ Provide a variety of materials and opportunities for student projects. These can include reference books, manipulatives, construction and drawing materials, computers with Internet access, and other audiovisual materials. Arrange the classroom so that workstations can be quickly set up when needed.

- ✓ Give students options to choose from several projects that cover the lesson objective. Choices should reflect various learning styles. For example, visually preferred learners may want the option of showing a poster or brochure to present what they have learned rather than just talking about it.

- ✓ The options should be at various levels of difficulty and complexity and involve different types of thinking skills. Bloom's Taxonomy (Revised) remains an effective model for designing activities at different levels of cognitive thought (Sousa, 2006).

- ✓ Vary your lesson delivery style during each class period to appeal to different learning styles. For example, use discussions for auditorily preferred learners, have handouts outlining the topic for visually preferred learners, and incorporate hands-on activities for kinesthetically preferred learners. Remember that all students benefit when they use a variety of modalities while learning.

- ✓ For each project and activity, consider grouping students according to ability or interest. During units on percent or graphing, for instance, several students may be interested in examining population growth.

✓ Consider using a variety of assessment tools and offer students several assessment options. Design assessments with various skill levels, learning styles, and thinking skills in mind. Show sample work and share with students the rubric or scoring criteria you will use to evaluate open-ended assessments and projects.

SIMPLIFIED INSTRUCTIONAL MODEL

Based on all I can gather from cognitive neuroscience, a reasonable model for teaching mathematics to children and adolescents would proceed through four major steps (Figure 8.2). The first step would be to build on young children's intuitions about numbers, subitizing, quantitative manipulations, and counting. These innate talents are strongly rooted in developing neural networks and

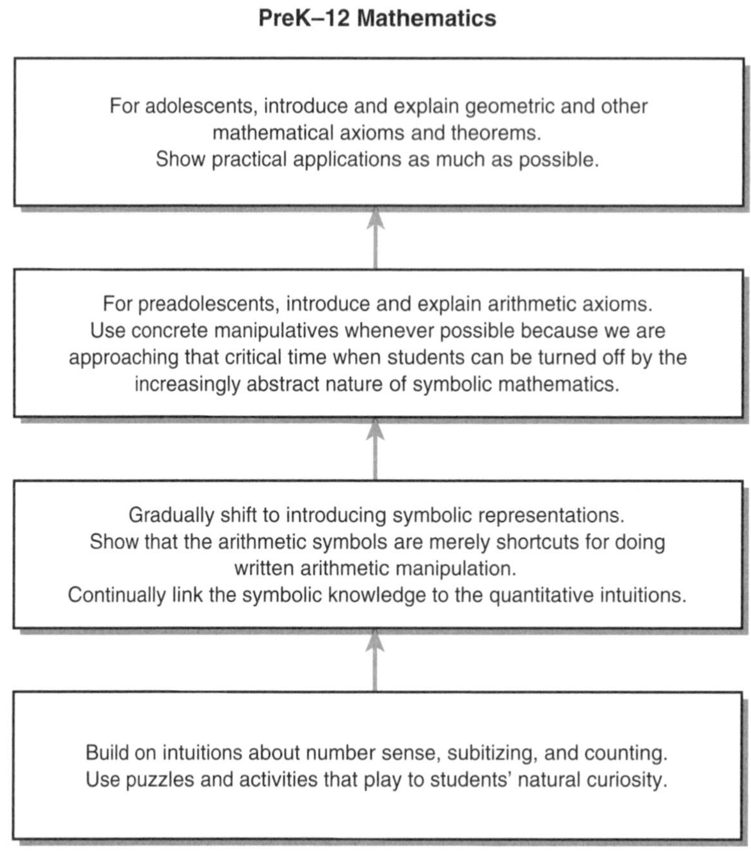

Figure 8.2 This is a simplified model of instructional considerations for teaching PreK through Grade 12 mathematics. The main considerations are to keep tying new information to intuitive concepts about number and quantity, and to include concrete manipulatives and practical applications as much as possible.

should be cultivated with concrete activities rather than stunted with paper worksheets. Activities and instruction should play to these students' natural curiosity with amusing number puzzles and problems.

The next step is to introduce them to symbolic notation in mathematics, emphasizing how it offers a powerful and convenient shortcut when manipulating quantities. It is important at this point to continue to tie the symbolic knowledge once again to the quantitative intuitions. In this way, the symbolic representations become part of the intuitive network instead of being memorized as a separate and unrelated language.

In step 3, introduce the preadolescent brain to arithmetic axioms. Appropriate concrete manipulatives should be used here as much as possible because we are moving into that critical time when students can be turned off by the increasingly abstract nature of symbolic mathematics. Later, as adolescents, their brain's frontal lobe becomes more adept at higher-order thinking and logic. So in step 4, introduce and explain mathematical and geometric axioms and theorems. But it is still necessary to show practical applications whenever possible. Remember, when students understand and recognize practical uses for what they are learning, they can attach meaning and thus increase their chances of retention.

I certainly recognize that this model may be simplistic. On the other hand, one reason that students get turned off to mathematics is that we often do not try hard enough to keep relating what they are experiencing in the classroom to concrete and practical applications. There are few school subjects in which teachers hear the lament "Why do I have to know this?" more than in mathematics. That observation alone should be ample warning that we have to work harder at meaning.

CONCLUSION

As research in cognitive neuroscience expands, we are very likely to discover more about how the human brain grows, develops, and learns. These discoveries offer educators and parents exciting opportunities for deciding what kinds of learning experiences children and adolescents should have to develop to their full potential. Research leads not only to new ideas but often validates past practices and questions some as well. Effective teaching strategies cut across all content areas. For the teaching of mathematics, I have suggested that some of the following notions should be kept in mind:

- Everyone has the ability to do mathematical operations. We are born with it.
- Rote learning without meaning impedes long-term application of mathematical knowledge.
- Learning mathematics is easier when it makes sense and is meaningful to the learner.

- Learning mathematics is easier when the learner can connect mathematical operations and concepts to solving problems in the real world.
- Talking and writing about mathematics improves the depth of learning and recall.
- Learning mathematics involves a progression from the concrete to the representational to the abstract.
- People learn mathematics in different ways.

Regardless of all the instructional strategies we develop, all the curriculum reforms we write, and all the materials we buy, no component is as important as the teacher. How the teacher views the learning process will largely determine that teacher's instructional practice and, consequently, how well students will learn mathematics. My purpose here was to present research from cognitive neuroscience to inform teachers of what we are discovering about the learning process in general and the learning of mathematics in particular.

And why is mathematics even worth learning? Our world is full of patterns. We see them in flowers, in snowflakes, in seashells, in the markings on animals such as zebras and leopards, in the distinctive songs of birds, and so on. If mathematics is truly the study of patterns, then teachers should help students recognize that the learning of mathematics will not only be useful in their future life but will also give them a window into understanding the wonders and beauty of our magnificent world.

Chapter 8 — Putting It All Together: Planning Lessons in PreK–12 Mathematics

Reflections

Jot down on this page key points, ideas, strategies, and resources you want to consider later. This sheet is your personal journal summary and will help to jog your memory.

Glossary

Abstraction. The process of extracting the underlying essence of a mathematical concept, removing any dependence on real-world objects to which it might originally have been connected, and generalizing it so that it has wider applications as, for example, the axioms of geometry.

Algorithm. A process or set of rules used in calculations or other problem-solving operations.

Associative memory. The brain's ability to detect patterns and to make associations between working memory and past experiences.

Associativity. A property of numbers whereby the sequence in which they are added or multiplied produces the same result. Thus, $(a + b) + c = a + (b + c)$, or $(a \times b) \times c = a \times (b \times c)$.

Cardinal principle (cardinality). The concept that the last number counted represents the size of the group in a collection.

Cerebellum. A major part of the brain, located in the rear above the brain stem, that is largely responsible for coordinating muscle movement.

Cerebrum. The largest of the major parts of the brain, it controls sensory interpretation, thinking, and memory.

Chunking. The ability of the brain to perceive a coherent group of items as a single item or chunk.

Closure. The teaching strategy that allows learners quiet time in class to mentally reprocess what they have learned during a lesson

Commutativity. A property of numbers whereby they can be added or multiplied in any order. Thus, $8 + 5 = 5 + 8$ or $4 \times 7 = 7 \times 4$.

Compensation. The idea that removing some items from one part of a collection and adding them to the other part leaves the whole quantity unchanged.

Constructivism. A theory of learning stating that active learners use past experiences and chunking to construct sense and meaning from new learning, thereby building larger conceptual schemes.

Corpus callosum. The bridge of nerve fibers that connects the left and right cerebral hemispheres and allows communication between them.

Cortex. The thin layer of cells covering the cerebrum that contains all the neurons used for cognitive and motor processing.

Covariation. The idea that a whole quantity increases (or decreases) if one of the parts is increased (or decreased).

Declarative memory. Knowledge of events and facts to which we have conscious access.

Distributed practice. The repetition of a skill over increasingly longer periods of time to improve performance.

Electroencephalograph. An instrument that charts fluctuations in the brain's electrical activity via electrodes attached to the scalp.

Episodic memory. Knowledge of events in our personal history to which we have conscious access.

Frontal lobe. The front part of the brain that monitors higher-order thinking, directs problem solving, and regulates the excesses of the emotional (limbic) system.

Functional magnetic resonance imaging (fMRI). An instrument that measures blood flow to the brain to record areas of high and low neuronal activity.

Gray matter. The thin covering of the brain's cerebrum also known as the cerebral cortex.

Guided practice. The repetition of a skill in the presence of the teacher, who can give immediate and specific feedback.

Immediate memory. A temporary memory in which information is processed briefly (in seconds) and subconsciously, then either blocked or passed on to working memory.

Independent practice. The repetition of a skill on one's own outside the presence of the teacher.

Limbic area. The structures at the base of the cerebrum that control emotions.

Long-term storage. The areas of the cerebrum where memories are stored permanently.

Massed practice. The repetition of a skill over short time intervals to gain initial competence.

Mnemonic. A word or phrase used as a device for remembering information, patterns, rules, or procedures.

Motivation. The influence of needs and desires on behavior.

Motor cortex. The narrow band across the top of the brain from ear to ear that controls movement.

Neuron. The basic cell making up the brain and nervous system, consisting of a cell body, a long fiber (axon) that transmits impulses, and many shorter fibers (dendrites) that receive them.

Nondeclarative memory. Knowledge of motor and cognitive skills to which we have no conscious access, such as riding a bicycle.

Number sense. In its limited form, this refers to our ability to recognize that an object has been added or removed from a collection.

Numerosity. The perception of approximate numerical quantities, such as more than and less than, without assigning an exact number.

Occipital lobe. A brain area located in the back of the cerebrum that is responsible for processing mainly visual information.

Parietal lobe. A brain area of the cerebrum, lying between the occipital and frontal lobes, that is involved in processing sensory information, including touch, taste, and movement.

Positron emission tomography (PET) scanner. An instrument that traces the metabolism of radioactively tagged sugar in brain tissue producing a color image of cell activity.

Practice. The repetition of a skill to gain speed and accuracy.

Prefrontal cortex. The area of the brain just behind the forehead that controls the planning, decision making, reasoning, and execution of behavior and that integrates information in working memory.

Primacy-recency effect. The phenomenon whereby one tends to remember best that which comes first in a learning episode and second best that which comes last.

Prime-time. The time in a learning episode when information or a skill is more likely to be remembered.

Procedural memory. A form of nondeclarative memory that allows the learning of motor (riding a bicycle) and cognitive (learning to read) skills.

Rehearsal. The reprocessing of information in working memory.

Semantic memory. Knowledge of facts and data that may not be related to any event.

Subitizing. The ability to determine the number of objects at a glance, without counting.

Temporal lobe. A brain area of the cerebrum located behind each ear, just under the parietal lobe, involved in the processing and interpretation mainly of sound and spoken language.

White matter. The support tissue that lies beneath the brain's gray matter.

Working memory. The temporary memory wherein information is processed consciously.

References

Adams, T. L. (2000, Winter). Helping children learn mathematics through multiple intelligences and standards for school mathematics. *Childhood Education, 77,* 86–92.

Ainsworth, L., & Christinson, J. (2000). *Five easy steps to a balanced math program: A practical guide for K–8 classroom teachers.* Denver: Advanced Learning Press.

Alarcón, M., Knopik, V. S., & DeFries, J. C. (2000, January-February). Covariation of mathematics achievement and general cognitive ability in twins. *Journal of School Psychology, 38,* 63–77.

Altermatt, E. R., & Kim, M. E. (2004). Can anxiety explain sex differences in college entrance exam scores? *Journal of College Admission, 183,* 6–11.

Ashcraft, M. H. (1995). Cognitive psychology and simple arithmetic: A review and summary of new directions. *Mathematical Cognition, 1,* 3–34.

Ashcraft, M. H. (2002). Math anxiety: Personal, educational, and cognitive consequences. *Current Directions in Psychological Science, 11,* 181–185.

Ashcraft, M. H., & Kirk, E. P. (2001, June). The relationships among working memory, math anxiety, and performance. *Journal of Experimental Psychology: General, 130,* 224–237.

Augustyniak, K., Murphy, J., & Phillips, D. K. (2005, December). Psychological perspectives in assessing mathematics learning needs. *Journal of Instructional Psychology, 32,* 277–286.

Baker, S., Gersten, R., & Lee, D-S. (2002). A synthesis of empirical research on teaching mathematics to low-achieving students. *Elementary School Journal, 103,* 51–73.

Barth, H., La Mont, K., Lipton, J., & Spelke, E. S. (2005, September 27). Abstract number and arithmetic in preschool children. *Proceedings of the National Academy of Sciences, 102,* 14116–14121.

Barton, M. L., & Heidema, C. (2002). *Teaching reading in mathematics* (2nd ed.). Aurora, CO: Mid-continent Research for Education and Learning.

Beilock, S. L., Kulp, C. A., Holt, L. E., & Carr, T. H. (2004, December). More on the fragility of performance: Choking under pressure in mathematical problem solving. *Journal of Experimental Psychology: General, 133,* 584–600.

Berch, D. B. (2005, July/August). Making sense of number sense: Implications for children with mathematical disabilities. *Journal of Learning Disabilities, 38,* 333–339.

Berger, A., Tzur, G., & Posner, M. I. (2006, August 15). Infant brains detect arithmetic errors. *Proceedings of the National Academy of Sciences, 103,* 12649–12653.

Bernardo, A. B. I. (2005, September). Language and modeling word problems in mathematics among bilinguals. *The Journal of Psychology, 139,* 413–425.

Berns, G. S., Cohen, J. D., & Mintun, M. A. (1997). Brain regions responsiveness to novelty in the absence of awareness. *Science, 276,* 1272–1275.

Bigelow, B. & Zhou, R. (2001). Relational scaffolding of school motivation: Development continuities in students' and parents' ratings of the importance of school goals. *The Journal of Genetic Psychology, 162,* 75–93.

Booth, J. L., & Siegler, R. S. (2006, January). Developmental and individual differences in pure numerical estimation. *Developmental Psychology, 42,* 189–201.

Brannon, E. M. (2003, July). Number knows no bounds. *Trends in Cognitive Sciences, 7,* 279–281.

Brannon, E. M. (2005, March). The independence of language and mathematical reasoning. *Proceedings of the National Academy of Sciences, 102,* 3177–3178.

Brosvic, G. M., Dihoff, R. E., Epstein, M. L., & Cook, M. L. (2006). Feedback facilitates the acquisition and retention of numerical fact series by elementary school students with mathematics learning disabilities. *The Psychological Record, 56,* 35–54.

Bruner, J. S. (1960). *The process of education.* Cambridge, MA: Belknap Press.

Buckner, R. L., Kelley, W. M., & Petersen, S. E. (1999, April). Frontal cortex contributions to human memory formation. *Nature Neuroscience*, *2*, 311–314.

Burns, M. (1998). *Math: Facing an American phobia.* Sausalito, CA: Math Solutions Publications.

Burns, M. (1998, January). Teaching math, thinking math. *Early Childhood Today, 12,* 29–35.

Burns, M. (2004, October). Writing in math. *Educational Leadership, 62,* 30–33.

Butterworth, B. (1999). *What counts: How every brain is hardwired for math.* New York: Free Press.

California Department of Education. (1999). *Mathematics framework for California public schools: Kindergarten through grade twelve.* Sacramento: Author.

Carpenter, T. P., Franke, M. L., Jacobs, V. R., Fennema, E., & Empson, S. B. (1998, January). A longitudinal study of invention and understanding in children's multidigit addition and subtraction. *Journal for Research in Mathematics Education, 29,* 3–20.

Carpenter, T. P., Franke, M. L., & Levi, L. (2003). *Thinking mathematically: Integrating arithmetic and algebra in elementary school.* Portsmouth, NH: Heinemann.

Carpenter, T. P., & Levi, L. (2000, October). *Developing conceptions of algebraic reasoning in the primary grades.* Research report. Madison, WI: National Center for Improving Student Learning & Achievement in Mathematics & Science.

Castelli, F., Glaser, D. E., & Butterworth, B. (2006, March 14). Discrete and analogue quantity processing in the parietal lobe: A functional MRI study. *Proceedings of the National Academy of Sciences, 103,* 4693–4698.

Clements, D. H. (1999, March). Subitizing: What is it? Why teach it? *Teaching Children Mathematics, 5,* 400–405.

Clements, D. H. (2001, January). Mathematics in the preschool. *Teaching Children Mathematics, 7,* 270–275.

Damasio, A. (2003). *Looking for Spinoza: Joy, sorrow, and the feeling brain.* New York: Harcourt.

D'Amico, A., & Guarnera, M. (2005). Exploring working memory in children with low arithmetic achievement. *Learning and Individual Differences, 15,* 189–202.

Danzig, T. (1967). *Number: The language of science.* New York: Free Press.

Dehaene, S. (1997). *The number sense: How the mind creates mathematics.* New York: Oxford University Press.

Dehaene, S. (2001). Author's response: Is number sense a patchwork? *Mind & Language, 16,* 89–100.

Dehaene, S., Dupoux, E., & Mehler, J. (1990). Is numerical comparison digital? Analogical and symbolic effects in two-digit number comparison. *Journal of Experimental Psychology: Human Perception and Performance, 16,* 626–641.

Dehaene, S., Molko, N., Cohen, L., & Wilson, A. J. (2004, April). Arithmetic and the brain. *Current Opinion in Neurobiology, 14,* 218–224.

Dehaene, S., Spelke, E., Pinel, P., Stanescu, R., & Tsivkin, S. (1999, May). Sources of mathematical thinking: Behavioral and brain-imaging evidence. *Science, 284,* 970–974.

Devlin, K. (2000). *The math gene: How mathematical thinking evolved and why numbers are like gossip.* New York: Basic Books.

Diezmann, C. M., & English, L. D. (2001, Fall). Developing young children's multidigit number sense. *Roeper Review, 24,* 11–13.

Dihoff, R. E., Brosvic, G. M., Epstein, M. L., & Cook, M. J. (2004). Provision of feedback during preparation for academic testing: Learning is enhanced by immediate but not delayed feedback. *The Psychological Record, 54,* 207–231.

Dobbs, J., Doctoroff, G. L., Fisher, P. H., & Arnold, D. H. (2006, March-April). The association between preschool children's socio-emotional functioning and their mathematical skills. *Journal of Applied Developmental Psychology, 27,* 97–108.

Ediger, M. (2006, June). Writing in the mathematics curriculum. *Journal of Instructional Psychology, 33,* 120–123.

Epstein, M. L., Brosvic, G. M., Dihoff, R. E., Lazarus, A. D., & Costner, K. L. (2003). Effectiveness of feedback during the testing of preschool children, elementary school children, and adolescents with developmental delays. *The Psychological Record, 53,* 177–195.

Farkas, R. D. (2003, September-October). Effects of traditional versus learning-styles instructional methods on middle school students. *Journal of Educational Research, 97,* 42–52.

Fletcher, J. M. (2005, July-August). Predicting math outcomes: Reading predictors and comorbidity. *Journal of Learning Disabilities, 38,* 308–312.

Flewelling, G. & Higginson, W. (2001). *A handbook on rich learning tasks.* Kingston, ON, Canada: Centre for Mathematics, Science, and Technology Education.

Forgasz, H. (2006, Spring). Factors that encourage or inhibit computer use for secondary mathematics teaching. *Journal of Computers in Mathematics and Science Teaching, 25,* 77–93.

Foss, J. M. (2001). *Nonverbal learning disability: How to recognize it and minimize its effects.* (ERIC Digest E-619). Arlington, VA: ERIC Clearinghouse on Disabilities and Gifted Education.

Fuchs, L. S., & Fuchs, D. (2002). Mathematical problem-solving profiles of students with mathematical disabilities with and without comorbid reading disabilities. *Journal of Learning Disabilities, 35,* 563–573.

Fuchs, L. S., Compton, D. L., Fuchs, D., Paulsen, K., Bryant, J. D., & Hamlett, C. L. (2005, August). The prevention, identification, and cognitive determinants of math difficulty. *Journal of Educational Psychology, 97,* 493–513.

Fuson, K. C., Wearne, D., Hiebert, J. C., Murray, H. G., Human, P. G., Olivier, A. I., Carpenter, T. P., & Fennema, E. (1997, March). Children's conceptual structures for multidigit numbers and methods of multidigit addition and subtraction. *Journal for Research in Mathematics Education, 29,* 130–162.

Gagnon, J., & Maccini, P. (2001). Preparing students with disabilities for algebra. *Teaching Exceptional Children, 34,* 8–15.

Gardner, H. (1993). *Frames of mind: The theory of multiple intelligences* (Rev. Ed.) New York: Basic Books.

Gazzaniga, M. S., Ivry, R. B., & Mangun, G. R. (2002). *Cognitive neuroscience: The biology of the mind* (2nd Ed). New York: Norton.

Geary, D. C. (2004, January-February). Mathematics and learning disabilities. *Journal of Learning Disabilities, 37,* 4–15.

Gersten, R., & Chard, D. (1999). Number sense: Rethinking arithmetic instruction for students with mathematical disabilities. *Journal of Special Education, 33,* 18–28.

Gersten, R., Chard, D., Jayanthi, M., & Baker, S. (2006). *Experimental and quasi-experimental research on instructional approaches for teaching mathematics to students with learning disabilities: A research synthesis.* Signal Hill, CA: Center on Instruction/RG Research Group.

Gersten, R., Jordan, N. C., & Flojo, J. R. (2005, July-August). Early identification and interventions for students with mathematics difficulties. *Journal of Learning Disabilities, 38,* 293–304.

Goldberg, E. (2001). *The executive brain: Frontal lobes and the civilized mind.* New York: Oxford University Press.

Gogtay, N., Giedd, J. N., Lusk, L., Hayashi, K., Greenstein, D., Valtuzis, A. C., et al. (2004, May 25). Dynamic mapping of human cortical development during childhood and early adulthood. *Proceedings of the National Academy of Sciences, 101,* 8174–8179.

Graham, D., & Meyer, L. (2007). Graphic organizers in mathematics. Available online at www.sw-georgia.resa.k12.ga.us

Griffin, S. (2002). The development of math competence in the preschool and early school years: Cognitive foundations and instructional strategies. In J. M. Rover (Ed.). *Mathematical cognition: A volume in current perspectives on cognition, learning, and instruction* (pp. 1–32). Greenwich, CT: Information Age Publishing.

Griffin, S. (2003, February). Laying the foundation for computational fluency in early childhood. *Teaching Children Mathematics, 9,* 306–309.

Griffin, S. (2004). Building number sense with Number Worlds: A mathematics program for young children. *Early Childhood Research Quarterly, 19,* 173–180.

Griffin, S. (2004). Number worlds: A research-based mathematics program for young children. In D. H. Clements, A. M. DiBiase, & J. Sarama (Eds.). *Engaging young children in mathematics,* (pp. 325–342). Mahwah, NJ: Erlbaum.

Griffin, S. & Case, R. (1997). Rethinking the primary school math curriculum: An approach based on cognitive science. *Issues in Education, 3,* 1–49.

Guerrero, S., Walker, N., & Dugdale, S. (2004, Spring). Technology in support of middle grade mathematics: What have we learned? *Journal of Computers in Mathematics and Science Teaching 23,* 5–20.

Gurganus, S. (2004). Promote number sense. (20 Ways to . . .). *Intervention in School and Clinic, 40,* 55–58.

Habib, R., McIntosh, A. R., Wheeler, M. A., & Tulving, E. (2003). Memory encoding and hippocampally-based novelty/familiarity discrimination networks. *Neuropsychologia, 41,* 271–279.

Harper, N. W., & Daane, C. J. (1998). Causes and reduction of math anxiety in preservice elementary teachers. *Action in Teacher Education, 19,* 29–38.

Hunter, M. (2004). *Mastery teaching.* Thousand Oaks, CA: Corwin Press.

Ifrah, G. (1985). *From one to zero: A universal history of numbers.* New York: Penguin Books.

Ischebeck, A., Zamarian, L., Siedentopf, C., Koppelstätter, F., Benke, T., Felber, S., et al. (2006, May). How specifically do we learn? Imaging the learning of multiplication and subtraction. *NeuroImage, 30,* 1365–1375.

Jackson, F. B., (2002, May). Crossing content: A strategy for students with learning disabilities. *Intervention in School and Clinic, 37,* 279–282.

Jones, G., Thornton, C., & Putt, I. (1994). A model for nurturing and assessing multidigit number sense among first grade children. *Educational Studies in Mathematics, 27,* 117–143.

Jordan, L., Miller, M., & Mercer, C. (1998). The effects of concrete to semi-concrete to abstract instruction in acquisition and retention of fraction concepts and skills. *Learning Disabilities: A Multidisciplinary Journal, 9,* 115–122.

Kaufmann, L., Handl, P., & Thöny, B. (2003, November-December). Evaluation of a numeracy intervention program focusing on basic numerical knowledge and conceptual knowledge: A pilot study. *Journal of Learning Disabilities, 36,* 564–573.

Klibanoff, R. S., Levine, S. C., Huttenlocher, J., Vasilyeva, M., & Hedges, L. V. (2006, January). Preschool children's mathematical knowledge: The effect of teacher "math talk." *Developmental Psychology, 42,* 59–69.

Kline, K. (1998, October). Kindergarten is more than counting. *Teaching Children Mathematics, 5,* 84–87.

Koehler, O. (1951). The ability of birds to count. *Bulletin of Animal Behavior, 9,* 41–45.

Krakauer, J. W., & Shadmehr, R. (2006, January). Consolidation of motor memory. *Trends in Neurosciences, 29,* 58–64.

Kroesbergen, E. H., & van Luitt, J. E. H. (2003). Mathematics interventions for children with special education needs: A meta-analysis. *Remedial and Special Education, 24,* 97–114.

Kucian, K., Loenneker, T., Dietrich, T., Dosch, M., Martin, E., & von Aster, M. (2006). Impaired neural networks for approximate calculation in dyscalculic children: A functional MRI study. *Behavioral and Brain Functions, 2.* Available online at www.pubmedcentral.nih.gov/tocrender.fcgi?iid=126977

Landerl, K., Bevan, A., & Butterworth, B. (2004, September). Developmental dyscalculia and basic numerical capacities: A study of 8-9-year-old students. *Cognition, 93,* 99–125.

Latterell, C. M. (2005, Fall). Social stigma and mathematical ignorance. *Academic Exchange Quarterly, 9,* 167–171.

Lawrenz, F., Gravely, A., & Ooms, A. (2006, March). Perceived helpfulness and amount of use of technology in science and mathematics classes at different grade levels. *School Science and Mathematics, 106,* 133–139.

Legault, L., Pelletier, L., & Green-Demers, I. (2006). Why do high school students lack motivation in the classroom? *Journal of Educational Psychology, 98,* 567–582.

Lemer, C., Dehaene, S., Spelke, E., & Cohen, L. (2003). Approximate quantities and exact number words: Dissociable systems. *Neuropsychologia, 41,* 1942–1958.

Luna, B. (2004, October). Algebra and the adolescent brain. *Trends in Cognitive Sciences, 8,* 437–439.

Luna, B., Thulborn, K. R., Munoz, D. P., Merriam, E. P., Garver, K. E., Minshew, N. J., et al. (2001, May). Maturation of widely distributed brain function subserves cognitive development. *NeuroImage, 13,* 786–793.

Maguire, E. A., Frith, C. D., & Morris, R.G.M. (1999, October). The functional neuroanatomy of comprehension and memory: The importance of prior knowledge. *Brain, 122,* 1839–1850.

Manalo, E., Bunnell, J. K., & Stillman, J. A. (2000, Spring). The use of process mnemonics in teaching students with mathematics learning disabilities. *Learning Disability Quarterly, 23,* 137–156.

Martin, A., Wiggs, C. L., & Weisberg, J. (1997). Modulation of human medial temporal lobe activity by form, meaning, and experience. *Hippocampus, 7,* 587–593.

McComb, K., Packer, C., & Pusey, A. (1994). Roaring and numerical assessment in contests between groups of female lions, *Panthera leo*. *Animal Behavior, 47,* 379–387.

McGlone, M. S., & Aronson, J. (2006, September-October). Stereotype threat, identity salience, and spatial reasoning. *Journal of Applied Developmental Psychology, 27,* 486–493.

McNeil, N. M., & Alibali, M. W. (2005). Knowledge change as a function of mathematics experience: All contexts are not created equal. *Journal of Cognition and Development, 6,* 285–306.

McNeil, N. M., Grandau, L., Knuth, E. J., Alibali, M. W., Stephens, A. C., Hattikudur, S., et al. (2006). Middle school students' understanding of the equal sign: The books they read can't help. *Cognition and Instruction, 24,* 367–385.

Mechner, F. & Guevrekian, L. (1962). Effects of deprivation upon counting and timing in rats. *Journal of the Experimental Analysis of Behavior, 5,* 463–466.

Micheloyannis, S., Sakkalis, V., Vourkas, M., Stam, C. J., & Simos, P. G. (2005, January 20). Neural networks involved in mathematical thinking: Evidence from linear and non-linear analysis of electroencephalographic activity. *Neuroscience Letters, 373,* 212–217.

Miller, K., & Paredes, D. R. (1990). Starting to add worse: Effects of learning to multiply on children's addition. *Cognition, 37,* 213–242.

Miller, K., Smith, C. M., Zhu, J., & Zhang, H. (1995). Preschool origins of cross-national differences in mathematical competence: The role of number-naming systems. *Psychological Science, 6,* 56–60.

Monuteaux, M. C., Faraone, S. V., Herzig, K., Navsaria, N., & Biederman, J. (2005, February). ADHD and dyscalculia: Evidence for independent familial transmission. *Journal of Learning Disabilities, 38,* 86–93.

Morge, S. (2005, Fall). High school students' math beliefs and society. *Academic Exchange Quarterly, 9,* 182–187.

Moyer, R. S., & Landauer, T. K. (1967). Time required for judgements of numerical inequality. *Nature, 215,* 1519–1520.

Murphy, M. M., Mazzocco, M., Gerner, G., & Henry, A. E. (2006). Mathematics learning disability in girls with Turner syndrome or fragile X syndrome. *Brain and Cognition, 61,* 195–210.

National Assessment of Educational Progress (NAEP). (2007, February). *The nation's report card: 2005 assessment results in mathematics.* Washington, DC: National Center for Educational Statistics.

National Council of Teachers of Mathematics (NCTM). (1995). *Assessment standards for school mathematics.* Reston, VA: Author.

National Council of Teachers of Mathematics (NCTM). (2000). *Principles and standards for school mathematics.* Reston, VA: Author.

National Council of Teachers of Mathematics (NCTM). (2006). *Curriculum focal points for mathematics in prekindergarten through grade 8.* Reston, VA: Author.

National Science Foundation. (2004). *Science and engineering indicators: Elementary and secondary education.* Arlington, VA: Author.

Ninness, C., Rumph, R., McCuller, G., Harrison, C., Ford, A. M., & Ninness, S. K. (2005, Spring). A functional analytic approach to computer-interactive mathematics. *Journal of Applied Behavioral Analysis, 38,* 1–22.

Nuerk, H. C., Kaufmann, I., Zoppoth, S., & Willmes, K. (2004). On the development of the mental number line: More, less, or never holistic with increasing age? *Developmental Psychology, 40,* 1190–1211.

Nunley, K. (2004). *Layered curriculum: The practical solution for teachers with more than one student in their classroom* (2nd ed.). Amherst, NH: Brains.org.

Nunley, K. (2006). *Differentiating the high school classroom.* Thousand Oaks, CA: Corwin Press.

Passolunghi, M. C., & Siegel, L. S. (2004). Working memory and access to numerical information in children with disability in mathematics. *Journal of Experimental Child Psychology, 88,* 348–367.

Paus, T. (2005). Mapping brain maturation and cognitive development during adolescence. *Trends in Cognitive Sciences, 9,* 60–68.

Pekrun, R., Maier, M., & Elliot, A. (2006). Achievement goals and discrete achievement emotions: A theoretical model and prospective test. *Journal of Educational Psychology, 98,* 583–597.

Petrosini, L., Graziano, A., Mandolesi, L., Neri, P., Molinari, M., & Leggio, M. G. (2003, June). Watch how to do it! New advances in learning by observation. *Brain Research Reviews, 42,* 252–264.

Piaget, J. (1952). *The child's conception of number.* New York: Norton.

Piaget, J. (1954). *The construction of reality in the child.* New York: Basic Books.

Piazza, M., Mechelli, A., Butterworth, B., & Price, C. J. (2002). Are subitizing and counting implemented as separate or functionally overlapping processes? *NeuroImage, 15,* 435–446.

Pintrich, P. (2003). A motivational science perspective on the role of student motivation in learning and teaching contexts. *Journal of Educational Psychology, 95,* 667–686.

Platz, D. L. (2004, Fall). Challenging young children through simple sorting and classifying: A developmental approach. *Education, 125,* 88–96.

Pugalee, D. K. (2001, May). Writing, mathematics, and metacognition: Looking for connections through students' work in mathematical problem solving. *School Science and Mathematics, 101,* 236–245.

Qin, Y., Carter, C. S., Silk, E. M., Stenger, V. A., Fissell, K., Goode, A., et al. (2004, April 13). The change of the brain activation patterns as children learn algebra equation solving. *Proceedings of the National Academy of Sciences, 101,* 5686–5691.

Rodriguez, D., Parmar, R. S., & Signer, B. R. (2001, Winter). Fourth-grade culturally and linguistically diverse exceptional students' concepts of number line. *Exceptional Children, 67,* 199–210.

Rose, S. (2005). *The future of the brain: The promise and perils of tomorrow's neuroscience.* New York: Oxford University Press.

Rouselle, L., & Noël, M-P. (2007, March). Basic numerical skills in children with mathematics learning disabilities: A comparison of symbolic vs non-symbolic number magnitude processing. *Cognition, 102,* 361–395.

Rubinstein, O., & Henik, A. (2005, September). Automatic activation of internal magnitudes: A study of developmental dyscalculia. *Neuropsychology, 19,* 641–648.

Ruffell, M., Mason, J., & Allen, B. (1998). Studying attitude to mathematics. *Educational Studies in Mathematics, 35,* 1–18.

Ryan R., & Deci, E. (1999). Intrinsic and extrinsic motivation: Classic definitions and new directions. *Contemporary Educational Psychology, 25,* 54–67.

Sabbagh, L. (2006, August-September). The teen brain hard at work. *Scientific American Mind, 17,* 20–25.

Sathian, K., Simon, T. J., Peterson, S., Patel, G. A., Hoffman, J. M., & Grafton, S. T. (1999, January). Neural evidence linking visual object enumeration and attention. *Journal of Cognitive Neuroscience, 11,* 36–51.

Sawyer, W. W. (1982). *Prelude to mathematics.* New York: Dover Publications.

Scharton, S. (2004, January). I did it my way: Providing opportunities for students to create, explain, and analyze computation procedures. *Teaching Children Mathematics, 10,* 278–283.

Schmandt-Besserat, D. (1985). Oneness, twoness, threeness. *The Sciences* (New York Academy of Sciences), 44–48.

Schwartz, C. E., Wright, C. I., Shin, L. M., Kagan, J., Whalen, P. J., McMullin, K. G., et al. (2003, May). Differential amygdalar response to novel versus newly familiar neutral faces: A functional MRI probe developed for studying inhibited temperament. *Biological Psychiatry, 53,* 854–862.

Schweinsburg, A. D., Nagel, B. J., & Tapert, S. F. (2005, September). fMRI reveals alteration of spatial working memory networks across adolescence. *Journal of the International Neuropsychological Society, 11,* 631–644.

Seo, K.-H., & Ginsburg, H. P. (2003). "You've got to carefully read the math sentence. . .": Classroom context and children's interpretations of the equals sign. In A. J. Baroody & A. Dowker (Eds.), *The development of arithmetic concepts and skills* (pp. 161–187). Mahwah, NJ: Erlbaum.

Serlier-van den Bergh, A. (2006). *NLD primary materials: Basic theory, approach, and hands-on strategies.* Paper presented at the Symposium of the Nonverbal Learning Disorders Association, March 10–11, 2006, San Francisco, CA.

Shaley, R. S., Manor, O., Kerem, B., Ayali, M., Badichi, N., Friedlander, Y., et al. (2001, January-February). Developmental dyscalculia is a familial learning disability. *Journal of Learning Disabilities, 34,* 59–65.

Sharma, M. (2006). *How children learn mathematics.* Framingham, MA: Center for Teaching/Learning Mathematics.

Shearer, C. B. (2004). Using a multiple intelligences assessment to promote teacher development and student achievement. *Teachers College Record, 106,* 147–162.

Shields, D. J. (2005, Fall). Teachers have the power to alleviate math anxiety. *Academic Exchange, 9,* 326–330.

Siegler, R. S., & Jenkins, E. A. (1989). *How children discover new strategies.* Hillsdale, NJ: Erlbaum.

Singh, K., Granville, M., & Dika, S. (2002). Mathematics and science achievement effects of motivation, interest, and academic engagement. *Journal of Educational Research, 95,* 323–332.

Smith, S. Z., & Smith, M. E. (2006, March). Assessing elementary understanding of multiplication concepts. *School Science and mathematics, 106,* 140–149.

Solomon, P. G. (2006). *The math we need to know and do in grades PreK–5: Concepts, skills, standards, and assessments.* Thousand Oaks, CA: Corwin Press.

Sousa, D. A. (2005). *How the brain learns to read.* Thousand Oaks, CA: Corwin Press.

Sousa, D. A. (2006). *How the brain learns* (3rd ed.). Thousand Oaks, CA: Corwin Press.

Sowder, J., & Schappelle, B. (Eds.). (2002). Research related to teaching: Introduction. *Lessons Learned from Research.* Reston, VA. NCTM.

Spelke, E. S. (2005). Sex differences in intrinsic aptitude for mathematics and science? A critical review. *American Psychologist, 60,* 950–958.

Spencer, S. J., Steele, C. M., & Quinn, D. M. (1999). Stereotype threat and women's math performance. *Journal of Experimental Social Psychology, 35,* 4–28.

Squire, L. R., & Kandel, E. R. (1999). *Memory: From mind to molecules.* New York: W. H. Freeman.

Starkey, P. & Cooper, R. G., Jr. (1980). Perception of numbers by human infants. *Science, 210,* 1033–1035.

Steffe, L. P., & Cobb, P. (1988). *Construction of arithmetical meanings and strategies,* New York: Springer-Verlag.

Steinberg, L. (2005, February). Cognitive and affective development in adolescence. *Trends in Cognitive Sciences, 9,* 69–74.

Stonewater. J. K. (2002, November). The mathematics writer's checklist: The development of a preliminary assessment tool for writing in mathematics. *School Science and Mathematics, 102,* 324–334.

Strauss, M. S., & Curtis, L. E. (1981). Infant perception of numerosity. *Child Development, 52,* 1146–1152.

Suresh, P. A., & Sebastian, S. (2000). Developmental Gerstmann's syndrome: A distinct clinical entity of learning disabilities. *Pediatric Neurology, 22,* 267–278.

Tang, Y., Zhang, W., Chen, K., Feng, S., Ji, Y., Shen, J., Reiman, E. M., & Liu, Y. (2006, July 11). Arithmetic processing in the brain shaped by cultures. *Proceedings of the National Academy of Sciences, 103,* 10775–10780.

Taylor-Cox, J. (2001, December). How many marbles in the jar? Estimation in the early grades. *Teaching Children Mathematics, 8,* 208–214.

Temple, E., & Posner, M. (1998). Brain mechanisms of quantity are similar in 5-year-olds and adults. *Proceedings of the National Academy of Sciences, 95,* 7836–7841.

Terry, W. S. (2005). Serial position effects in recall of television commercials. *Journal of General Psychology, 132,* 151–163.

TIMSS Video Mathematics Research Group. (2003). Understanding and improving mathematics teaching: Highlights from the TIMSS 1999 video study. *Phi Delta Kappan, 84,* 768–779.

Tomlinson, C. (1999). *The differentiated classroom: Responding to the needs of all learners.* Alexandria, VA: Association for Supervision and Curriculum Development.

Wagner, A. D., Schacter, D. L., Rotte, M., Koutstaal, W., Maril, A., Dale, A. M., Rosen, B. R., & Buckner, R. L. (1998, August 21). Building memories: Remembering and forgetting of verbal experiences as predicted by brain activity. *Science*, *281*, 1188–1191.

Witzel, B. S., Mercer, C. D., & Miller, M. D. (2003, May). Teaching algebra to students with learning difficulties: An investigation of an explicit instruction model. *Learning Disabilities Research and Practice, 18,* 121–131.

Woodruff, G., & Premack, D. (1981). Primitive mathematical concepts in the chimpanzee: Proportionality and numerosity. *Nature, 293,* 568–570.

Wynn, K. (1990). Children's understanding of counting. *Cognition, 36,* 155–193.

Young-Loveridge, J. (2002, November). Early childhood numeracy: Building an understanding of part-whole relationships. *Australian Journal of Early Childhood, 27,* 36–42.

Zaslavsky, C. (2001, February). Developing number: What can other cultures tell us? *Teaching Children Mathematics, 7,* 312–319.

Zorzi, M., Priftis, K., & Umiltá, C. (2002). Neglect disrupts the mental number line. *Nature, 417,* 138.

Resources

Note: All Web sites were active at time of publication.

Ask Dr. Math

http://mathforum.org/dr.math/

This site began as a project at Swarthmore College that used university students to answer questions in mathematics. There are now hundreds of volunteers from colleges around the world who answer mathematics questions. The Frequently Asked Questions page makes interesting reading, especially "A Crash Course in Symbolic Logic."

Assessment in Math and Science

www.learner.org/resources/series93.html

This site is sponsored by Annenberg Media and contains free (with registration) online video workshops on Knowing versus Understanding, Scoring, Embedded Assessment, Connections Across the Disciplines, and Assessment Reform.

Calc101.com Automatic Calculus and Algebra Help

www.calc101.com

This site offers free and passworded help for finding derivatives, integrals, graphs, matrices, determinants, and systems of linear equations. The solutions are provided in simple terms and use standard mathematics notation, and show the steps used.

Calculus Help.com

www.calculus-help.com

This fun site for calculus includes a problem of the week, tutorials, an interactive cheat sheet, calculus music (the touching "Quadratic Formula Song," the catchy "Day Before Notebooks Are Due Blues," and calculus holiday carols). The site updates often with new material.

Coping With Math Anxiety

www.mathacademy.com/pr/minitext/anxiety/index.asp

This site takes a constructive look at math anxiety, its causes, its effects, and at how students can learn to manage this anxiety so that it no longer hinders their study of mathematics. It includes special strategies for studying mathematics, doing homework, and taking exams.

Geometry Junkyard

www.ics.uci.edu/~eppstein/junkyard

Created by David Eppstein, a professor of computer science at the University of California-Irvine, this site contains clippings, web pointers, lecture notes, research excerpts, papers, abstracts, programs, problems, and other information related to discrete and computational geometry, presented in a unique and entertaining format.

Interactivate Math Activities

www.shodor.org/interactivate/activities/

From the Shodor Education Foundation, this site includes a curve generator, a bounded fraction finder, and an impressive list of games for geometry, algebra, probability, statistics, and modeling.

Interactive Mathematics Miscellany and Puzzles

www.cut-the-knot.org/content/shtml

An entertaining site with hundreds of problems in all areas of mathematics presented in an interactive format.

Interactive Resources

www.globalclassroom.org/ecell00/javamath.html

This is a portal to interactive mathematics sites designed for grades one through six. It includes algebra patterns and function, place value, money, arithmetic operations, time graphing, measurement, fractions, decimals, and geometry.

Karl's Calculus Tutor

www.karlscalculus.org/calculus.html

This site provides extensive help with all areas in calculus, including number systems, limits, continuity, derivatives, applications of derivatives, exponentials and logarithms, trigonometry functions, and downloads for calculator programs.

Layered Curriculum®

http://help4teachers.com

This is Kathie Nunley's site, which offers information about her methods for layering the curriculum in mathematics and other subject areas.

MacTutor History of Mathematics

www-groups.dcs.st-and.ac.uk/~history/index.html

Maintained by the University of St. Andrew in Scotland, this site is an excellent source of material on the history of mathematics. It has an extensive list of biographies of famous mathematicians and is rich in information on a wide variety of topics, including ancient Babylonian, Chinese, and modern-day mathematics.

Math Cats

www.mathcats.com

This is a site for primary elementary grade students that uses attractive animation to teach arithmetic operations, conversions, measurement, estimation, geometry, and other related topics.

Mathematical Interactivities—Puzzles, Games, and Other Online Educational Resources

http://mathematics.hellam.net/

Students here can play unique mathematical games, and find out how to do number tricks and more on this interesting site. Teachers should preview the games before assigning them because some of the sites are not self-explanatory and do not provide adequate feedback.

The Math Forum

http://mathforum.org

Sponsored by Drexel University, this site offers answers to many questions in mathematics, plus weekly puzzles and games.

Math Homework Help

www.phoenix.k12.ny.us/jcb/staff/math/mathhelp.htm

This site offers an extensive listing of homework help sites for algebra, pre-algebra, AP statistics, precalculus, calculus, computer science, conversions, calculators, and graphing. The math glossary is excellent.

The Math Playground

www.mathplayground.com

This graphically appealing site offers elementary and middle school students an entertaining way to learn word problems, logic games, and mathematics games. The site also contains printable worksheets, interactive quizzes, and practice facts.

Math Teacher Link: Classroom Resource Bank

http://mtl.math.uiuc.edu/classroom_resources.htm

Sponsored by the University of Illinois at Urbana, this site connects to teacher-created classroom projects, algebra, geometry, calculus, and probability and statistics links. Project-based Internet lessons and sample mathematics lesson plans are also available.

Math2.org

www.math2.org

This site features reference tables, an open mathematics encyclopedia, a collection of mathematical theorems and formulas, and over one hundred graphical JAVA applets that demonstrate mathematical concepts.

Mr. Calculus

http://homepages.roadrunner.com/askmrcalculus/index.html

This site provides assistance with AP Free Response tests and links to tables on derivatives, convergence tests, logarithms, exponents, and other useful college mathematics and calculus sites. Included are interactive lessons and calculators for all types of mathematical operations, as well as lessons and worksheets, a prime numbers chart, a perfect squares chart, and study tips.

National Council of Teachers of Mathematics: Principles and Standards

http://standards.nctm.org/

The NCTM document from 2000 that recommends the processes and standards of mathematics instruction for grades preK–12.

Number Worlds Elementary Mathematics Program

http://clarku.edu/numberworlds/

The *Number Worlds* program is a research-based PreK–6 curriculum that teaches the specific math concepts and skills needed for later mathematical learning. The program has been evaluated with children from low-income populations and proven effective in enhancing computational fluency, number sense, mathematical reasoning and communication, as well as performance on standardized mathematics achievement tests.

Online Quizzes

www.edselect.com/quizzes.htm

Here is an extensive listing of quiz sites and quiz creators, including a free-to-nonprofits software programs that allow you to create interactive multiple-choice, short-answer, jumbled-sentence, crossword, and matching exercises.

PBS Teachers: Math

www.pbs.org/teachers/math

This is a curriculum data bank in all areas of PreK–12 mathematics provided by the Public Broadcasting Service with links to books, media, and online professional development courses.

Practical Uses of Math and Science (PUMAS) NASA

http://pumas.jpl.nasa.gov

This site offers dozens of suggestions on how to show the practical and everyday uses of mathematics and science.

Professor Freedman's Math Help

www.mathpower.com

This site was created by Ellen Freedman, a professor from Camden Community College in New Jersey. It provides information about basic mathematics, algebra, study skills, math anxiety, and learning styles and specifically addresses the needs of the community college adult learner. There are musical videos illustrating different mathematical operations, tutorials, homework assignments, interactive games, and links to many more resources.

Purplemath

www.purplemath.com/internet.htm

This award-winning site provides links to lessons and tutoring, quizzes and worksheets, and a collection of downloadable information on mathematics.

SuperKids Math Worksheet Creator

www.superkids.com/aweb/tools/math/index.shtml

This site helps teachers easily customize worksheets for arithmetic operations, fractions, percentages, greater than/less than, odd or even, rounding, averages, exponents, factorials, prime numbers, and telling time.

Index

CORWIN
PRESS